MORE PRAISE

"I deeply appreciate how Professor Martin has redefined retirement as a time of continuing contribution to society, whether that contribution is helping a neighbor or starting a business or a nonprofit. Also, as a marathoner and tai chi practitioner, I appreciate her emphasis on wellness and the mind-body connections."

> —Dr. E. Percil Stanford, PhD, president of Folding Voice, professor emeritus, founder of the University Center on Aging, the Department of Gerontology, and the National Institute on Minority Aging at San Diego State University; inaugural senior vice president for diversity and inclusion at AARP; and member of multiple White House Conference on Aging advisory committees

"As I approach retirement age, I'm frequently asked 'Where will you live?' and 'What will you do?' Professor Martin's excellent text walked me through the more important questions of 'Do you know what makes you tick?' and 'What roles and activities are most valuable to you personally?'"

> —Dr. Bruce Andrus, MD, MS, cardiologist

The
Inspired
Retirement

The Inspired Retirement

PURPOSE AND PASSION IN YOUR NEXT ADVENTURE

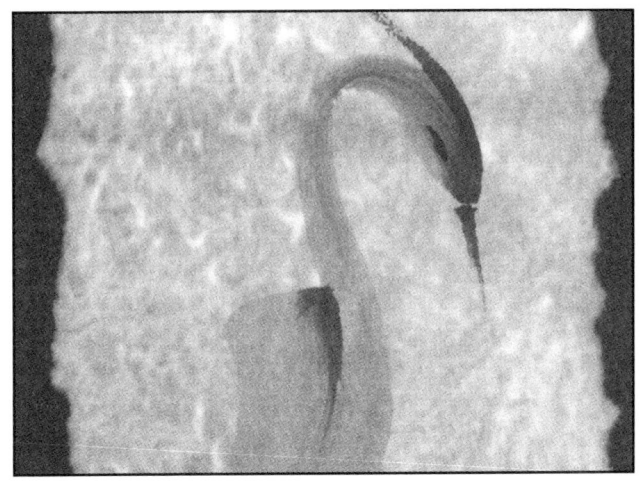

Nathalie Martin

The Inspired Retirement © 2025 by Nathalie Martin

All rights reserved. No part of this book may be reproduced in any form whatsoever, by photography or xerography or by any other means, by broadcast or transmission, by translation into any kind of language, nor by recording electronically or otherwise, without permission in writing from the author, except by a reviewer, who may quote brief passages in critical articles or reviews.

Image on p. 285 reprinted with permission from www.cartoonstock.com.

Cover art by Pat Marsello
Book design and typesetting by Jim Handrigan
ISBN 13: 978-1-64343-528-2
Library of Congress Catalog Number: 2025901492
Printed in the United States
First Edition 2025
29 28 27 26 25   5 4 3 2 1

Beaver's Pond Press
939 West Seventh Street
Saint Paul, MN 55102
(952) 829-8818
www.BeaversPondPress.com

To contact the author, email martin@law.unm.edu.

To Stewart and Mi Hita.
You two are my everything.

CONTENTS

Foreword xi
Introduction 1

PART I: PREPARING FOR THE ADVENTURE
1. Living the Inspired Life 11
2. Rediscovering the Natural Rhythm and Flow of Life 25
3. Mindset: Our Most Valuable Real Estate 41

PART II: EMOTIONAL BARRIERS TO AN INSPIRED RETIREMENT
4. Dealing with Difficult Emotions: Grief, Anxiety, and Anger, Oh My ... 57
5. Learning to Love and Forgive 83

PART III: CREATING AND MAINTAINING WELL-BEING IN MIND, BODY, AND SPIRIT
6. Connecting the Mind and Body through Yoga 103
7. Coming to Terms with the Older Body 111
8. Physical Movement 121
9. Nutrition and the Older Body 135
10. Sleep, Socializing, Stress, and Devising Your Individual Health Plan . 149

PART IV: CREATING THE INSPIRED RETIREMENT LIFE
11. Discovering Your Broad Retirement Life Objectives 169
12. Discovering Your Skills, Values, and What Brings You Joy 177
13. The Nuts and Bolts of the Inspired Retirement 199
14. Reinvention Stories 213
15. The Relocation Equation 235

PART V: YOUR MONEY AND YOUR INSPIRED RETIREMENT

16. A Mindful Money Mindset Part I: Staying Inspired When
    Money Is Tight 253
17. A Mindful Money Mindset Part II: The Symbolic Role of Material
    Wealth in Our Lives 285

PART VI: CONCLUSION

18. Putting It All Together: Living the Inspired Retirement 307

Acknowledgments 311
Endnotes 313
Index 327

FOREWORD

The Spanish word for retirement is *jubilación*, which evokes thoughts of great happiness and joy. Compare that to our own culture's musings about retirement, which envision bored people with deteriorating bodies and minds. Yet retirement needn't be like this. It can be a time filled with good health, joy, happiness, and purpose.

In *The Inspired Retirement*, Professor Nathalie Martin shows us how, and the timing for this book could not be more apt. Over thirty million Americans will retire in the next decade, far more than at any other time in history.

Yet it is unclear what we're supposed to do with our newfound time. A recent *New York Times* article entitled "What Does Retirement Really Mean?"[1] demonstrates the need for this book. The vast majority of those featured in the *New York Times* story were searching for renewed purpose in life. This search poses questions like the following:

> What will this new life look like?
> Will golfing and fishing be enough?
> Will I be healthy enough to enjoy life?
> How will I recreate my identity?
> How will I balance doing with being?
> Finally, how can I make sure I stay relevant well beyond the jobs that have defined me for centuries?

The Inspired Retirement helps answer these questions at the precise moment that millions of people are asking them. As an author, law professor, and meditation teacher, Professor Martin shares her expertise through mindfulness and contemplative exercises that get to the bottom of what matters most to each of us. In her previous books and articles, Professor Martin has written about purpose and meaning at the beginning of a career. She now shares her expertise with those nearing the end of their careers.

In a helpful combination of information and purposeful exercises, Professor Martin encourages us to become still so we can explore that unique sweet spot in which our overall lifespans are shorter, but our day-to-day lives allow us the luxury of determining how we want to spend our limited time on earth.

This delightful book takes us on a wild ride, first inviting us to slow down and find out what is in our hearts, then asking us to improve our mindset and shore up our emotional, mental, and physical well-being, and finally taking us on a deep dive into our own unique search for purpose and meaning in life.

After working in the aging space for six decades, I cannot say enough about the contributions of this exceptional book.

—Paul Nathanson, founding executive director of the National Senior Citizens Law Center, past president of the American Society on Aging and Justice in Aging, and past secretary of the Gray Panthers

INTRODUCTION

If you have ever wondered what retirement might be like, or what else life has in store for you, you are not alone. This question of "what next" is the core question considered throughout this book. To prepare to write it, I spent a year interviewing people from all walks of life about what brings them joy, happiness, and purpose post-career. There is one thing that a former postal worker, a waitress, a ski resort executive, and a university president all have in common. If they are retired or retiring soon, they are stepping into one of life's largest abysses and biggest adventures.

Retirement can be anything we want it to be, but we need to figure out *what* we want it to be. Over the next decade, over thirty million Americans will retire, the largest number in history. Individually and societally, this is both a monumental challenge and a remarkable opportunity.

Aging in our society is stigmatized, as is retirement. This stigma results partly from the limitations of aging itself, and partly from American society's biases against aging people. As a result, retirement sometimes also gets a bad rap, both in our own minds and the minds of others. Recall that ski executive I mentioned above. In my interview with her, she reported so looking forward to retirement and to having lots of time to ski ski ski! Yet within a week of retiring, she said she felt "old." Never mind that she can still ski the pants off anyone I know. Her mindset told her, "I'm retired, therefore I'm old."

The goal of this book is to help readers overcome the actual and perceived limitations of aging and retirement to create their happiest and most meaningful life going forward. As Atul Gawande explains in *Being Mortal*, aging is frequently accompanied by three plagues: boredom, loneliness, and dependence.[2] Both retirement and aging can be accompanied by failing health; a lack of challenge, purpose, and meaning; and an absence of joy in life. Here, in this book, I take on the three plagues and help readers create the life they want.

We close the gap on the type of retirement planning few of us know to do: the planning of our lives rather than the planning of our finances. We are trained to save enough money for retirement and to look forward to not having to work, but few people think about what day-to-day life will be like in retirement; how we will spend the days, weeks, months, and years; and how we will stay healthy—mentally, emotionally, and physically.

While doing interviews for this book, I found it hard to keep people off the subject of money. Perhaps this is because money is the only aspect of retirement for which we actually plan. This is a shame as there is much more to the inspired retirement than saving money. There is also the vision of what we want our lives to look like in retirement and the planning that will get us there. I call this "retirement life planning."

While there are money chapters toward the end of this book, this book is mostly about planning the non-monetary side of retirement. Many of us look forward to retirement all our adult lives but don't give much thought to what we will actually be *doing* in retirement, particularly what we will do to find purpose and challenge.

Aging, which often accompanies retirement, also brings unique emotional and physical challenges. The better we cope with these challenges, the more inspired our lives will be. In the pages that follow, we will learn how to navigate these challenges and design the life we want post-retirement.

To accomplish this, we will use visualization, journaling, and other mindfulness techniques. What we focus on in life is what flourishes in our life. This book helps us figure out what we want to make flourish in our lives. Buddhist nun Pema Chödrön recently wrote that how we live is how we die.[3] Similarly, how we live is how we retire. How we live and how we retire are within our control. We can make choices now that will improve the rest of our lives and bring inspiration to retirement.

The Three-Legged Stool of the Inspired Retirement

Like the financial side of retirement,[4] planning for the inspired retirement life involves three interrelated components: (1) purpose, (2) mental, physical, and spiritual well-being, and (3) joy.

These three components create the sweet spot of healthy aging. In these pages, I aim to help readers develop and tap into these life forces and use them to create a plan for maximum enjoyment later in life.[5] Through your own reflections and the stories of others, you will learn what will lead to a happy and fulfilling retirement.

Discovering Life Work

At some point, many of us can choose whether we want to continue working for pay. Once retired, some people feel no need to work at all. They have worked all their lives helping family, friends, and others, and it is time to truly relax and be who they want to be and do what they want to do. For these people, their focus for the future might be planning meaningful leisure, health, and overall happiness rather than meaningful work.

For many people, however, continuing to work brings purpose, passion, and happiness. In my interviews and in the retirement stories I have read, many people are not satisfied to live through past accomplishments and want to continue doing some form of work throughout life. Indeed, studies show that without some ongoing contribution to society, many people falter, un-retire, or simply become ill and die.[6]

Assuming we want to keep living well *and* doing some form of work, how do we decide what to keep working at or on? We may find we want to continue doing what we've been doing since we entered our professions. Many jobs allow for part-time work, and some people (especially in academia) continue to work at the same job until the end. This is not everyone's choice, however, even if it is available. Some people decide that what they've done so far is fabulous for what it was, but now, they seek to do something else as icing on the cake of a fulfilling life.

Fortunately, aging clarifies things. We can see how we have spent our professional lives and find new ways to spend our remaining time. This process can be enjoyable and can bring us joy. It is, however, a process. We never permanently answer these questions but continue to explore our options throughout life. In that way, the inspired retirement is a practice rather than a destination.

Discovering Joy, Happiness, and Well-Being

In addition to thinking about and planning for our ongoing life work, we can also plan for more guilt-free indulgence and joy. While indulgence is often present in our lives, it is rarely guilt-free, and joy is often entirely missing from retirement plans. Tapping into joy can feel inaccessible after a life of working so hard for so long, yet joy can be learned once we understand that we deserve it. So can guilt-free indulgence, such as reading a book during the day or sitting outside in the sun and doing nothing. We can learn to recognize and experience joy, so why shouldn't we choose joy?

Finally, to live life with maximum joy and purpose, we need to be as healthy and happy—emotionally, mentally, and physically—as possible. This subject is also addressed in this book.

The Voice and Format of This Book

This book is written in the "I," "we," and "you" voice. It makes you an active participant in creating your inspired retirement. This is accomplished through exercises that ask you to pause and reflect and sometimes write. I call these *Purpose Practices*, as they help you learn what makes you tick and what you want from life. If you like to learn about yourself and what interests you, using these tools is the ultimate self-indulgence. After all, who is more interesting than you?

It is up to you whether to do the exercises, but I have practiced them and tested them out on others. I've found that people who do the exercises tend to get the most out of their holistic-life retirement planning. Some exercises help clarify goals and determine what steps to take next. Others simply create opportunities to slow down and savor life, something that makes all of us happier.

The exercises in this book involve journaling, breathwork, meditation, gentle movement, and visualization. Science shows that journaling, and all expressive writing, has particular benefits for the mind and body. All of these practices help clarify what we want and need. And don't worry, the writing is casual and just for your eyes. You need not share it.

The Other Tools You'll Want

You'll also want two additional tools besides this book: a notebook or journal and a favorite pen. I have used many kinds of notebooks and journals in the past and suggest one that you will feel comfortable carrying and writing in. Fancy or simple, it's no matter, but often simplest is best. It won't feel so precious or permanent. Again, this is a journey. What you write is up to you, and you can write new things later. We will start journaling soon, so you may want to grab those tools as you read on.

The Defining Question of This Book

To get a flavor for the journey ahead, pause and consider this question:

> What is likely to bring me joy and satisfaction in the coming decades?

Take a moment to write down the question and today's answers in your notebook or journal.

Throughout these pages, we will explore this question through stories, examples, excerpts from interviews, and most importantly, additional exercises designed to get to the bottom of these answers for you. The answers will change over time, but you will learn how to re-ask the questions when you need to.

Like the saying that you never dip your toe in the same river twice, we are all different and we are always changing. Our goal is to embrace the search. Life can be one fabulous adventure after another. If you have reached or will soon reach retirement age, you are on the cusp of one of life's most exciting adventures. American poet Mary Oliver once said, "Tell me, what is it you plan to do with your one wild and precious life?" In these pages we explore that question, as well as ways to stay emotionally, mentally, and physically healthy and happy, for all of your days.

The Organization of This Book

To start, this book asks you to remember and access your past experiences of joy. Joy and gratitude can counter many of the painful things that aging can bring us, things like grief, loss of mobility, and loneliness. Developing a joyfulness practice can make life more fun.

Next, this book explains how mindfulness and rest can be a clarifying salve and healer in a life filled with stress, caretaking, and external and self-imposed busyness. It explores how stillness and mental rest can help us to figure out what we truly care about, what we have been running from, and where we would like to go. These first two chapters explore how much freedom of time and space we can create in our lives and how we can use this newfound time and space for our own happiness and for the well-being and benefit of others. In chapter 3, we examine the role of mindset in creating a healthy and happy life.

Next, in chapters 4–10, we explore how to create maximum health in mind, body, and soul in retirement. We start by exploring how to work with difficult emotions, such as grief, sadness, anxiety, and guilt, and next explore how to share our feelings and nurture relationships that sustain us. This part of the book explores self-compassion and the role of forgiveness and emotions in staying happy and healthy. Next, there is a chapter on the benefits of yoga, particularly for the aging body. Yoga combines mind and body health into one practice, and this chapter connects our discussion of emotions with our consideration of the needs of the physical body. We reintroduce mindset and coming to terms with the aging body, and then discuss how to stay healthy physically, by moving the body, eating well, maintaining an active social life, getting good sleep, and managing stress.

In the chapters that follow, chapters 11–15, we more deeply explore our largest retirement objectives, our strengths, our core values, and the times in life we have experienced joy and purpose through vocations or avocations. We identify activities that make us feel most alive, activities that could meaningfully replace the time and effort we once spent on work, and the goals that will bring the most value to our lives. Since our goals change over time, these practices teach us how to continually inquire about our skills and values. We then explore stories of reinvention from retirees who have created meaningful post-retirement lives. We also consider the pros and cons of relocation and how to tell if a community you are considering will meet your needs.

Near the end, in chapters 16–17, we explore the role of money in an inspired retirement. We discuss how our physical surroundings and material wealth impact the quality of our lives. For those for whom money is tight, we briefly discuss how to live within one's means, cut expenses, and perhaps earn more money working part-time. We then discuss how to divest ourselves of unwanted and unnecessary things and ideas for maximum clarity and joy. These chapters have nothing to do with investment strategies and everything to do with understanding how to put money to its best use in our own lives and in society. We discuss the kinds of expenditures that lead to joy and the kinds of giving that can lead to real change in our society. Finally, in the last chapter, we distill what we have learned about ourselves, create a plan for the future, and create a roadmap for revisiting these questions as we age and change.

PART ONE

Preparing for the Adventure

CHAPTER 1:
LIVING THE INSPIRED LIFE

Suddenly at retirement you go through a door to an empty room and have to furnish it and decorate it yourself, with only yourself to judge how well you did.[7]
—Dr. Michael MacMillan

Have you ever wondered what else life has in store for you, what else you might do with this beautiful life of yours? Me too, which is why I wrote this book. The thought of retirement can bring joy to the hearts of some, and fear or confusion to the hearts of others. All of us who have not yet retired or who have retired but aren't sure how we'll spend our time, have one thing in common. We aren't totally sure what happens next.

We are not sure where this next adventure will take us but we know it will be an adventure. Whether you choose to slow down or switch up your work life, or whether retirement is forced on you, if you have picked up this book, you have reached a milestone. You can retire if you want to. This creates endless possibilities and unthinkable freedom. Many of us have looked forward to the end of work as we have known it for years. That does not mean we know what to do with ourselves. No doubt, you will live an inspired life in retirement. But first, you need to figure out what *will* inspire you.

Finding Inspiration

Will your inspiration be the sky, the sun, the ocean, or the forest? Family and friends? That hobby you always wanted to pursue, or that big purpose project? Or perhaps it is the relaxation and peace you always pictured? Maybe you have no idea what will inspire you, and that is fantastic too. Discovering what inspires you is fun, and you finally have time to figure it out.

So, what does it mean to be inspired? According to *Merriam-Webster*, inspired means "of extraordinary quality, as if arising from some external creative impulse." Inspired is the opposite of feeling meh or mediocre. You can find what inspires you by asking questions and listening to the answers.

The Contemplative Process and Its Benefits

This book uses contemplative practices to ask those questions and listen to the answers, to get to the heart of what matters most. While we need to actively pursue our retirement dreams, before we do, it helps to slow down and think about what we want from life. Finding purpose and meaning post-career is an inside job. We can ease into retirement by working part-time, or we can jump right into a whole new life, but before we do anything, it helps to give the situation some quiet thought. As we age, we can see that our time is limited. There is no reason to waste any more of it.

Time spent thinking about and planning for our best next life is never wasted. To get your creativity flowing, I suggest various contemplative exercises throughout this book, which provide a host of mental and physical benefits. To start, mindfulness techniques can help us clarify our life goals and dreams. While the word "mindfulness" has become so overused that it is almost meaningless, many proven mindfulness practices can clarify our thinking. Using them to devise our unique retirement life can help us make the most of the life we have left.

Mindfulness is more than just a practice. It is also a way of life, a way of looking at the world and yourself. Eventually, if you practice regularly, the practice seeps into all aspects of your life, slowing you down and allowing you to experience more of your life because you are present for it. For this reason, mindfulness can become both a formal practice like sitting or walking in meditation, as well as an informal practice, where you practice in the tasks of everyday life. This informal practice is like a program running in the back of your mind. At the same time, it is the opposite of a program running in the back of your mind because it is clearing away debris, acting like one of those Pac-Man memes, eating the thoughts and beliefs you no longer need. Mindfulness clears the mind, slows down thoughts, and gives us a chance to experience life in the present moment.

Mindfulness is far from new. It has centuries of science behind it. To name just a few of the benefits proven by scientific studies, meditation lowers the production of carbon monoxide in the body and decreases heartbeat and respiration rates. It also reduces lactate levels in the bloodstream. Elevated levels of lactate in our blood cause anxiety, tension, and fatigue. Following meditation, blood pressure also drops, and the skin gets a more elastic look and feel. Meditation also improves mental health and creates a sense of well-being.[8] One of the most important benefits of mindfulness techniques is improved thinking and focus, something we need more as we age.[9] We can use mindfulness to slow down and learn things about ourselves and others, perhaps without much effort.

On the other hand, when we move through life quickly without pausing, we often get in our own way. We make life harder than it is. While there are many examples of ways in which we unnecessarily complicate our lives and get in our own way, this story from a vet friend is a favorite. A client of the animal clinic was chasing his dog around the house every morning to give the dog liquid fish oil. To administer it, he would position himself above the dog, force the dog's mouth open, and squirt the fish oil in the dog's mouth. The dog hated it so much that she would run away from her own beloved owner! Then one day a bit of the fish oil spilled on the floor. Can you predict the punch line? Sure enough, the dog lapped it right up.

One way we get in our own way is by letting our thoughts control us, rather than seeing them for what they are, just thoughts. When we allow our thoughts to become very concrete, as if they were reality, we create drama in our own lives through these thoughts. If we can somehow remember that these thoughts are just thoughts and not let them run us around, we can reduce drama in our lives, which will ripple out to those around us and reduce some of their suffering too.[10] We can learn to get out of our own way.

Sometimes we need help getting out of our own way. We need to challenge our assumptions and learn to swim with, rather than against, the current. Mindfulness can help us do that. Optimism helps too.

Journaling as Contemplation

Besides meditation, we can also clarify our thoughts by writing them down. For many people, this is easier because meditation seems too foreign. Writing down our ideas has many benefits. It clears the mind, prepares us for decision-making, helps us to deal with stress, clarifies our emotions, and helps us to take action. Here is an exercise to try:

> Take a minute to just breathe, nice and slow. Then take a few moments to picture your life ten years from now. What would

you like to be doing? How would you like to be spending your days? Write down a brief description of that life.

An answer could be something like this:

> It's early in the morning and I am up because I want to be. I have a loose agenda for the day, but most of the things on the agenda are things I choose to do, not things I am forced to do because of external forces such as a job, extended family obligations, or guilt trips. I get to choose my own schedule, but I do have a schedule.

Or your answer could be more specific, which may be even more helpful. For example, mine would sound something like this:

> I would wake up, meditate, do a bit of stretching, walk the dog, do some work that I find meaningful, exercise, do some errands and a bit more work, have dinner—perhaps with friends, go for an evening walk, and go to bed.

Even this description leaves out an important piece of information, namely what this meaningful work might entail. It also leaves open the question of whether life would feel satisfying without at least some meaningful work. We'll explore these questions in the chapters that follow through pausing, writing, and engaging in other contemplative practices.

Discovering Your Gifts

In these pages, you will discover your unique skills, gifts, and values, as well as what you love most. We will then explore how to use our skills and knowledge in new ways, ways that could positively impact other people's lives as well as our own.

Your experience is unique as we each bring something different to the table. For example, consider this story about the artist Picasso. According to legend, Picasso scribbled a sketch one day in a café and then tossed it in the trash. Another patron asked for it and he quoted her a huge sum of money for the sketch. When she said, "But it took you less than five minutes," he said, "No, dear lady, that took me a lifetime." This story could describe you. Over the past twenty, thirty, or forty years, you have developed enormous knowledge and skills. You can do more now than you could thirty years ago and do it in less time. Sharing that experience can bring a unique sense of joy.

No matter what it is you want to do, every day of your life so far has prepared you for this choice. In addition to wisdom and skills, you now have, or will soon have, the time to do whatever it is you want to do.

Discovering Joy and Openness

It is fun to have fun but you have to know how.
—Dr. Seuss

Preparing for retirement is not all about work. We can also have fun! But as Dr. Seuss says, we need to know how. We can learn or relearn how to have fun by developing a joyfulness practice. We all want to be happy, to be healthy, and to live life with ease.

Finding and feeling joy can be easier said than done. Aging can lead to many changes in our lives, including repeated grief and a sense of loss over physical, mental, cognitive, and societal changes. These changes can make it hard to picture and experience joy. But, like any other habit, regular joyfulness practice builds more joy, more appreciation, and more happiness.

What will bring each of us joy is different. Maybe your joy is found by taking care of your family and yourself or your physical body. Maybe you find joy in working for a nonprofit, or in a bookstore so you can discuss books with patrons. Perhaps watching movies or sitting in the sun brings you joy.

We can find joy in everyday moments once we develop a joyfulness practice. We can also go searching for joy. For example, when my family was going through a rough time recently, we pulled out an old journal from a time when we had a new-to-us cabin in the woods and first became birdwatchers. The happiness and beauty of our past jumped off the page and reunited us with things basic and essential to our well-being. We were reminded of how healing it is to be in nature, learning something new, and embracing a challenge with awe and a sense of purpose in that new pursuit. Like our old journal, the following exercise reconnects us with past experiences of joy.

It also shows that we can be contemplative about anything we choose. We can contemplate how to have fun and be joyful. Since joy and fun are part of the inspired retirement, we will try a joyfulness practice now.

PURPOSE PRACTICE 1.1

Allow yourself to daydream about some true fun you've had. If not much comes to mind, see if you can find an old journal or photo album (remember those?) and use the memories to bring back that feeling of joy.

Once you find joy, take a few extra minutes to relish it. Recall the details and internalize the feelings that joy creates in the physical body. Write down what you felt and how this past experience still provides joy.

Finding Joyful Activities by Picturing the Ideal Day

The visualization below, in Purpose Practice 1.2, helps us learn what we love as well as what we love to do. Visualization creates

CHAPTER ONE

intention, and setting intentions helps us reach our goals, even goals like happiness and joy. Additionally, the more we learn about what makes us happy, the more likely we will be to gravitate toward those things because we have set an intention to do so.

Both Oprah Winfrey and happiness doctor Tim Sharp suggest making a physical vision board, a piece of poster board that shows drawings or pictures of the life you want.[11] While I have not made one myself, you might consider it. According to Dr. Sharp, this visual aid brings the pictured things into your life almost subliminally and increases happiness. It might be fun to buy a big Post-it pad from an office supply store and have a vision-board party with a few friends and wine or coffee.

The exercise below is not a vision board exercise but a visualization in words. I am a lawyer by trade and have never quite connected with my artistic self, so for me this one is easier than a visual aid with pictures. It is modified from Talane Miedaner's book, *Coach Yourself to Success*.[12]

As background, Miedaner tells the story of Marjorie, a successful woman who was having trouble getting out of bed in the morning. Miedaner told Marjorie to plan the perfect morning. Marjorie did so. She planned to awaken, meditate, go for a walk in the woods, shower, and have a fresh-baked muffin and coffee on her veranda while writing in her journal. Marjorie discovered two things through this exercise: one, she really needed her own downtime in the morning; and two, to her delight, she could fit many of the elements of the perfect morning into her everyday routine.

Do this exercise without much thought. Just do it lightly with playful curiosity. Curiosity keeps us young. As mentioned in the introduction, expressive writing of any kind has a myriad of mental and physical benefits. The process of writing helps us regardless of what we write. If that writing is also clarifying, all the better.

> ### PURPOSE PRACTICE 1.2
>
> Use your journal to write down in vivid detail what your best morning would look like, and when you get a chance, try it out. How much of that best morning, or evening for that matter, can you bring to your day-to-day life?
>
> You can extend this principle and plan an entire ideal day. You can wake up and tell yourself, "Today will be an ideal day." Much of the time, it will be ideal in some way because you planned and built in as many elements of the ideal day as you could.
>
> Write it all down. Then go back and look at the activities in the ideal morning or day. See how many of those activities you could put into today and each day.

This exercise is a starting point for how you want to spend your time going forward. Feel free to daydream as much as you like. Learning what you love is engaging and insightful and doesn't have to be hard. If you're curious, the process can roll right through you. The things you identify are part of your journey to joy. You may find you are already having many ideal days but just haven't stopped to appreciate them. When you gain that appreciation, life is often better and brighter.

As we move though our inquiries about purpose and joy, we want to remember that time is our most valuable asset. We won't want to squander it. Meditation teacher Jack Kornfield has this wonderful idea about life: everything in it is either meditation on the one hand, or tending the garden on the other.[13] What Kornfield considers meditation is what we can consider joyful, fun, and purposeful. When Kornfield speaks about tending the garden, he means doing the tasks of everyday life—washing the dishes, taking out the trash, going to traditional jobs—all the things we need to do to survive.

We will always need to tend the garden because life includes tasks we need to do just to live, but when considering the question "what next," it is helpful to ask whether this thing you think you want to do with your newfound retirement time is more like meditation or more like tending the garden.

It makes sense to voluntarily take on only new things that feel like meditation or flow. You'll need to tend the garden, but we can limit new garden-tending tasks by being aware of what we love and what we do for other reasons. We can also make choices based upon our preferences, rather than the preferences of others.

This exercise will help you articulate these choices.

PURPOSE PRACTICE 1.3

Stop and make a list of things that make you feel like you are in flow or the zone, something akin to meditation.

Post this list where you will see it daily. Read the list often. We all know what tending the garden is, and we can make those tasks more enjoyable and purposeful too, but for now, see if this classification system helps you get more "flow" time, more time in joyful and purposeful activities. You might also consider making a short list of things you'd rather not do in your retirement.

Finally, to find more joy we can practice gratitude. Having a regular gratitude practice, in which we focus on the positive parts of life, enhances mental wellness, reduces sadness and anxiety, improves sleep, and improves heart health.[14] These practices usually involve redirecting our thoughts from negative to positive ones when we are feeling down or frustrated, stopping and pausing to practice gratitude, and writing down what we are grateful for. Sharing gratitude with others can exponentially increase that joy.

Below, we provide a simple but powerful gratitude practice.

> **PURPOSE PRACTICE 1.4**
>
> List three things in your life for which you are grateful.

This gratitude exercise makes us happier, in addition to providing the physical enhancements noted above.[15] If you like it, set up a time to do this practice daily, perhaps at bedtime or first thing in the morning. It takes less than a minute. You can use a special page in your journal or notebook for this practice. Or you can write three things you are grateful for in a calendar each day.

Yoga for Joy and Long Life

Throughout this book, I will try to pique your interest in yoga. You'll find various yoga practices, as well as text about its benefits. Studies of people who practice yoga regularly show that the practice can lengthen the tips of the DNA (the telomeres) and help reverse years of undue physical and mental stress, and perhaps even lengthen life.[16] A little yoga is good for most people, but the choice is yours, of course.

As an introduction to yoga, we'll end this chapter with a breathing exercise designed to connect us with joy, followed by a simple heart-expanding pose. Breathing more deeply is healing, and this exercise combines deep breathing with gentle movement. Yoga has many mental and physical benefits, including calming the mind, improving balance and flexibility, and improving sleep. Anyone can practice it, making it especially good for the aging mind and body.

CHAPTER ONE

Yoga for Joy and Openness

PURPOSE PRACTICE 1.5

This breathing exercise is called *breath of joy*.

Stand with feet hip-width apart and smile.

Raise your arms out to the side and above your head. Place them in prayer pose and drop them to your heart, thumbs touching your chest. Take three deep breaths.

Now raise your arms above your head as you inhale, then as you exhale, swoosh the arms to your sides and behind you as you bend your knees and drop your torso down toward the floor. Do this three or four times, lifting and swooshing, inhaling on the way up and exhaling on the way down.

If standing is difficult, you can also do this exercise sitting up straight on the edge of a chair with no arms. The results are the same whether standing or sitting. We are creating an open feeling of possibility.

Now, we will practice the yoga posture, gate pose.

Seated or Standing Gate

Now, sit or stand with your feet out wide and raise your arms to your sides parallel with your shoulders. Reach those arms out as far as you can away from your torso, as if you were reaching for the walls around you. Lift your chest up and bring your shoulders up and then down, rolling them toward your back.

Now, keeping the torso straight and upright with the chest up, reach to the right and down the right leg. Keep the body straight as if between two panes of glass. Now lift the left arm up. Smile and reach that top arm slightly back, opening up the entire side of the body. Breathe.

Return to center and reverse. Now, the left arm moves down the left leg and the right arm reaches for the sky. Smile and move that top arm slightly back to open the body up to the side. Open heart, big smile. Breathe.

Try this one or two more times.

Now, enjoy three deep healing breaths.

Now that we have read about, journaled about, and practiced joy, we will turn our attention to slowing down. We will begin to release our tendencies toward workaholism and self-imposed busyness and clear the decks for more enjoyment and purpose in life.

We will also open our eyes to the benefits retirement can bring. Just as author and midlife thought leader Chip Conley suggests we reclaim the word *elder*, we also need to reclaim the word *retirement*, which originally derived from a middle French word meaning "to go into seclusion."[17] Retirement can be filled with purpose and awe. We can use our unique gifts and plan the retirement life of our dreams.

CHAPTER 2:
REDISCOVERING THE NATURAL RHYTHM AND FLOW OF LIFE

In this chapter, we practice slowing down so we can silence the noise and busyness around us and get to know ourselves better. We also learn to get out of our own way.

Make Life a Journey Rather than a Destination

Where are you going? Where are you going in such a hurry? Life can either be vast or fast but you have to choose at some point. See if you can look at life as a journey rather than a destination. We spend a great deal of time coming and going from place to place, anticipating what it'll be like to get there. This time is wasted if we don't enjoy it.

Recently, a neighbor told me about a road trip he had planned between Albuquerque and Chicago. It did not sound inspiring to me because it is all highways and cities, but to my neighbor, it is not all cities and highways. It is historic Route 66, small towns, and lovely state parks. He was over the moon about hitting every tiny town in Kansas and Missouri.

In addition to making life more of a journey than a destination, see if you can use your downtime, say in an airport security or supermarket line, to focus on the breath and the present moment. Meditate on the sweater of the person in front of you. Feel your feet on the ground. Be here now, or as Jack Kornfield says parroting signs in Las Vegas, "You must be present to win."

As it is, we live in a frenetic world that leaves us no time to ask big questions. We are often so preoccupied with the business of daily living that we don't pause to ask ourselves, "*What do we want our lives to mean? What do we want to leave behind as our legacy?*"[18] We need answers to these questions if we want to take stock of, and direct, our lives. We cannot take stock of or direct our lives if we don't slow down.

On average, those of us over sixty have one thousand more weeks to live.[19] How will we spend these thousand weeks? Time is our scarcest resource. The irony is that we need to slow down to figure out what to do with our limited time. We have many choices in this world, and starting right now, we can each make one choice that will improve our life. We can vow to move fast, slow, or medium, but never to hurry.

We can choose to do things at the pace that feels most natural for us. If you always move fast, go ahead and move fast. Just don't hurry. If you enjoy moving slowly, move slowly. Just don't hurry. Give yourself plenty of time. Explore the luxury of showing up early for things and not having to worry about being late. See if you can sync your own movement with the rhythms of nature by creating a life without rushing. This simple step may help you discover how to spend your thousand weeks.

Addiction to Work and Busyness

I know, I know. You're thinking, "I am too busy to slow down." After a lifetime of busyness, slowing down is easier said than done.

Most of us have spent decades rushing to catch our own breath. Our lives have been filled with obligations, external and self-imposed, and we have learned to rush through the moments of our lives. If we have a few moments to spare, we fill them with activity, trying to get more done, ticking things off our "to-do" list, being productive. We climb mountain after mountain but are not really sure we are climbing the right mountains, the ones we care about.

We don't really know why we do what we do, or whether any of it really matters in the end. We eventually become addicted to this busyness, which somehow defines us as productive human beings. Addiction to work and to success are real phenomena. As Arthur Brooks explains in his book *From Strength to Strength*, the desire to acquire more and more material possessions, and more honors and awards, keeps us hooked.[20] We want more money and more success, but these extra professional honors and material things don't make us happier.

The desire for more and more professional success is seductive, not to mention highly addictive. One woman Brooks interviewed said she could not work less because leisure seemed less valuable than working, and that to be "successful" in the eyes of herself and a bunch of other people (many of whom were now dead), she had to keep at it. She didn't even like the work anymore but was scared to change her workaholic habits for fear of what would happen. Her hard work and her job made her, in her own words, "special." This is what an addiction to work looks like. Does it sound familiar to you?

According to Brooks, Winston Churchill, Saint Augustine, and Abraham Lincoln all suffered from work and success addiction, and in Lincoln's case, it almost led him to suicide.[21] Brooks wrote the heartfelt prayer below to relieve us of work addiction. If work addiction is something you suffer from, which might be evidenced by sneaking around to work in the evening, perhaps you can recite this prayer:

> From putting my career before the people in my life, deliver me.
> From distracting myself from life with work, deliver me.
> From my desire to be superior to others, deliver me.
> From the allure of the world's empty promises, deliver me.
> From my feelings of professional superiority, deliver me.
> From allowing my pride to supplant my love, deliver me.
> From the pains of withdrawing from my addictions, deliver me.
> From the dread of falling into decline and being forgotten, deliver me.[22]

As Brooks explains, shedding a false image of an extremely special self, based upon worldly accomplishments, is scary but worth it. To start, see if you can slow down and embrace this moment.

How Rest Heals Us

We sacrifice so much of ourselves through busyness. When we remain frantic and exhausted, it is hard to think straight. In his book *Sabbath: Restoring the Sacred Rhythm of Rest*, author and theologian Wayne Muller describes how, as a society, we have lost the rhythm between work and rest. Noting that our culture values action and accomplishment over rest and replenishment, we favor doing something, anything, over doing nothing.[23] By doing all of these things without giving a thought to why, "we miss the compass points that would show us where to go. . . . We miss the quiet that would give us wisdom."[24]

We want more of everything: influence, money, recognition, power, love, and possessions.[25] Yet even when we live our lives in service to others, if our mind is not clear, we reduce ourselves to robots.[26] We sometimes blind ourselves with frantic overactivity, and cause harm that theologian and activist Thomas Merton describes as violence to ourselves and others.[27] As Muller explains, in Chinese, the word "busy" is an apt combination of the characters for "heart" and "killing."[28]

Perhaps not surprisingly then, all major world religions incorporate the idea of a sabbath or rest day. Muller draws his own ideas about slowing down through the Jewish tradition of Sabbath or Shabbat. Though not Jewish himself, Muller uses the Jewish Sabbath as a metaphor for a more balanced life.[29] For traditional Jews, observing the Sabbath means engaging in no work for a full twenty-four hours. This retreat from the busyness of our lives replenishes balance and rests the body and the mind. Apparently, the Almighty was quite serious about the need for this rest, as observing the Sabbath is a commandment on equal footing with not committing murder.[30]

Drawing on nature, Muller observes that all of nature follows a certain rhythm of rest and renewal:

> The fruit contains the seed, and the seed contains the fruit. What we harvest in this season provides the seed for the next season. In Sabbath time, we taste the fruit of our labor and prepare the seeds for the weeks to come. If we are too busy, if we rush, we missed this rhythm. One day we look up and it is winter, and where are all the fall days, brisk and clear, leaves ablaze? How did we spend them? What were we doing?[31]

As Muller further explains:

> When we live without listening to the timing of things—when we live in work in 24 hour shifts without rest—we are on war time, mobilized for battle. Yes we are strong and capable people, we can work without stopping, faster and faster, electric lights making artificial days, so the whole machine can labor without ceasing. But remember: *no living thing lives like this.* There are greater rhythms that govern how life grows: circadian rhythms, seasons, and hormonal cycles, and sunsets and moonrises, and great movements of seeing stars. We are part of the creation story, subject to all its laws and rhythms.
>
> When we rest, we can relish the seasons of a moment, a day, a conversation. In relationships, we sense the rhythms of

> contact and withdrawal, of giving, and receiving, of coming close, pulling away, and returning. To surrender to the rhythm of the seasons and flowerings and dormancies is to savor the secret of life itself.[32]

We all want to make a difference in this world, yet filling our days with meaningless activity can keep us from seeing what we can do to *make* that difference. We are simply too busy to see it. While we might know we are stressing out our body with all this frantic activity, this harm to the body is not all that is lost. Without a restoration of the balance between work and rest, we also lose the ability to think.

Suggestions for Gradually Slowing Down in Everyday Life

Here are a few suggestions for slowing down. You don't have to do them all at once, or even do them all at all. For now, just read about them and try one or two if you feel moved. I have tried them all, and they improve concentration and bring a sense of calm and well-being if you do them regularly.

Take Time Away from Devices

What we pay attention to is how we spend our lives. I know it sounds impossible, but try to separate yourself from your electronic devices. Start with small time periods, just an hour or two. Consider this both a serious challenge and an important goal for personal growth. If you put your mind to it, you can do it. Then, see if you can dedicate some time to live *each day* without your devices.

Cell phones bring us closer to people far way, but further away from those people right near us. Can you recall the last time you dilly-dallied with your cell phone when you were with other people? When was the last time you found yourself in the presence of one person while emailing or texting another? Dr. James A. Roberts wrote an entire book on phone addiction called *Too Much of a Good Thing*,[33] and Suffolk law professor R. Lisle Baker and Harvard Medical School professor Daniel Brown dedicated seventy pages to a law review article entitled "The Lost Art of Paying Attention."[34]

If giving up devices for even one hour seems daunting, I get it. Most of us are addicted to our personal technology to one degree or another. However, we can create more meaning in our lives and be happier if we dare to train ourselves to *not* use technology while in the presence of others. If you want to take on a more advanced challenge, set aside time alone without devices as well. This type of "retreat" is soothing to the soul.

Take Some Time to Be Silent

See if you can use some of your time for silence. Silence is where we really open up. I don't mean just silence around the house but also silence of the mind, letting the mind slow down enough to see what's actually inside. It can be uncomfortable, and I sometimes have trouble doing it myself, but when I do, the rewards are significant.

Pick a Daily Activity to Do Slowly

By choosing just one or two daily activities to perform slowly, we can begin to slow down and pay closer attention to all the parts of our lives. In Purpose Practice 2.1 we will try this activity on a small scale.

Don't try to do everything you do in a day slowly. Rather, pick one activity to purposefully do slowly. Perhaps it is watering the plants. Or maybe you slowly fold laundry or unload the dishwasher. Perhaps you just drink a cup of coffee very slowly with attention to each sip. Right now, I have a seventeen-year-old dog, so it is a blessing to her if I slow down our walks. It is a blessing to me too.

> **PURPOSE PRACTICE 2.1**
>
> Briefly write down what you did slowly in your notebook. This takes just a moment or two but will keep you motivated to try doing other things more slowly, more intentionally, and more joyfully.

Accept Multitasking for What It Is

Multitasking seems productive, but in reality, it merely allows us to, as one source says, screw up several things at once.[35] Multitasking decreases productivity by causing us to do things shallowly rather than deeply. Virtually nothing can be done well while doing something else.[36] The science supports this, as multitasking has repeatedly been shown to decrease concentration and reduce creativity and performance.[37] Try to pick one thing to do at a time and really focus on that one thing. See how this changes the results you get as well as your frame of mind.

Focus on the Breath

Take on some informal but consistent mindfulness practices. For example, find times throughout the day to connect with your breath. Try making the exhale a bit longer than the inhale. This lengthened exhale technique has been shown to reduce blood pressure and improve overall heart health.[38] Also, don't hold your breath but do find that little space between the in breath and the out breath. Since you may not be used to pausing for anything, see if you can consider that space a mini-meditation.

Focus on Transitions

Now see if you can notice the little spaces of time between tasks. Just pause briefly and let there be some space and time. As Lao Tzu says, "Nature does not hurry, yet everything is accomplished." This pause will help you clear the mind a bit. Decisions may become easier to make. Intractable problems might seem less daunting and you might even think of a solution to them, much like when you get a great idea in the shower. Pema Chödrön calls this "the pause" and instructs us to find it wherever we can.[39]

More Involved Practices

Below, we describe some more involved mindfulness practices to help you slow down and become more aware of your desires and the world around you. This section is written mostly for those new to meditation, and these practices are meant to be ongoing practices you can choose to do as you move through life.

I have tried all of these practices and many of them have changed my life, even when I have been less than consistent. There is no need to change your whole life, only to make small changes. Anything helps. Feel free to explore a few of these practices. Just like physical activity, try something you can practice on an ongoing basis for a while, and see how you feel.

Start Your Own Simple Meditation Practice

We are not actually living when we dwell on the past or ruminate about the future. The only time we have is this moment, and it is gone as quickly as it comes. Our time is a nonrenewable resource. When it is gone, it is gone forever.[40] As Jon Kabat-Zinn explains, "We live our lives in moments, not hours, days, or months."[41] And, as an octogenarian yoga student once told me, Eleanor Roosevelt said this:

> Yesterday is history
> Tomorrow is a mystery
> Today is a gift and that is why we call it the present.

Being present is a goal of meditation because it is in the present moment that we are most ourselves and most alive. Indeed, times when we are present are the only times we are truly alive. At all other times, we are living in the past or the future. And, while our future time on this earth is limited, we can expand the time we spend in the present.[42]

People often say that meditation is hard and requires a lot of work. In reality, it only requires dedication and time. It is not hard. It just has to be done to work. Meditation teacher and author Paul Wilson was once asked to identify a group of people that would not benefit from meditation. His answer? Lazy people.[43]

Beginning to meditate can be as simple as setting a timer, sitting in a quiet place at the same time each day, and watching or counting your breath. It is as simple as that. It may be boring at times, or you may feel sleepy, but at its most basic, this is meditation. You just keep returning to the breath.

There is no need for classes or apps or special techniques. Having said that, I do elaborate on some other practices below in case just sitting there seems intimidating. The important thing is to try. There is no way to do it wrong. There is no such thing as a bad meditator, just people who meditate and people who don't.

Take a Meditation Class or Use a Meditation App

If you have not meditated before and want support for this endeavor, consider taking a class like Jon Kabat-Zinn's "Mindfulness-Based Stress Reduction" (MBSR) program. You can also download the Insight Timer or another free mindfulness app and listen to some guided meditations. Start slowly. Pick a fifteen- or twenty-minute meditation to begin, and do it while walking. Work up to listening without walking so that you're just sitting, and then add a few minutes a day just sitting in stillness. You can sit on a chair or a cushion; just keep your back upright to help you breathe fully and deeply. Your posture determines your level of alertness.

Even small bouts of meditation can be life changing. A study of lawyers found that by meditating for just six minutes a day, they experienced improved concentration, sleep, and interpersonal relationships, and even got more work done in less time.[44] The six-minute meditation study of lawyers is a humorous riff on the time increment some lawyers use to charge their clients.

Assuming you are not one of those people who bills time in six-minute increments, you can add another gratitude practice to this foray into meditation. You can feel lucky that you don't have to keep track of your time in six-minute increments!

The exercise below helps develop a meditation practice if you don't already have one.

PURPOSE PRACTICE 2.2

To get started in meditation, give it a try. Make it a goal. For example, commit to meditating for just six minutes a day for twenty-one days, the number of days needed to establish a new habit. You are accomplished, so we know you can do it. Just try it and make a note in your journal of any changes you notice. If your mind wanders, so what. Just bring it back. Start slowly. Build up. If you don't like it, you can always stop, but first give it a try.

Meditate with a Mantra

I have an overactive mind. As such, my favorite type of formal meditation practice is mantra practice. Mantra practice is not prayer but rather just the repetition of a phrase over and over to calm the mind. Traditionally a mantra was a phrase or sound used in religious settings to prepare the mind for concentration in meditation. Lately though, the word mantra has been used colloquially to mean a statement or slogan repeated frequently. As I use it here, the word mantra means a practice used to affirm a belief and calm and clear the mind. Mantra practices calm the mind and are easier than most forms of meditation because they give the mind something to do.

I was always reluctant to suggest mantra practice in my work with lawyers because it seemed too odd or new age for some. I was emboldened, however, by Jeena Cho and Karen Gifford's book *The Anxious Lawyer*, which contains an eight-week meditation program, in which a new technique is introduced and practiced each week.[45] The results are recorded in a journal. The practices include a body scan, following your thoughts, a METTA or loving-kindness meditation, a forgiveness meditation, a self-compassion meditation, and a mantra practice.

Mantra practice is among the easiest forms of meditation because reciting the mantra keeps the mind from wandering off. Despite this ease, the results are excellent. To start a mantra practice, you first choose a mantra. You have many options, including an English mantra, a chakra seed sound mantra, or a classical Sanskrit mantra. It is a matter of personal preference. In some ways, it doesn't matter what you choose. The mantra gives the busy mind something to do and directs us toward an intention.

Mantra practice is simple once you have chosen a mantra. You learn the mantra and repeat the mantra for either a set period of time, or for 108 repetitions per day. Many religious traditions ask that rituals be performed a certain number of times, and in the Indian Vedic tradition, the number 108 has mystical and religious significance. The number 108 also happens to be two times around the Catholic rosary, which has fifty-four beads. It is also six times the number eighteen, which has special significance in Judaism, standing literally for the concept of life. You can do your mantra for more than 108 times, in your formal "sit," after your formal "sit," or throughout your day. You just want to hit 108 times. I use a set of beads called a *mala* which has 108 beads, but if I don't have it with me and want to do my mantra, I recite the mantra for ten minutes. If I have recited my mantra for at least ten minutes, I don't worry about the number. I know I have done more than 108 repetitions. Also, to start, you might try reciting yours while walking slowly. Just watch out for oncoming traffic!

According to Paul Wilson in *The Calm Technique*, it is simplest to choose a mantra and stick with it forever.[46] On the other hand, don't pressure yourself. You might need to experiment a bit. Don't stress, just have fun. Also, remain light and calm as you repeat the mantra. Don't grip the mantra, just repeat it playfully. Mantra practice is fun because it is easy. You don't need to try to think, not think, or do anything else. You just repeat the mantra and this simple repetition calms and focuses the mind.

I was taught to repeat my mantra out loud, though both Cho and Gifford, as well as Wilson, suggest you repeat it silently. It is up to you, and you can mix and match. Just do the mantra, if you can, every day. It is hard not to feel calm after reciting the mantra.

Cho and Gifford claim that mantra practice is especially good for improving concentration. They also claim that mantra practice connects us to inner joy. Perhaps that is why I love it. One of my highest values is joy, though I lean toward being serious and not always toward fun, so I often work on this value.

Choosing a Mantra

Like I said, it is probably easiest to start with an English mantra, one that addresses an issue of importance to you or one that you work toward in your life. My yoga teacher, Kali Om, works hard and needs to remind herself to relax, so she uses "relax and enjoy." I struggle to focus on the positive, so I often use "I am surrounded by love and beauty." Lawyer and yoga teacher Bonnie Bassan works with self-acceptance, in both others and herself, so she likes "I have enough, I do enough, I am enough." My husband, Stewart, works on physical health and strength, so his mantra is "Every day is a step, either one step forward or two back." Interestingly, when Stewart started working with his mantra, he had never even heard of a mantra or a mantra practice. It was just an affirmation that kept him going. You too may already be unknowingly engaging in a mantra practice.

English mantras can also be more generic. For example, Cho and Gifford suggest the English mantra "let go" and Paul Wilson likes "calm." While English mantras are easy, no muss no fuss, with nothing to memorize, you might enjoy what is called a seed sound or Sanskrit mantra simply because these ancient mantras have been in use in meditation for so long. You can find these on the Internet, but I will share just one, *so hum*. So hum means *I am that*. This ancient mantra is said to bring about ultimate self-knowledge and growth. It is both simple and healing. To use this mantra in a traditional way, say *so* on the inhale and *hum* on the exhale. As you repeat *so*, inhale and imagine a line of energy drawing up the front of the body from the root of the spine to the area between the eyebrows. As you repeat *hum*, exhale and imagine that energy running from the area between the eyebrows down to the back to the tailbone.

Career Transition Meditation

This chapter finishes with my own guided meditation on career transitions. If you like, you can read it into your voice notes on your phone and then listen while you practice it.

This meditation helps clear away the many things that you may have been telling yourself about yourself and your life. It lets you see a glimmer of what is inside you. We will strip away some of the constructs we and society have created for ourselves, to see what is inside our true selves.

PURPOSE PRACTICE 2.3

Find a comfortable position with your back upright. Close your eyes and bring your hands to your heart space and your feet to the ground.

Once you get into a comfortable seated position with your eyes closed and your hands at your heart space, begin to focus on your breath. Take the time to do this over several rounds of breath. Perhaps you want to breathe normally but focus your attention on the exhale. Next begin to focus on the silence or space. See if you can find that silence or space even briefly.

Begin to let the thoughts that are hanging out in your mind just gently float away like clouds in the sky. As these thoughts begin to gently release, form in your mind's eye some of the different identities that you have created for yourself. Think about your job, your family, your spouse or children, your friends, even your clothes, your house, and your car. Just begin to imagine these things that you identify with in your life.

Now begin to separate yourself from those things.

Just imagine you are being moved away, for example from your job, just creating a little bit of space between you and your job, and then on the exhale moving a little bit further away from that job.

Do that again with another role or job you have, again separating yourself from the ego associated with that role, and on the exhale, separating yourself a bit further from the ego associated with that role.

Now, begin to do the same thing with other things that are important to you. Start with material things. Imagine separating yourself from your home and exhaling, beginning to move a little further away from that home, and then keep going with your car and your clothes and your other material possessions.

Then move on to the people in your life. Separate yourself from your family, inhaling, separating, exhaling, inhaling, separating more, exhaling again, and so on. Then move on to your friends and other very important people in your life.

When you are done, sit quietly, and focus on your breath.

Now write down your reactions to this meditation.

Do not worry, you will not be separating yourself in real life from these jobs, roles, people, or things. You are simply trying to realize that the ego you have created for yourself is not your entire identity. You are so much more than all of this and you have the ability to create a positive mindset, the topic of the next chapter.

CHAPTER 3:
MINDSET: OUR MOST VALUABLE REAL ESTATE

We have many freedoms in life, but the most valuable one is that we get to choose what occupies our minds. What we think about is how we spend the moments, the days, and the years of our lives. What we think about is also what flourishes and grows in our lives. As one interviewee explained eloquently, "Worrying about something is like praying for what you don't want or meditating on %^&*."

For a humorous example of the power of thoughts, in *The Thought Exchange*, David Friedman shares a story about how he and his partner Shawn had the same strange buzzing vibration in their bodies for four months.[47] Shawn was certain this was a sign that his chakras were finally aligning. David, who has a history of hypochondria, said he was sure he had developed an aortic aneurism. David lived through four months of "Oy, I am dying," and Shawn, four months of "Ah, I am growing."

We are not our thoughts, yet our thoughts drive most of our experience because our lives unfold through them. Our thoughts also deeply impact our emotional lives as well as our physical bodies. Thankfully, we have the ability to change our thoughts when they are not serving us.

Retirement can throw our thoughts for a loop. One ski executive, or as she likes to call herself, snow farmer, planned her retirement down to the day, to coincide with a big bonus she would receive after a certain number of years of service. She counted the days. To her surprise however, she felt unmoored in retirement. Something in her mindset changed when she actually retired. Yet keeping an optimistic mindset around our future exciting adventures in retirement is within our control. We can also watch what our mind is telling us, consciously and subconsciously.

Thought-Watching Exercise

Most of us are not fully aware of the thoughts we tell ourselves, but we can listen and find out. Thought watching is a form of meditation. As Pema Chödrön explains, the point of meditation is not to get rid of thoughts but to see their true nature. She even goes so far as to say that meditation has three parts: posture, a focus point like the breath, and watching our thoughts. As she further explains, "Thoughts will run us around in circles if we buy into them, but really they are like dream images. They are like an illusion—not really all that solid. They are, as we say, just thinking."[48] If we allow these thoughts to solidify, we create drama and more suffering for ourselves.

When I first heard about thought watching as a meditation practice, I was dubious. I assumed the point of meditation was to slow down, empty the mind, and get rid of as many thoughts as possible. I did the meditation anyway and it was illuminating.[49] As I watched my thoughts and made a mental note of them, I saw that many of my thoughts were negative and repetitive. They were sometimes unkind to others but most frequently unkind to me. Some of you will recall the 1967 book *I'm OK—You're OK* by Thomas Harris. These thoughts were clearly expressing the opposite, essentially that "I'm not OK, and you're not so great either."

The value of thought watching is seeing what is running in the back of your mind. You can see if you are subconsciously hurting yourself with repetitive, negative self-talk. As Bruce Lipton explains in *The Biology of Belief*, the subconscious mind is hundreds of times more powerful than the conscious mind because the subconscious mind was created while we were in our first years of life in a state of mind likened to hypnosis.[50] We had little control over the messages we received, and many of these early messages are still unknown to us. Yet they are there, lurking in our heads.

Lipton estimates that we operate most of our time using *only* the subconscious, yet the subconscious mind often tells us harmful lies about ourselves that we picked up as children.[51] If we can discover what these subconscious thoughts are, we can eventually eliminate these negative messages. Knowing what these thoughts are gives us the power to rewrite the story behind these thoughts and to change our subconscious thoughts into more beneficial self-stories. In Purpose Practice 3.1., we practice thought watching.

PURPOSE PRACTICE 3.1

Sit quietly in a chair or on a cushion with your back straight and your feet on the floor. Bring your hands to your lap and become relaxed but alert. Set a timer for five or six minutes and begin to focus on your breath.

Now expand the exhale a bit longer than the inhale as you just sit and breathe. Gently focus on your breath, without grasping the breath or judging yourself.

Sit back and watch your thoughts. Let them come and go like clouds in the sky.

Alternate between focusing on your breath and watching your thoughts.

You might even become tired of the many thoughts that keep imposing on your breath practice. If that happens, you are making progress toward calming and clearing the mind.

When the timer goes off, jot down a few of the more repetitious thoughts.

Now examine those thoughts. Are they true? Are they kind? Are they helpful to you? Is it helping you to keep replaying them?

Write a journal entry about what the thoughts were and what you learned.

What *did* we learn here? First, we are not our thoughts. Rather, we can choose our thoughts, choose what occupies the valuable real estate of our minds. This is never truer than toward the end of a career. We have the power to see much more as we age. We can choose whether to use our minds to continue working and living exactly as we are now, or whether to choose to do something else with our lives, whether to work part-time at this job or another, or whether to stop working entirely and spend our time on other life activities. This is true freedom.

Again, the mind is the most valuable real estate in the world. We can choose to allow the mind to be filled with anxiety, loneliness, and other painful conditions, or we can choose to let it be occupied with other things. These are the choices we are free to make as the lives of Elie Wiesel, Viktor Frankl, and others show us. The power inherent in this choice is life changing.

We have more control over our lives than we think we do. If our thoughts don't serve us, we need not be attached to them. And while control gets a bad rap in yoga circles as it is the opposite of letting go, like all things in life, balance is the key. We have control over our minds to a great degree as long as we can recall that we are not our thoughts. We can choose to release negative thoughts and live the life we want even if life seems difficult right now. Here is a list of things we can, with practice, control:

Our

> thoughts
> speech
> response to adversity
> perspective
> effort
> habits
> work ethic
> beliefs
> priorities
> actions

How often we

> exercise
> take risks
> express gratitude

How much time we spend

> worrying
> dwelling on the past[52]

What a freeing realization.

Mindset Research

Dr. Carol S. Dweck, author of *Mindset*,[53] pioneered the concept of growth versus fixed mindsets. According to Dweck, a growth mindset is affiliated with success while a fixed mindset is not. This is true whether a person is talented, gifted, super-intelligent, or just average. In other words, your mindset is more important than your skill or your intelligence.

So, what are these mindsets? A fixed mindset assumes abilities and talents are given, limited, and minimally subject to improvement. People with fixed mindsets believe they were born with certain qualities, positive and negative, and that these qualities are largely fixed throughout life. As you can imagine, a fixed mindset is not very motivating.

A growth mindset, on the other hand, is one held by people who believe they can constantly improve, expand, and enhance their lives regardless of the lot they were cast. People with growth mindsets beat the odds to achieve things that seem impossible, in large part because they believe they can. As Henry Ford purportedly said, "Whether you believe you can do a thing or not, you are right." Ford also believed that nothing will hold you back as much as your own belief that you can't do something.

The benefits of a growth mindset include the willingness to embrace new experiences, changes, and challenges, to accept feedback, and to learn from mistakes. A growth mindset can also give people motivation, drive, and enhanced creativity.

Conversely, fixed mindsets are limiting. Those who have them possess several unhelpful traits. People with fixed mindsets are often threatened by feedback, avoid challenges, give up easily, and see little point in making any real effort toward a goal. As you can see, these are not traits possessed by most successful people, let alone happy ones.

Ways to Develop a Growth Mindset

Limiting beliefs result from a fixed mindset, which is why it is worth developing a growth mindset. Is it possible to develop a growth mindset? Absolutely. Forbes ran a story on developing a growth mindset, and many of their suggestions are found below, along with a few of my own:[54]

1. Listen to your thoughts again, and identify and work to eliminate self-defeating and self-limiting ones. Cross-examine these thoughts. Are they true? Are they kind? Are they encouraging? Do these thoughts disparage you in a way that you would never disparage others? Treat yourself like you would treat a good friend.

2. Fight anxiety with a mantra such as "everything's gonna be all right" or "this too shall pass." Try not to waste time worrying about things that might not happen or over which you have no control. Also, believe that sometimes things just go right without a lot of work.

3. Adopt a beginner's mind. Be curious. Acknowledge what you don't know, and embrace this lack of knowledge as an opportunity to grow and learn. If you don't know something, you have something to look forward to: finding out more. Beginners have the most fun and the most awe. They also make the deepest and quickest progress, so join in and be a beginner at something.

4. Try not to blame others for your mistakes and shortcomings. If you take responsibility, you can learn from the mistakes and grow from them. If you blame others, you are stuck in a victim mentality. You never improve because you haven't taken personal responsibility and have ceded all control for change to others. Take control, take responsibility and use mistakes to change for the better. This is within your control and the best evidence of a growth mindset.

5. Allow yourself to fail. It is critical to fail, as only failure leads to growth. As I tell my students, "Win or learn." We don't learn much from success. Yet every failure is a stepping stone on the path to success, and so many success stories begin with failing miserably again and again, only to succeed in the end. If you give up before you let yourself fail, you have robbed yourself of the opportunity to succeed.

6. Leave your comfort zone and become comfortable operating outside it. For many of us, the comfort zone is a refuge, a place to go to be free from hardship and

challenge. However, "free from challenge" also means "free from growth." Challenge is often the secret sauce of healthy aging. Push yourself, bear the discomfort, and grow. I struggle with this and work on it with my therapist. I have become good at certain things and just want to keep doing them. Yet this does nothing to promote growth. Try to be brave. Dr. Sharp, aka Dr. Happy, suggests jumping out of a plane. That is a bit radical for me, but you get the idea.[55]

7. Also, and related to number 6 above, try not to let your ego come between you and changes that could make you happier and more successful. A growth mindset will push you into places where you feel less comfortable, less accomplished, and less certain. The ego will protest, but success (or even failing but having fun) in new arenas will be worth it. You can grow more and have more fun if you are willing to challenge your ego.

We Are Not Our Thoughts but Our Thoughts Can Help or Harm Us

Bruce Lipton's *The Biology of Belief* helps explain how much our perceptions and thoughts impact our physical and mental well-being. Like many other people, I thought most physical illness resulted from our DNA, the biological cards we were dealt, plus a few lifestyle choices. In reality, DNA contains the blueprint of our cells, but exerts less control over our health and lives than our environments. Lipton found while studying and creating stem cells in the lab that DNA itself has much less impact on what happens in our lives than the environment in which the cells grow.[56]

Most disease and poor health outcomes, Lipton argues, result from the impact of our thoughts on our DNA, not the DNA itself.[57]

Not to get too technical here, but DNA is covered with a protective sheath of protein. Without the influence of the external environment that permeates that sheath, DNA is more or less inactive. External stimuli, such as chemicals and other material outside the cell, move DNA into its role of influence. These external environmental stimuli have a more significant influence on how the DNA responds than what is inside the DNA itself.[58]

As a result, Lipton contends that external stimuli, namely our thoughts, beliefs, and emotions, things we can control, play a huge role in our physical health. According to Lipton, the breakdown of actual physical cells causes just 5 percent of illness.[59]

The Effects of Toxins, Trauma, and Negative Thoughts on the Brain

Under a microscope, cells know how to tell friend from foe. For example, if a toxin is put into the petri dish with the cells, the cells move away. When a growth hormone is put in the dish with the cells, the cells move toward it.[60] Cells can also be manipulated by other forms of trauma that negatively impact the cells.[61] This negative impact can be observed under the microscope. Since individual cells don't think, to understand the impact of thoughts on cells, one must examine images of the whole brain. The brain as a whole operates like its individual cells, embracing good things and resisting bad ones.[62]

Prolonged stressful and traumatic thoughts cause changes in the brain that hurt the cells because the brain cannot move away from the chemicals released by the thoughts. The brain is the central organ that responds to stress when it perceives and determines things it sees as threatening.[63]

The brain also manages the behavioral and physiological responses to stressors, and the brain can adapt and show remarkable resilience in response to stressful experiences, but only when it is trained to do so through meditation and other practices.[64]

Conversely, when stress continues without interruption, stress hormones flood the brain with toxins that interfere with cognition, decision-making, anxiety, and mood. They literally interfere with clear thinking. What's more, parts of the brain like the amygdala, the hippocampus, and the prefrontal cortex are damaged and shrunken by prolonged exposure to stress. In other words, troubled, anxious, negative thoughts measurably harm our brains and the rest of us.

Thoughts Derive from Our Mindset

This science reinforces the importance of mindsets on our health and well-being. Lipton includes many examples of the importance of environment on cells, and among the most poignant and heartbreaking are the studies of Eastern European orphanages. These studies show that when you give infants everything they physically need, but withhold love and tenderness, virtually all the babies get sick and many die.[65] Of those who survive, a large proportion have autism and other medical challenges.[66] This demonstrates the direct connection between physiological condition and perceptual experiences.

Lipton provides other examples of how stress influences what happens to cells. For example, Lipton describes how when an organ is transplanted, the immune cells typically try to destroy the new organ because it is seen as a foreign threat. During transplant surgery, doctors inject stress hormones into the body to suppress the immune system and keep it from rejecting the new organ, thus allowing the new organ to be accepted over time.[67]

Lipton and other scientists have written extensively about how stress hormones released during the fight-or-flight response deplete the immune system. Lipton claims that we all have many germs in our system already, but it is only when stress takes over and reduces the immune system that these disease-causing toxins take hold in the body and create physical illness. While certain food choices are helpful to boost the immune system, stress can at times be so strong that no food can help. Just as they say you cannot exercise your way out of a bad diet, you can't eat your way out of a highly stressful life.

A great deal of the stress we experience results from our own negative thoughts and our reactions to our environments, not the environments themselves. Moreover, we think of DNA as the director of our lives, but it is our thoughts, not our DNA, that create much of the health or illness in our lives. Lipton's work demonstrates the direct impact our thoughts and perceptions have on the way the body operates, including when the body becomes strong and vital, as well as when it becomes susceptible to illness and disease.

Building a Growth Mindset

Let's now put to work some of the techniques we read about in creating a growth mindset.

PURPOSE PRACTICE 3.2

Open your journal and reread the ideas you had when you did the thought-watching exercise. Now apply some of the techniques to create a growth mindset to those thoughts. They are paraphrased here:

1. Evaluate the truth and compassion of your thoughts.
2. Try not to worry about things outside your control that have not yet happened.
3. Don't give up your power by blaming others for your shortcomings.
4. Adopt a beginner's mind.
5. Allow yourself to fail at something in order to grow.

6. Leave your comfort zone to promote personal growth.

7. Don't let your ego stand between you and your growth.

If there is truth to any of the negative things you said about yourself, address those issues. Make a plan to change your behavior. On the other hand, if these thoughts are just doubt, fear, anxiety, or other useless negativity, see them for what they are and work to cast them aside. Dislodge and cross-examine these negative or unproductive thoughts.

Embracing Disruptors

Finally, know that things will happen to disrupt your peace of mind and recognize these things as another challenge in life. Use this knowledge to your advantage. As they say, "compost happens" and it is unrealistic to think otherwise. In *Life Is in the Transitions: Mastering Change at Any Age*, Bruce Feiler explains that in the average lifetime we face many high points, low points, and turning points. He calls things that switch up our world "disruptors." In the average lifetime, we each have thirty to forty disruptors, one every twelve to eighteen months.[68]

Disruptors are things like having a best friend or relative move away, losing a friend to cancer, having a pet pass away, losing a job or having a spouse lose a job, or moving to a new community. Sometimes, several disruptors hit us at once. These things can really shake us up. Not surprisingly, they don't stop when we get older.

Feiler's discussion of disruptors helps us appreciate that these things are going to happen to all of us. It is easier to understand them and to live with them if we know they are inevitable. This knowledge can help us accept things we cannot change. For example, my family moved to Oregon for the purpose of researching and writing this book. While there, my husband suffered an incredible injury, my dog had to have an operation, my aunt had over $100,000 stolen from her, and then my father-in-law died. All of these things happened at once. It was overwhelming and depressing, a combination of many disruptors, but also part of life. If we know they are coming, we don't need to feel such deep disappointment and anxiety every time a disruptor hits. We can recognize them as they come and say, "Oh, there's a disruptor, another rough patch in life."

How we handle the disruptors is key and the question is, will this disruptor become a major low point, what Feiler calls a "lifequake"? Or will it be a blip on the path forward, or perhaps an opening for something new? We can use our mindsets to control not the disruptors but our reactions to them. We can work toward thinking of these disruptors as openings for something new. That is within the power of our mindset. Our mindset can literally make us physiologically and psychologically stronger, healthier, and happier. In the next chapter, we tackle emotional health in greater detail.

PART TWO

Emotional Barriers to an Inspired Retirement

CHAPTER 4:
DEALING WITH DIFFICULT EMOTIONS: GRIEF, ANXIETY, AND ANGER, OH MY

Speaking of disruptors, bad things happen, and we need to deal with those bad things. Sometimes, though, we worry about bad things that might never happen. These are catastrophes of our own making.

How We Create Unnecessary Drama

In *The Wizard of Oz*, when Dorothy, the Tin Man, and the Scarecrow hear crunching noises in the woods, Scarecrow wonders if there are any animals out there who might be interested in eating things like, um, straw. Dorothy throws in "Oh My" and the crew repeats "Lions and tigers and bears, oh my" throughout the forest.

These lions and tigers and bears represent an unknown and feared predator that may or may not exist, fears that are often bigger in our minds than in real life. Things that scare us most often are things we've made up in our heads, and there are things we can do to reduce these imaginary fears.

As Pema Chödrön explains, since the beginning of time, humans have been trained to create drama in their lives and to turn every thought into a big deal. We can train ourselves to not allow these thoughts to become such a big deal. We can operate in the dichotomous place of openly acknowledging our thoughts but not allowing them to create our own World War III.[69]

Coping with Real Difficulties in Life

Of course, we also face real difficulties, such as the loss of loved ones, the loss of mobility, a failing memory, societal ageism, and other real impediments that make us angry, hopeless, and scared. There is also sadness that feels pervasive and enduring. As noted in the last chapter, we will experience an average of thirty to forty serious disruptors in our lives and they don't stop coming as we age.[70]

We need courage to face our imagined lions, tigers, and bears, as well as the real fears and disappointments in our lives. We often try to hide from these feelings but eventually, we need to feel what we feel.[71] There is no joy without sadness, no success without challenge, no inner peace without struggle. If we want to live fully and experience real happiness, we have no choice but to experience the full range of human emotions. These include anger, grief, and sadness, which can increase as we continue to suffer loss after loss as we age.

Aging, Grief, and Sadness

Difficult life experiences are what make us who we are. When teaching mindfulness to college students, I ask them to recall experiences in which they felt the most accomplished and alive. Inevitably they report on life's most difficult moments even though that is not part of the instructions. Many point to times when they faced huge obstacles and emerged whole from the other side of pain and struggle. For example, one adult student described rescuing his drug-addicted mother from a dangerous encounter. Another student described saving a friend from death in a rushing river. While most of the students' stories are less dramatic, people feel most alive after facing and surviving something difficult. These struggles enhance confidence, resilience, and resolve.

This means that most difficult experiences have silver linings of sorts, but it would be trite to imply that these ancillary benefits somehow make it worth the loss of valued and beloved parts of our lives and ourselves. After losing both of my parents within seven months, I could not see one good thing that came out of those deaths, not one. And I missed them so badly my heart and entire body literally ached. Today, several years later, I see that my father was struggling and that his death was a relief for him. As for my mother, I see that she died doing what she loved. There is sadness, yes, but also life and love in their deaths.

But getting to this point was and still is a process. It takes time. The older we get, the more familiar grief becomes. By the time we reach our fifties and sixties, we have faced a great deal of grief from the loss of loved ones and the dreams that died with them. We also continue to grieve the loss of physical capabilities and changes in society that seem intractable. While grieving these losses, we don't need to look for any "good" that comes out of them. We just need to sit with the grief and sadness and realize that life can be challenging.

As we continue to age, these feelings of grief and sadness become more familiar. As we sit with them, so too can we live with them. As a close friend said after an unthinkable loss, "I don't think this will be more than I can handle." As crushing as the experience was, it was not more than she could handle, as long as she allowed herself to grieve.

Because these experiences of deep sadness and grief multiply as we age, we must truly experience our emotions, our grief, and our sadness. We can't skip this step, however much we would

CHAPTER FOUR

like to. We need to work through the entire hot mess, or as Jon Kabat-Zinn would say, the full catastrophe of living.[72]

As David Friedman explains in *The Thought Exchange*, we need to feel and tolerate the feelings that come up, to withstand them, or as he says *stand with them*.[73] He suggests we feel the emotion in the body, note the tightness, the tingling, the shortness of breath, and try to stay with it, sit with it, feel it. He recommends that we try not to push it away or direct it at someone. This poem expresses the same sentiment:

> This being human is a guest house
> Every morning a new arrival.
> A joy, a depression, a meanness,
> some momentary awareness comes
> as an unexpected visitor.
>
> Welcome and entertain them all!
> Even if they are a crowd of sorrows,
> who violently sweep your house
> empty of its furniture,
> still treat each guest honorably.
>
> He may be clearing you out for some new delight.
> The dark thought, the shame, the malice,
> meet them at the door laughing,
> and invite them in.
>
> Be grateful for whoever comes,
> because each has been sent
> as a guide from beyond.
>
> —Rumi

It heals to let the feelings come and to welcome them in. As we sometimes say in yoga, "Feel here, heal here." Of course, no one really wants to feel sadness, but the only way out is through. We may feel the sensations will overtake us, that we won't be able to come back, to crawl back out. I have felt this myself while grieving so many times. Yet we have no choice but to feel what we feel.

Pushing the feelings away can make those really dark feelings come back even stronger later. It is best to suffer through, sit with, and live through them because that is what it means to be human. Letting these feelings in also prevents us from falling apart in public or at some other inopportune time. Getting in touch with sadness and loss is a process, an art form. If you loved someone or something and then lost it, you still had that love, and what else is life but love?

No matter who you are, sadness will at some point come for you as it does for all of us. How will you react? Again, if you allow yourself to truly experience the sadness rather than pushing it away, you can process the sadness and keep it from materializing into depression.

One way to create a sadness buffer is to plan in advance how we will take care of ourselves when things fall apart.

PURPOSE PRACTICE 4.1

Spend a few moments thinking about and perhaps writing down what you will do today to be good to yourself, to help you hold things together even when they seem to be falling apart. Do some of the things on the list today, even if you don't feel like it.

We can also create other rituals around letting sadness come. For example, my friend and collaborator Todd Petersen suggests creating a "sad" playlist to listen to when you need to work through and truly experience sadness. As you listen, ask yourself, "Why am I sad? What is the triggering effect? What can I experience here?"

Let sadness come. Experience it and then, like intrusive thoughts during meditation, let it go like a cloud passing in the sky. The story below, from author and master trial attorney Randi McGinn, exemplifies this best for me. Randi has a strict rule of "no

CHAPTER FOUR

crying in court" even for clients during a trial,[74] but acknowledges that everyone in the office cries outside the courtroom for the very same reason, to process the overwhelming emotions that come up in court. To ensure that she keeps her rule of no crying in court, she says this:

> How do you keep from crying in front of a jury when you are dealing with the saddest facts imaginable in a case? You cry the first day your client tells you about her lost child. You cry when you visit their home to see that, months or sometimes years after that child's death, her bedroom remains untouched, the same as it did the day she died. You cry at night when you are preparing your witnesses to testify at trial. And if you are still not cried out by the time you walk into the courtroom, you pinch yourself or bite the inside of your cheek until it bleeds to keep from crying in front of a jury before the verdict comes in.[75]

Keep in mind this crying is done to process the sadness. We have all been there, that place where the sadness engulfs us. Three weeks after my dad's death, I suffered the loss of a pet, and I am a huge animal lover. With no children to distract me, a dead father, and a dead pet, I was in bad shape. My solution? Get in my car, get on the highway, and scream my head off. It did not take away all my sadness, but it did create a temporary release of that pent-up despair.

While no "good" comes out of losing the people we love, we do develop empathy and compassion through these losses. It is hard to have true empathy, as opposed to sympathy, for someone who is going through something you yourself have never experienced. While my own grief has caused me to pity myself and ask *why me*, it also taught me that we all suffer. To be part of humankind, we must suffer. Through this recognition comes renewed empathy, compassion, and even gratitude. Eventually, we can also experience joy.

We must experience the range of emotions that fill this messy life, but once we have, we can recall what we are grateful for and the reasons we have loved deeply. At the end of the day, it always pays to focus on what we have rather than what we don't have. We can practice recognizing and being mindful of the positive, just like practicing any other skill. We can consciously focus on the positive, the bright side of life, which brings more positive thoughts. The mind multiplies whatever we bring to it, and if we bring it appreciation, gratitude, and love, we will get more of each.

Sadness and Grief versus Depression

There is a big difference between sadness and grief on the one hand, and depression on the other. Sadness and grief are emotions we all feel eventually. They are part of the human condition.[76] We all experience sadness in response to difficult, hurtful, challenging, or disappointing events, experiences, or situations. We all experience grief after loving deeply and losing our loved ones. When we experience sadness, we feel sad *about something*. The same is true of grief. We are grieving something or someone. These feelings of sadness and grief come and go. The sadness eventually dissipates a bit. While grieving can go on for a long time, it has a very specific cause.

Depression, on the other hand, is a mental illness that affects our thinking, emotions, perceptions, and behaviors in chronic ways. When we're depressed, we feel sad about *everything*. Depression is not necessarily triggered by an event. It is a general malaise that permeates our very beings. Experts say that experiencing five or more of these at a time indicates that one is likely depressed and could benefit from professional help:

1. A depressed or irritable mood most of the time.

2. A loss or decrease of pleasure or interest in most activities, including ones that had been interesting or pleasurable previously.

3. Significant changes in weight or appetite.

4. Disturbances in falling asleep or sleeping too much.

5. Feeling slowed down in one's movements or restless most days.

6. Feeling tired and sluggish, and having low energy most days.

7. Having feelings of worthlessness or excessive guilt most days.

8. Experiencing problems with thinking, focus, concentration, creativity, and the ability to make decisions most days.

9. Having thoughts of dying or suicide.[77]

Despite being psychologically abnormal, clinical depression is extremely common in our culture. Between 6 and 7 percent of the US population suffers from it. Growing up with a bipolar mother prone to periodic suicidal ideations, I know that clinical depression can be fatal. As we sometimes say in my family, suicide is a long-term solution to a short-term problem. Yet this is inaccurate too as depression, left untreated, is a very long-term problem.

While sadness and grief do not require professional help, depression does need to be treated professionally. If you have doubts about yourself or a loved one, go see someone. Personally, I think everyone benefits from therapy, depressed or not. It is the ultimate self-indulgence.

As we leave this discussion of depression and sadness, it helps to remember that sadness will come for all of us. Just like grief and aging go hand in hand, so do sadness and aging. As explored by Atul Gawande in *Being Mortal*, aging is often accompanied by three plagues: boredom, loneliness, and dependence.[78] All three plagues can make us sad. Staying active and connected helps fight the plagues, but there will always be some sadness. If you like music, consider creating your own sad playlist now. Also, reread your response to Purpose Practice 4.1 and create a preemptive plan for self-care to use when you feel really sad.

Dealing with Fear and Anxiety

Continuing with our discussion of dealing with difficult emotions as we age, we now turn to fear and anxiety. Fear and anxiety are common at any age, but with so many things going wrong, they can increase with age. We can't escape fear or anxiety, nor would we want to. None of us would survive without fear and anxiety. We would take unnecessary risks and get eaten by the modern-day equivalent of a saber-toothed tiger.

In prehistoric days, we needed to be able to run from tigers and other predators. Since life depended on it, we became hardwired to watch out for danger through fear and anxiety.[79] Today, though, we utilize this biological flight, fight, or freeze response on much smaller stressors that are not life or death. We face mini stresses all day, things like driving in traffic, dealing with difficult colleagues, minor health problems, and other little life annoyances. We unnecessarily create more lions and tigers and bears, oh my!

By now we have also faced some really terrorizing realities: death, disease, poverty, and addiction, as well as societal ills like ageism, racism, sexism, violence, and homelessness, not to mention multiple wars, attacks on democracy, and climate change. All activate our flight, fight, or freeze response, but the flight, fight, or freeze response does not help with these modern life stressors. It usually makes things worse.

One goal of mindful practices is to neutralize the flight, fight, or freeze response caused by fear and anxiety, and reduce their frequent byproducts: sleeplessness, weight gain or loss, and reduction in overall health. As we discussed in chapter 3, the hormones released by anxiety, fear, and stress in general weaken the immune system and can lead to major health catastrophes like heart attacks, cancer, and disabling accidents. As we age, these threats are more pronounced because the body is weaker. As such, healthy aging requires managing anxiety.[80]

Anxiety also wastes a lot of energy, another thing that can be in short supply as we age. Neuroscientist Alex Korb give a great example of how anxiety wastes time in his book *The Upward Spiral: Using Neuroscience to Reverse the Course of Depression, One Small Change at a Time*.[81] He worked himself into a lather over a dinner party he was throwing when he realized he needed to shower and clean his apartment in addition to making the food. His anxiety slowed him down and cost him an extra twenty minutes in wasted time. While stressing out over the party, he also missed a call from his guests saying they'd be half an hour late. Without the anxiety attack, he would have had more than enough time.[82] This is a small, relatively unimportant example of how anxiety hurts us.

Throughout my interviews, anxiety was a subject that came up a lot, even though I did not ask about it. From these interviews, I have seen that some of the things that cause us anxiety are minimal and fleeting, like the dinner party. Others are more serious. Whether these experiences are small or significant, they always feel like a big deal to the person experiencing them.

For example, one of my interviewees, Lucia, an accountant in a big-five accounting firm who retooled into a career in real estate, said she worries all the time about hurting people. She is super sensitive and I find it hard to believe she survived big-five accounting as long as she did. Lucia was beating herself up over an incident involving an attorney who made a mistake in one of her deals. Lucia could have corrected it if she had noticed. While the mistake was harmless in the end, the other agent in the deal told Lucia she needed to turn the lawyer in because he was not doing an adequate job. Lucia felt like it was her fault that she did not catch the error. She had repetitive, negative, doomsday thoughts for days. She just could not forgive herself. She even thought she might lose her license when she held her ground and refused to turn in the lawyer. It worked out in the end, but she was still distraught weeks later. Yet the anxiety did not serve any purpose.

Another interviewee said that because her mother lived in Germany during World War II, her mother saved everything and was imbued with a permanent scarcity mentality. Her daughter, my interviewee, hated these habits but could not shake them. She had running anxiety about wasting time, material things, food, and so on, no matter what she did. However, talking about it and recognizing the anxiety helped. By recognizing where these thoughts came from, and by watching her subconscious mind berating itself and then talking back to that voice, she was able to separate herself, at least somewhat, from these fears. Being conscious of her anxiety did not eliminate it but did release its hold on her, and she felt much better.

Emotions Are Experienced in the Physical Body First

We often blame our thoughts for our emotions, but we have it backward. This image, from a *US News* article entitled "Study

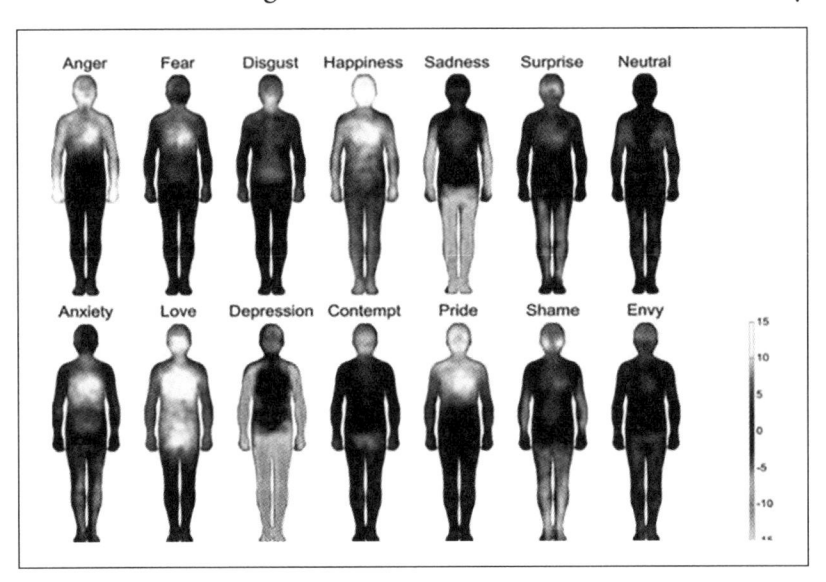

Finds Emotions Can Be Mapped to the Body," shows how the body changes when we experience various emotions. The image visually demonstrates that emotions are experienced in the body, not as thoughts in the mind.[83]

After emotions originate in the physical body, we later create thoughts around these emotions that manifest as experiences of the mind. In scientific terms, we can observe the limbic system of the brain and actually see where excitement, fear, anxiety, memory, and desire originate.[84]

Scientists who study the brain design studies that measure the impact of stress on the brain and cognition. As a result of these studies, they can provide advice on how to reduce unnecessary stress and anxiety. For example, depressed people have high activity in the amygdala portion of the brain, which regulates fear and anxiety. People can learn to reduce amygdala activity and relieve stress and anxiety, and even mild depression.

Being anxious is the brain's natural reaction to perceived danger, so don't be too hard on yourself for being anxious. Just watch out if it seems chronic. Remind yourself that anxiety impedes clear thinking and is bad for your brain and the rest of your body.[85] Below, we provide some tips on reducing anxiety and fear in your life that can also help reduce grief and mild depression.

Tips on Reducing Anxiety, Sadness, Grief, and Depression

As we have seen, anxiety activates the fear circuit, the same neural circuitry that keeps us out of danger from saber-toothed tigers.[86] This fear circuit can be mediated by calming and placating the amygdala and the hippocampus, the parts of the brain activated by our emotions.[87] We can develop mindful, conscious awareness of anxiety as it arises. We can name it "anxiety" and try to identify its cause.[88]

Based upon the knowledge that things will happen in life to disrupt our status quo, see if you can move toward mindful acceptance that anxiety will happen. See if you can see it and name it as you experience it.[89] Try to focus on the present moment.[90] Worry is never in the present tense. It is always about something that happened in the past or might happen in the future.[91]

Staying present and self-examining the triggers of an emotion can activate the prefrontal circuits of the brain, which can in turn calm the limbic system and the prefrontal cortex. To do this, Korb suggests we put our emotions into words.[92] He suggests we feel the emotions without attaching emotional reactivity to them. Just feel them and write it down.[93] Use your notebook for this.

> **PURPOSE PRACTICE 4.2**
>
> Take Korb's advice. Next time you experience anxiety, fully feel that anxiety, and then name it in your journal. Don't judge it or react emotionally, just write about the experience for what it is.

The exercise in Purpose Practice 4.2 above can improve our brain's function, not to mention make life a little easier. This is mindfulness in action. As Korb explains, all mindfulness activities reduce worry and anxiety by temporarily cutting off worry and anxiety at the source.[94] While Korb writes mostly about helping relieve clinical depression, his tips are also useful for allaying anxiety and sadness, both of which—if left unchecked—can lead to clinical depression.

Here are a few more of his anxiety and sadness-busting tips, mixed in with some of my own.

1. Move your body. Moving your body will create new neurons in the hippocampus and relieve negative emotions. Hate exercise? Call it something else. Just get outside and move for some other reason, to see a friend,

watch a sporting event, watch birds, whatever it takes. Do not just sit inside. Go out. Bring a friend for accountability.[95] Remember that exercise improves sleep and being outdoors calms the soul.[96]

2. Do some yoga. Korb suggests that yoga, in particular, can provide your body with immediate biofeedback, giving the brain useful and calming information about how the mind and body are connecting.[97] Yoga can also help open the front body (avoid slumping) and help you to stand up straighter, which improves mood.[98]

3. For another tip on keeping the back straight, which improves mood, put a pillow or a blow-up lumbar roll behind your low back at the base of your chair, as well as your car seat. While seated at a desk, sit on an exercise ball for part of your day. You can buy a stand-up desk or, if you really want to go for it, explore getting a treadmill desk. Standing up helps, as does sitting up straight. Your posture determines your level of alertness.

4. Breathe and relax, whatever that takes. While there are many breathing exercises throughout this book, one easy way to reduce anxiety is to lengthen both the in-breath and the out-breath, taking a moment to notice the little pause between the in-breath and the out-breath. Then, as you feel ready, begin to lengthen the exhale so it is longer than the inhale. The longer exhale will calm the nervous system, reduce the fight, flight, or freeze response, and improve brain function, something we all appreciate.[99]

5. Fight perfection. Accept that you will not be perfect. Imperfection is the human condition. As Korb says, "It is better to do something only partly right than to do nothing at all."[100] In other words, perfection is the enemy

of good. If you are out there making some mistakes, it means you are out there doing something. Keep going!

6. Develop long-term goals. Long-term goals create good habits and fire up the brain in all the right ways.[101] The reasons for this are technical, so bear with me. The part of your brain that creates emotion (your amygdala) evaluates the degree to which the goal is important to you.[102] It and the frontal lobe work together to keep you focused on, and moving toward, situations and behaviors that lead to the achievement of that goal, while simultaneously causing you to ignore and avoid situations and behaviors that don't.[103] Due to neuroplasticity in the brain (the brain's ability to rewire itself in response to learning and stimuli), goal-setting literally changes the structure of your brain so it's optimized to achieve your goal. This phenomenon was discovered in a study of multiple sclerosis (MS) patients, which found that MS patients who set ambitious wellness goals had fewer negative MS-related changes in the brain than a control group. Goal setting literally helped heal these MS patients' brains and can help you ignite your brain as well. You don't need to have MS to benefit from a goal-setting practice, and the goal can be anything. You need not aim to win a Pulitzer Prize or find a cure for cancer. Any goal will fire up your brain.

Try to incorporate as many of Korb's suggestions into your life as you can, and for starters, try this breathing exercise.

PURPOSE PRACTICE 4.3

Take ten long, deep breaths in and out, and really sigh out the mouth on the exhale. Make it loud and fun. Count them and keep your focus on these breaths. As other thoughts arise, acknowledge them, and let them go, bringing your attention back to your breath.

Practice this throughout your day today and notice any changes in your body.

One last tip for alleviating anxiety is to assign someone or something else to worry about the thing that is vexing you. This could be another person or perhaps a symbolic assignee like a worry doll. Andean women make little thread dolls called *worry dolls* and sell them in bamboo boxes. My mother and I used these when times were tough, especially when her partner Saul almost died of sinus cancer. To use the dolls, you take them out of the box at bedtime and assign one doll to worry about each thing that is bothering you, or if it is a big worry, they can all worry about the same thing. While I don't always like to think about worries right before bed, so do not use this as a regular bedtime ritual, sometimes the mind will not let go of the worry at bedtime. The worry dolls give you a place to leave that worry while you get a good night's sleep.

It is all about intention here and this exercise sets an intention to get that stubborn brain to let go of that worry for the night. Worst case scenario, you'll play with some dolls for a few moments and get relief from your worries while you do. Best case scenario, you'll get a longer break from your worries and get a good night's sleep.

Dealing with Anger

Having discussed sadness, grief, depression, anxiety, and fear, we will now turn to one last emotion for this chapter: anger. Anger can sneak up on us and can harm others. Again, we have all been there. Even renowned Buddhist nun Pema Chödrön tells a story of blowing up at her granddaughter and then cheekily asking the little girl not to tell anyone, especially someone carrying one of grandma's books.[104]

When you're experiencing a negative emotion like anger, it can help neutralize the emotion to picture an emotion inconsistent with the negative one, such as picturing compassion to replace anger. While you can only replace a negative emotion with a positive one *after* you have allowed yourself to truly feel the original emotion, replacement frees you up to feel positivity. The exercise below suggests another effective way to neutralize anger, from Mirabai Bush, in her CD *Working with Mindfulness*.[105]

PURPOSE PRACTICE 4.4

This exercise is called the ninety-second feel. Bring a recent situation to mind that made you really angry. Set a timer for ninety seconds. Tighten your fists as much as you can. Force yourself to feel that anger as hard and as much as you possibly can for the full ninety seconds. Do not let go and keep squeezing. At ninety seconds, release the fist and release the thought. Pretty cool, right? You can try this with sadness too if you, like me, are more prone to sadness than anger. You can also try it with any emotion that is causing circular, repetitive, or negative thoughts. It is amazing how sick of that emotion you can become after ninety seconds.

The ninety second feel is a favorite because it is so active. We can be proactive about addressing anger.

Like all other emotions, anger is sending us a message. In his book, *Overcoming Destructive Anger: Strategies That Work*, Bernard Golden explains that anger lets us know that we are suffering from distress and can motivate us to address our underlying needs, desires, or perceived threats.[106] Because *unprocessed* anger can lead to "conflict, social isolation, problems at work, substance abuse, depression, shame, and even incarceration," Golden describes what triggers anger, how it affects our bodies and our minds, and what we can do to manage it.[107] We all feel anger. It is what we do with it that matters.

CHAPTER FOUR

Some people are biologically or socially predisposed to feel more anger than others, but we all feel anger and deal with it somehow, often through one of three unconstructive ways: to get outright aggressive, to get passive aggressive, or to turn that anger on ourselves.[108] To deal with anger more productively, Golden offers the following tips:

1. Manage your expectations. Try to figure out what expectations you have of others and think about those. For example, Golden says you may feel that your family or friends should always be available to help you or that you should never feel the effects of aging. Expectations like these will lead to disappointment because they are unrealistic.

2. Assess how you appraise or view a triggering event. We often attribute deeper meaning to events than these events actually have. This occurs most when we are focused exclusively on ourselves and our own needs and insecurities, rather than also considering the needs and insecurities of others. Golden uses the example of a partner who comes home late from work. This lateness feels disrespectful to the partner waiting at home, unless you consider it from the late, stuck-in-traffic spouse's point of view. Getting caught in traffic is a real pain.

3. Consider whether the anger is connected to some other emotion or event, or perhaps even hiding a more subtle emotion such as sadness, hurt, disappointment, anxiety, embarrassment, shame, or loneliness. Golden suggests we use mindfulness techniques to identify the root of the emotions underlying the anger.[109]

Mindfulness can help with anger. If we are paying attention, we get the opportunity to choose how to respond to the events around us. Studies show that mindfulness helps us differentiate between different emotions and, as a result, better regulate negative emotions. In one study, Daphne Davis and Jeffrey Hayes found that high levels of mindfulness predict "relationship satisfaction, ability to respond constructively to relationship stress, skill in identifying and communicating emotions to one's partner, amount of relationship conflict, negativity, and empathy."[110] In addition, people with higher mindfulness "reported less emotional stress in response to relationship conflict and entered difficult discussions with less anger and anxiety."[111] In this context, being mindful just means pausing to think about how you feel and pausing before you respond. These are excellent results for just doing a bit of pausing, feeling, and thinking before acting.

In summary, getting in touch with our emotions helps us regulate our behaviors and respond with thought and compassion rather than anger. Just creating space between the emotion that is first experienced in the body and our reaction to this emotion can help us to avoid harmful behaviors. Learning to watch our breath and to notice the space between the in breath and the out breath can train us to experience the emotion first before reacting to it.

To practice this, see if you can breathe for a short time and again, take note of that little pause between the in breath and the out breath. See if this noting can become part of your everyday experience. Use this pause between the in breath and the out breath as a break before you react to a difficult situation. Respond, don't react. This one practice can improve the quality of your life.

Developing Body Awareness and Emotional Mindfulness

Being aware of our feelings can help us resolve them and also help us respond to our feelings less harmfully. Sometimes things just feel off and we don't know why. We feel sad or upset but the precise feelings are unknown. We just don't feel happy or at peace. Remember that emotions are experienced in the body, not the mind. The mind only experiences *the thoughts* associated with an emotion. For every negative emotion, even ones of which we are unaware, there is a physiological response—often pain, tightness, agida,[112] and constriction.

One place we store negative emotional energy, such as anger, anxiety, and sadness, is in the hips. To release some of that energy and help identify an emotion being experienced, I suggest this modification of the yoga pose, pigeon:

PURPOSE PRACTICE 4.5

Start in an upright seated position in a chair with your feet on the ground and your hands at your sides. Reach down and grab your right ankle. Place the right ankle above the left knee. Sit up nice and tall, with your shoulders back and your chest lifted. Keep your neck straight and head looking forward.

Gently hinge forward at the hip crease with a neutral spine. Do not force the right knee to drop; it may be very high, but that just means you need a good hip stretch. (Make sure you feel sensation in the hip or thigh, not in the knee. You may even hug the knee in toward you if that helps you avoid knee strain.)

Gently twist your ribcage to the right and the left, gazing gently in the direction of the twist. Allow the tension in the hip to release. Hold for five long breaths and switch to the other side. Feel the release. Go slow and allow the body to really release the emotion.

You can also do this figure-four pose on your back. These are seated and prone versions of pigeon or half pigeon. Pigeon pose relieves and releases emotions held in the hips. It is not uncommon to cry while in this pose, which I consider a home run. The point, after all, is to identify and relieve an emotion. Even if the emotion is not identified, relieving and releasing the emotion improves our mood.

Doing this pose recently, I identified an emotion I did not know I had. I was feeling out of sorts but not really angry, sad, or anxious. The emotion turned out to be disappointment, following a series of small setbacks. As Bruce Feiler explains in *Life Is in the Transitions*, small setbacks combined can feel like one large setback.[113] Yet small setbacks are hard to explain to others because it is not any one big thing. It is hard to garner much compassion or even feel worthy of compassion or understanding when, for example, my husband has a bad back and our dog is getting old and frail.

In our case, our disappointment stemmed from missing part of the only full-year sabbatical we would ever have, during which we were supposed to be focusing on important work outside of our everyday life, including writing this book. Everything seemed to be going wrong. The activities of daily living were overwhelming due to the need for medical care that was unavailable. The dog was aging, perhaps dying. The weather was bad. We were living in a community without friends and did not know the community norms so were not fully accepted. There was no social safety net, and it was unclear how long the situation would last. We were not really angry or depressed or grieving, but we were disappointed that things were not going the way we had anticipated. This was supposed to be the "best time of our lives" and was turning out to be the opposite.

Identifying these disappointments in detail was helpful because it made us grateful for our regular, everyday lives, the New Mexico community in which we normally live, the friends we have, our knowledge of community norms, the weather in our town, the doctors we know, the veterinarians we know, and the sheer abundance of good things in our lives we often take for granted. We were able to rewrite our disappointed victim story into one of gratitude and perseverance. We were also able to see that while the situation was hard, it wasn't the worst, and it wouldn't last forever.

CHAPTER FOUR

Tamping Down Negative Emotions through Recognition and Rewiring

While we need to experience our emotions in order to work through them, there are also times when we need to redirect an emotion in order to avoid hurting ourselves and others. Mindfulness can help us recognize emotions but also neutralize them, an emotional intelligence technique. Psychologist Robert Plutchik's wheel of emotions helps us identify the emotion we are experiencing. It is reproduced and described here:

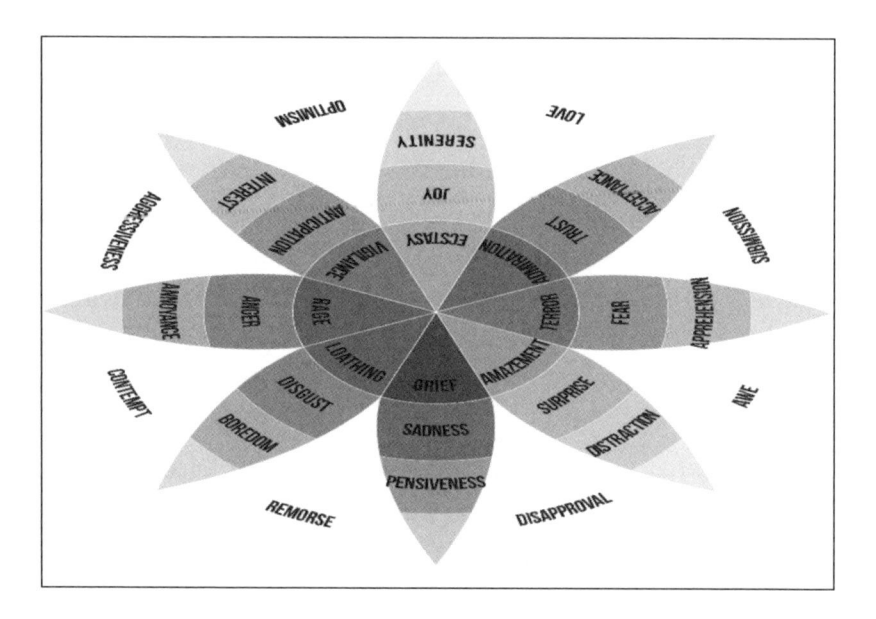

The wheel identifies eight basic emotions: joy, trust, fear, surprise, sadness, anticipation, anger, and disgust. Its framework helps bring clarity to emotions, which can sometimes feel mysterious and overwhelming. We can use the wheel to identify emotions and deescalate them so we can function and think before we act.

The cone's vertical dimension represents intensity—emotions intensify as they move from the outside to the center of the wheel, which is also indicated by the shading. The darker the shade and the closer to the center, the more intense the emotion. For example, anger at its least level of intensity is annoyance. At its highest level of intensity, anger becomes rage. Similarly, a feeling of boredom can intensify to loathing if left unchecked.

As discussed above, you need to experience an emotion in order to work through it. But once you *have* experienced and identified an emotion, you can often move a negative emotion such as rage, grief, or loathing from the center circle of emotions into the emotions found in the middle area of the chart, meaning anger, disgust, or sadness. You may even be able to neutralize that emotion into the outer circle of emotions, such as annoyance, boredom, and pensiveness.

To neutralize the emotion, journal about the emotion and how it feels to really face it. Include in detail both the body's and the mind's reaction to the situation, the facts, why you feel angry or sad, and so on. If there is another person involved, write down what you would say to that person and what you think they would say back. In other words, visualize it. Play it out in your mind. Then sit and breathe slowly. Note the effects of this intentional breath on the body and the mind. Calm down and see what you're feeling. Let some time pass and imagine how you will feel about this situation in six months or six years. Depending on what the situation and the feeling is, you may feel the emotion lessening its grip and neutralizing to the outer emotions on Plutchik's wheel. Now that it is all down on paper, see if you can let it go entirely.

This neutralizing process is a practice that gets easier with time. It is helpful to practice the process before engaging with others. You can respond later or more slowly, rather than in the moment, which will allow you to respond but not react. After enough observation and experience with these difficult emotions, they may eventually be felt only briefly and then just go away, almost on their own. Chade-Meng Tan, who ran Google's mindfulness program and wrote the book *Search Inside Yourself*, describes this process as feeling an emotion and watching it disappear like writing on water.[114] Acknowledge the emotion, feel it, live it, and then let yourself leave it.

Keep in mind there will always be some conflict and the need to manage conflict. For example, working with retirees in the fight against homelessness, one told me, "There are two camps when it comes to solutions for the unhoused. Some say you need to get clean first, then you can live inside. Others say, give people housing first, so they can get clean. I am in the housing first camp." Who knew there were camps in the coalition to help the unhoused?

Dealing with People Who Are Difficult to Love

Finally, the last topic we will cover in this chapter is dealing with people who are difficult to love. Few things are more unpleasant than dealing with difficult people. We all know people like this. Also, at one time or another each of us has been that difficult person. This exercise helps remove some of the judgment behind dealing with a difficult person. Nonjudgment is a yoga principle and practice that frees us from much suffering by letting us see things as they are, without (you guessed it) judgment.

Before we address how to deal with "difficult people," consider this story from Jack Kornfield's *After the Ecstasy, the Laundry*, in which he recounts a story of one Buddhist nun's difficulty with two other nuns:

> In my second community there were only a dozen nuns. I liked all but two. One was lazy and the other was self-absorbed. After my first year I was in the kitchen complaining to a friend, who said, "You know these are really not bad people. What is it that gets to you?" I said, "One is lazy and the other takes too much care of herself," and she replied, "Well, you ought to be more lazy and take better care of yourself!"[115]

Do you see the point of this story? Before we label someone difficult, we should try to find our own part in the difficulty. It takes two to tango, as my mother-in-law used to say. For example, I am sometimes in conflict with a colleague who is meticulous and detail-oriented and a strict follower of rules. I, on the other hand, am flexible about almost everything and not a detail person, both sometimes to a fault. Is it surprising that we are at odds?

Turning to your own situation, are you sure that the person you are having difficulty with is the difficult one? Could you be the difficult person? Might you be at least part of the problem? Recall that fixing *part* of a problem is far better than fixing nothing at all. Fixing your part is the only part within your control.

> **PURPOSE PRACTICE 4.6**
>
> Pick out someone with whom you have had difficulties at work or in another setting. How do you two differ? Are there ways in which the problems are just a matter of style? Do others seem to get along fine or at least better with this person? Even if not, see if you can use this exercise to learn something new about yourself. Write a paragraph or two about these issues.

Sometimes people are difficult for anyone to deal with. Sometimes it really *is* the other person and has nothing to do with you. In these situations, you should try not to be defensive and not to take the other person's comments and actions personally. Try to differentiate between situations in which you are part of the problem and situations where the other person is just being difficult. Go back and reconsider the last Purpose Practice.

After you have taken these steps, if the difficulty remains, consider these two questions:

1. What can you do to protect yourself without engaging in activity (or inaction) that harms you, harms others, or pushes you to do something out of character?

2. Is there anything you can do to help the other person?

Notice the order of these questions. Put your own mask on first before assisting others. If the answer to question two is no, and it is possible to limit your interactions with this person, do your best to disengage and move on.

If you cannot disengage because future interactions are required, remind yourself that this person is difficult to love, but don't give up on them. Just don't spend much mental energy thinking about the person. Remember that your mind is valuable real estate. Accept the situation for what it is and give it as little airtime as possible.

Parting Thoughts on Dealing with Difficult Emotions

Just as Rumi says in his poem reproduced above, this being human truly is a guest house. Emotions come and they go and we must experience them. After we experience them, we have a choice about how to react. We can choose to react in kind, we can do very little in reaction, or we can try to improve situations through our own insights and emotional intelligence. We will not have the energy to take on every battle, nor should we. Just know that, as long as we are mindful of the choices we are making, we have the capacity to do what is best.

We can train ourselves to work through difficult emotions and create more peace in our lives and the lives of others. Thankfully, we are better at this as we age because our vast experience tells us that these things will pass. We just need to remind ourselves of that fact. In the next chapter, we will tackle how to love and forgive.

CHAPTER 5:
LEARNING TO LOVE AND FORGIVE

In this chapter, we practice loving both ourselves and others. We also learn how to express love before it is too late. We discuss how and why we might want to reduce guilt and forgive ourselves and others.

The Importance of Self-Compassion in Dealing with Negative Emotions

In the last chapter, we discussed how to deal with negative emotions. Here we add self-compassion. Consciously weaving self-compassion into our daily practices can reduce negative emotions and improve your relationships, including your relationship with yourself. I work on self-compassion with my therapist because this practice does not come easily for me. Often, the easiest way for me to feel better about myself is to work more and harder. My logic is that if I work a lot, I will feel less busy and feeling less busy will be self-compassionate. This is not an ideal self-compassion practice, however. As my therapist likes to say, something more direct might work better.

CHAPTER FIVE

Self-compassion is a secular construct drawn from Buddhist psychology. More specifically, it is a way of relating to the self with kindness. Self-kindness is the opposite of arrogance. In fact, arrogance and conceit are signs of a lack of self-love.

Dr. Kristin Neff was the first person to measure and define the term "self-compassion."[116] She describes self-compassion as kindness toward the self, which entails being gentle, supportive, and understanding. As she explains, rather than harshly judging oneself for personal shortcomings, we can offer ourselves warmth and unconditional acceptance. By being kind to ourselves in good times and bad, in sickness and in health, even when we make mistakes, we turn ourselves into kinder and more compassionate people. This improves our relationships and benefits ourselves and others.

For years I have wondered why these practices are so difficult for almost everyone. It is likely because we have so few good role models in our lives for these practices. Many of us got the message as children that we were not good enough and were not worthy of love or compassion, and many of our parents were also sent the same messages. If this is true, it is not hard to see why most people don't cherish themselves in a way that would create self-love. This lack of self-love also makes it more difficult to love others.

According to Dr. Neff, having self-compassion means being able to recognize the difference between making a bad decision and being a bad person. When you have self-compassion, you understand that your worth as a person is unconditional.

Dr. Neff researches the mental differences between people with high self-esteem and those with high self-compassion. Here is how Dr. Neff differentiates between the two:

> *Self-esteem* means the extent to which we evaluate ourselves positively. It represents how much we like or value ourselves and is often based on comparisons with others. In contrast, self-compassion is not based on positive judgments or evaluations, it is a way of relating to ourselves. [Self-compassion]

> emphasizes interconnection rather than separateness. This means that with self-compassion, you don't have to feel better than others to feel good about yourself. It also offers more emotional stability than self-esteem because it is always there for you when you're on top of the world and when you fall flat on your face.[117]

Dr. Neff's research shows that self-compassion creates more benefits and fewer detriments than mere self-esteem.[118] Neff's research demonstrates that self-compassion increases emotional resilience and stability, and decreases negative self-evaluations, defensiveness, and the need to see oneself as better than others.[119]

Compared to people with high self-esteem, self-compassionate people are less likely to compare themselves to others. They are also less likely to get angry at others for perceived offenses.[120] People high in self-compassion also think about negative events in ways that reduce the effects of these negative events,[121] and self-compassionate participants have more thoughts of self-kindness, common humanity, and mindful acceptance.[122] All of this helps process and neutralize anger and leads to greater success and happiness in all aspects of life.[123]

But how do we practice self-compassion? These practices include things like developing a growth mindset, cross-examining and rejecting negative self-talk, treating ourselves like we would treat a friend or a small child, and celebrating ourselves in some way when we make a mistake, in recognition that we are human, and imperfect. Recall that perfection is both unattainable and boring. People don't even like other people who seem perfect, so be happy that you make mistakes in your life.

It helps to actually label these practices as self-compassion. That way, we can remember them. Recalling this discussion, we can remember the benefits of these practices and know that we are improving our lives. Self-compassion is very practical. Once we master it, it feels good!

CHAPTER FIVE

Self-Compassion Tips

Self-compassion can be harder for people who derive most of their sense of worth from their professional accomplishments. Those tendencies to compare ourselves to others can make us feel lesser. According to Dr. Neff, these three steps can help us connect with self-compassion:

1. Find ways to be kind to ourselves and to soothe and comfort ourselves when we are in pain. Suggestions are to put ourselves first in our priorities and be as kind to ourselves as we are to others.

2. Accept that to be human is to suffer. Without it, we would not be human. Also, we are not alone in this. We all suffer. This recognition can help us feel connected to other people, rather than disconnected and alone.

3. Use our mindfulness practices to sit with and acknowledge our own pain and validate it. Ignoring our pain keeps it with us. Feeling it helps us move it through our systems. The only way out is through. We need to notice our suffering before we can move beyond it and do something about it. When we see clearly and accept the things in life over which we have no control, we can respond wisely to our challenges. We can change our story.[124]

Self-compassion falls into the broader category of self-care, which also includes slowing down and noting moments of joy. Chip Conley calls these underlooked moments. Here is a list of some of his:

> Sunset walks with my dog Jamie in Baja, playing hide-and-seek with my sons in our tropical palm orchard, listening to *The Miseducation of Lauryn Hill*, slow rambles through Balinese rice fields, the Telluride Film Festival, the scene

with the swirling plastic bag in *American Beauty*, reading the Sunday *New York Times* in the bath while listening to any Ennio Morricone soundtrack, my mom's spaghetti.[125]

While Conley does not call these practices self-care, or even really a practice, any time you allow yourself time and space to savor life, you are engaging in valuable self-care. Conley's list reminds us, for example, to never be too busy to enjoy a sunset.[126]

If you are or ever have been addicted to work, you might fall into the trap of feeling that you don't deserve a nap, a bath, or an hour with a good book, until you have accomplished something. See if you can loosen your grip on that thought. You deserve to be well taken care of regardless of what you have accomplished today.

More on the Beauty in Mistakes

You will need humility to practice self-compassion. Humility is another trait people love in others. How will you choose to respond to your mistakes? With self-compassion? With humility? With worthwhile knowledge from which you can learn? See if you can celebrate imperfection, humility, and growth.[127]

Mistakes make us human. While making mistakes is our quickest path to self-improvement, it takes courage and work to learn from our mistakes. Yet making mistakes is human. Put simply, mistakes happen, but the pain does not have to be wasted. We can live and learn. Often the seemingly biggest mistakes come with the biggest rewards.

PURPOSE PRACTICE 5.1

Write a few sentences about a big mistake that ended up creating personal rewards for you.

I recall a time when I mixed up the days of the week and did not show up for my very first class of the semester. I was sitting in my office in sweatpants when a student arrived at the door and asked me if I was coming to class. I was mortified and had no choice but to go to the class in my sweatpants and teach a class for which I had not prepared. The same student later told me that this class session was one of her favorites in law school. She said it was the first time she realized that professors are real people, just like everybody else. The memory still makes me shudder a bit, but also demonstrates what our mistakes can do for us and others.

It is hard to celebrate mistakes, but it is a skill worth mastering. My friend and collaborator, Bonnie Bassan, says that every time she makes a mistake, she tells herself, "I'm sexy." The idea is to accept that you will make mistakes and not beat yourself up over it. You can also just tell yourself, "Thank goodness I made that mistake. Now I can learn something that will really help me in my life."

Dealing with Guilt, Shame, and Regret

Of all the unpleasant emotions out there, guilt and its relative shame are my least favorite. I feel guilty about all sorts of things, even though I know guilt is a genuine joy robber. They say that guilt is what you feel inside yourself and shame is what you feel when you fear others have or will find out about all those terrible things you have done.

Guilt often results from one of two things: first, the things we shouldn't have done, and second, the things we could've or should've done or done better. There is always regret. These feelings plague many of us and get in the way of a happy healthy life. It is absolutely true that there are things we shouldn't have done and things that we could've done or done better, but beating ourselves up over it doesn't help anybody. It's good to note what we could do differently or what we wish we had done better, but wallowing in guilt serves no purpose.

We can benefit by forgiving ourselves for things we did in the past. The sooner the better as these feelings don't help us. In terms of what we could have done better or more of, let's face one reality. We cannot do everything we want to do. We have limitations. Accepting these limitations is a form of humility and self-love. Conversely, feeling guilty about not doing more in situations in which we have already done a lot exaggerates our importance in the world and is a form of savior complex. Much in these stories is untrue. We really have done enough. Repeating this mantra can help:

> "I do enough, I have enough, I am enough."

But believe me, this is not easy. We fail to forgive ourselves in situations in which another person *would* forgive us. For example, one interviewee told me this story. In his first year of college, his mother passed away. He regretted staying enrolled in college, rather than returning home to help support his father and take care of his younger brother. His mentors at college suggested his mother would want him to continue, so he did, but here he is, sixty years later, still feeling badly about this. He was just eighteen at the time, had just lost his mother, and had no one from whom to seek advice but his professors. They had their own reasons for wanting him to stay in school, and it was heartbreaking to think of all the hours of regret this man had endured in his nearly eighty years. This is a classic example of guilt over a long-passed event that serves no purpose and continues to cause pain.

I can relate to this story as I still experience guilt related to how I cobbled together care for my elderly father. His body failed him, but his mind was as sharp as a tack. When I had to move him to a small care home from his beloved independent living community where he played bridge and hung out with other fellow academics, he looked up at me and said, "So this is it, huh? The last stop." I remain crushed by this comment. Then, a year or so later, the day he went on hospice, I went home for the night. My regret was deep when he died alone the very next morning. If I had known, I would have stayed the night. How could I have known, though? We always think we have more time. In any case, it hasn't helped me to continue to berate myself about this.

Ironically, after he died, several people told me they respected the way I cared for him, yet I repeatedly told myself I could have done more. This shows how hard it is to stop beating ourselves up about being human. We eventually need to let go of things that we wish we had done differently. Guilt helps no one. We deserve our own forgiveness. This is especially true when the person we have harmed is already deceased. We can no longer apologize but we can forgive ourselves.

People sometimes say that their relationship with someone who has already died actually strengthens and improves after their death. This may sound impossible given that the dead person is gone, but it is our role in the story that we can rewrite. In order to heal, we need to rethink our relationship with those who have departed. We need to leave the guilt and turn our focus to the living. This is how we heal.

Healing can take many forms if we can remember that guilt never serves us. This reminds me of another story from my own life, this time dealing with my mother's death. She had bipolar disorder and, in my childlike perception, "abandoned" my father and me when I was six or seven years old. Like many of us, on one level or another, I have spent my life working though this feeling of abandonment.

At my mother's memorial, one of her cousins explained that when I fell and cut my knee doing a task she had asked me to do, my mother concluded that being around me in her depressed and sometimes suicidal state could harm me. She felt she was a danger to me, which is why she left. Hearing this story changed my perception of her "abandonment" but it was, of course, too late to tell her that I understood.

While it is too late to express forgiveness to her, I can certainly work through it myself. There are ways in which I showed my love for my mother, and I can choose to focus on those when I feel I didn't do enough. I can rewrite my own story about giving and forgiving, even though I can't tell her.

Guilt from things that we should've done or shouldn't have done is hard to release but can be done through the practice of self-compassion. Through these practices, we change our self-illusions from stories of guilt to stories about compassion and gratefulness. We heal ourselves by changing our own perceptions about the past.

Human beings hurt one another, and there are no exceptions.[128] We all hurt others and as a result, we all suffer. We all have felt regret, shame, guilt, self-hatred, and self-blame for breaking our word and hurting others. Once we can truly forgive ourselves, we are on our way to forgiving others.

> **PURPOSE PRACTICE 5.2**
>
> Think of something you're still beating yourself up about, some past act. Describe the act in one phrase on a scrap of paper. Just before the phrase, write "I forgive myself for _____." Read it out loud several times. Use it like a mantra until you start to forgive yourself. After some time has passed, pay very close attention as you burn the paper and consider yourself forgiven.

Hopefully this technique can be used when needed to heal past regrets. Let's move on to apologizing and forgiving others.

Apologizing to the Living

Many movie and book plots involve people who have done terrible things and seek to right the wrong while the people involved are still alive. This plot runs through our own lives too. If there is a way to right a wrong, do it. Then celebrate what you did to make it right.

Acknowledging we are wrong and apologizing is almost always beneficial. But the key is not having any expectations about whether your apology will be accepted. You are apologizing to heal yourself, for the sake of your own heart and soul, not for the other person. It is the other person's choice whether to forgive.

Forgiving Others

The weak can never forgive. Forgiveness is the attribute of the strong.
—Gandhi

Switching to the subject of forgiving others, just as we have all hurt others, we have all been wronged by others. In most cases, we have received no apology for these wrongs. Although it is never easy to forgive a past act that is still haunting us, sometimes forgiving is the only way to move on. Choosing to forgive is just that, a choice. Forgiveness can never be coerced, nor can you fake it. The time must be right to forgive, and for some relationships, it may be too soon.

Still, holding a grudge causes pain. Religious texts and modern psychologists all agree that forgiving frees us from emotional turmoil. Despite what we may have been told, we *can* change our past, and one path to changing our past is forgiveness. We cannot change what happened to us, but we can change our emotional relationship to what happened. Unresolved and unfelt emotions lock us into a lifetime of pain, a habit that steals happiness.

So why do we so often choose not to forgive, to endure this pain over our happiness? Perhaps we think the other person should apologize or change. Perhaps we still seek vindication for things that happened decades ago. We think it might still be coming, that apology, that new piece of information that explains everything, so we wait. The subconscious part of the brain, the more powerful part, fights our more sensible self. We choose being right over being happy, and remain in a form of self-imposed bondage, which assures continued misery.

To begin dislodging this pain, we can start by changing our story. We can replace our victim story with a new one in which we may not forget but we forgive. We can create a more satisfying narrative in which we are in control of our own feelings and how we react to our past. We can grieve the loss of the imperfect parent, child, or friend we are finally forgiving. We can even grieve the loss of our old, injured self in favor of a new one. Maybe then forgiveness can come. We won't know until we try.

The Power of Forgiveness

Before tackling how to forgive, it makes sense to discuss how forgiveness helps us. In *The Book of Forgiving*,[129] Desmond Tutu and his daughter, Mpho, share their view that everyone deserves forgiveness, regardless of the atrocities they have committed. Under South African apartheid, the Tutus and their entire community experienced unthinkable violence and dehumanization on a daily basis, yet they still believe everyone deserves forgiveness. Indeed, in his work on the Truth and Reconciliation Commission after the fall of apartheid, based on his deep belief in forgiveness, Desmond Tutu encouraged the entire nation to move forward in forgiveness rather than revenge and violence.

As the Tutus explain, forgiving is in our self-interest. Without it, we remain emotionally tied to the person who harmed us and unable to experience healing and freedom. They insist that forgiving can release us from continuing trauma and hardship and can help us reclaim our lives and our stories. In this way, forgiveness is an act of self-love and self-preservation. Forgiving is

CHAPTER FIVE

healing. Because dislike, hatred, and resentment always eat us up, we are the primary beneficiaries of our choice to forgive. When we forgive, we benefit more than the one we are forgiving.

Failing to forgive, on the other hand, is caustic. It interferes with our work and our personal lives, yet forgiving is hard work. Maintaining the status quo seems simpler. Unforgiven acts allow us to tell our story without taking full responsibility for our own actions.

Failing to take responsibility comes in handy. As long as it is someone else's fault, we don't need to address the problem. We can just let the blame lie elsewhere, thinking, "We have done our best."

But have we? Blaming others gives them all the power over change. We can only control ourselves and our own reaction, never anyone else's. If it is someone else's fault, that person continues to hold all the power. We can recognize our role in the situation and move toward healing, in an act of self-love. Again, forgiveness heals.

For example, Jack Kornfield tells a story in which soldiers rescue a man held in captivity for decades. The rescuers asked him, "Have you forgiven your captors?" and he said, "No, never." The soldiers then asked him, "So they still have you imprisoned then?"[130] Nelson Mandela said the same thing when, after his release from prison, Bill Clinton asked Mandela if he hated his captors. Mandela said, "I felt hatred and fear, but I said to myself, if you hate them when you get in that car, you will still be their prisoner. I wanted to be free, so I let it go."[131]

Family situations are often the toughest to forgive. How many times have you heard people blame troublesome attributes of their adult selves on their parents? Kornfield describes another situation in which a mindfulness teacher describes his stepfather's harshness growing up. The teacher became aware that his stepfather's death was imminent and thankfully realized this about his stepfather:

> I realized that for all these years, he had tried to love me, but because of his own harsh father he could never let his feelings show; he was too afraid. In his own awkward way, he had raised me as his boy. And in my own awkward way I forgive him. I went back to visit him. So much in my own life lightened up after that. Thank God for forgiveness.[132]

Some acts may seem so unforgivable that they do not deserve our forgiveness, but recall that the one hurt by our failure to forgive is not the enemy. It is us, drinking the poison and hoping our nemesis will die. This story demonstrates this principle.

A fourteen-year-old boy killed another teen to prove he was worthy of gang membership. At trial, the victim's mother sat impassively silent, until the verdict was announced. At that point she stood up and said to the killer, "I am going to kill you." The youth was then taken to a juvenile detention center, where he had no visitors, none except . . . the victim's mother, who began visiting him. The imprisoned boy had been living on the streets and had no friends or family.

The mother would visit, eventually bringing small gifts. Near the end of his term, the mother asked the imprisoned boy what he planned to do when he got out. The question confused the boy as he had no plans. She offered to help him get a job at a friend's company, and eventually, to let him live in her spare room. He lived there for eight months, eating her food and working at the job she got him. One evening, she called him into the living room and said, "Do you remember in the courtroom when I said I was going to kill you?" The boy said, "I sure do, I will never forget that moment." The mother continued:

> Well, I did [kill you]. I did not want the boy who could kill my son for no reason to remain alive on this earth. I wanted him to die. That is why I started to visit you and bring you things. That's why I got you the job and let you live here in my house. That's how I set about changing you. And that old boy, he's gone. So, I want to ask you, since my son is gone and that killer is gone, if you'll stay here. I've got room and I'd like to adopt you.

She became the mother of her son's killer, the mother he never had. In *The Book of Forgiving*, Desmond and Mpho Tutu share numerous similar stories of victims' families befriending and even working with their children's perpetrators.[133]

Abraham Lincoln said something similar two centuries before, when he expressed sympathy for the plight of the south following the civil war. A Yankee patriot asked him how he "dared to speak kindly of our enemies when you ought to be thinking of destroying them." Lincoln responded by saying, "But do I not destroy my enemies when I turn them into friends?"[134]

PURPOSE PRACTICE 5.3

In *Getting to Yes with Yourself*, William Ury recounts this Lincoln story and then asks if there are "enemies" that we might be able to destroy by making them our friends. Think of a couple of people you don't care for much and write a journal entry on how you might turn each into a friend, if you chose to. You don't have to do it, just write about how you would do it if you were going to do it.

How to Forgive

In *The Book of Forgiving*, Desmond and Mpho Tutu propose four steps to forgiveness: tell the story, name the hurt, grant forgiveness, and renew or release the relationship.[135]

1. Tell the Story. According to the Tutus, telling our story is how we get back our power and self-worth after we have been harmed. They suggest writing down the story in enough detail to relive the story. This alone relives a burden.

2. Name the Hurt. Once we have told our story, the Tutus suggest we name the emotions and really feel these feelings. Giving voice to this pain, again writing it down first, will begin to heal it. It is hard to move forward without naming and experiencing this pain because the pain remains hidden. Again, the only way out is through.

3. Grant Forgiveness. Once we have told our story and named the hurt, we can release the story and the hurt through forgiveness. This is how we move from victim to hero. It is how we rewrite our stories with us in control of our own lives. When we have suffered trauma, we might need professional help to come to terms with what has happened and accept it as reality. Once that acceptance is present, there is some relief, but forgiveness provides more.[136] You can tell the perpetrator you forgive him or her, or you can just write it down and feel it in your heart. If you do tell the perpetrator, you can't expect anything back. Remember, you are doing this for yourself, not the other person. You'll know you have truly forgiven when you experience freedom from resentment, bitterness, and demand for justice or revenge. This will help rewrite the story.

4. Renew or Release the Relationship. Once you have forgiven, you can choose whether to renew or release the relationship with the one who has harmed you. Releasing is very symbolic. Even if you never speak to the person again, even if the person is no longer alive, they still impact your life until you release them.

Remember that you deserve to be happy, to be healthy, and to live life with ease. Feeling the feelings and then forgiving is one way out.

We will practice rewriting our victim story in a more general way here.

> **PURPOSE PRACTICE 5.4**
>
> Write a story about a past hurt. Now write a new story about the situation and life going forward. Read it twice a day for the next week.

Learning to Express Love When It Doesn't Come Naturally

For many people, expressing emotions seems almost impossible. After a lifetime of never saying *I love you, you matter to me, I am sorry*, etc., expressing emotions can be a tremendous challenge, not to mention just plain terrifying. If this is you, perhaps you can see this as a new challenge. Challenges keep us young and engaged. Challenges help us fight boredom, one of the three plagues of aging.

Challenges can be mental, physical, and emotional, and in this subsection, we explore the challenge of expressing emotions. Much of this book focuses on identifying activities that bring us intellectual and physical challenge, but what about emotional challenges, challenges of the heart? Here too there are many opportunities to grow.

This chapter has dealt so far with healing and resolving behaviors and emotions that are causing *us* harm, but what about the potential harm we cause others by not sharing our feelings, especially feelings of love and appreciation? Perhaps now is the time to take on this emotional challenge before it is too late. Challenging ourselves to become emotionally open and to express our love and gratitude has deep rewards. For one, we can avoid one of life's deepest regrets, not saying "I love you" before someone else dies or before we do.

In her book, *The Top Five Regrets of the Dying: A Life Transformed by the Dearly Departing*, Bronnie Ware describes the most heartbreaking regret, not telling people how you feel about them before they or we die. In more than one case, she suggested that her dying clients tell their family members they love them. Commonly, the client said, "He knows. My son knows I love him." Often, however, these children, spouses, friends, and other family members did not know, and in fact, lived all of their lives trying to gain that love.

Words like love can never be implied. They must be spoken. Speaking these words is priceless and can save years of pain. Countless children also regret not explicitly telling a parent that they love them before the parent died, or not asking real questions as that parent faced their death in the final hours. If this is you, don't feel ashamed, as it is me too, but if it is not too late, share the love now.

If you are not used to saying these things, how can you start? Perhaps by putting the words in writing first, before making plans to say them. Dr. Happy (Dr. Tim Sharp) suggests writing a gratitude letter that you then read.[137] Either way, writing feelings down can build courage to say what you need to say in just the right way.

PURPOSE PRACTICE 5.5

Write a short letter to someone expressing feelings you want them to know. Now practice saying the words and see how that feels. Imagine what it would feel like to actually say the words.

If you want to actually say these things, imagine that you have made the choice to do so. How does it feel to have made that decision? If it feels right, make a plan to share the words. If not, wait but try to imagine the benefits of being courageous and saying it. You don't want to regret not sharing your feelings while you still can. You are doing this mostly for yourself so don't seek any particular reaction.

Parting Thoughts on Self-Compassion, Forgiveness, and Expressing Love

We can learn to practice self-compassion, to apologize and forgive, and to express love. It is not easy but well worth it. These practices create meaningful challenges that enrich and improve our lives. Know that you are worth it. You will benefit and so will those around you.

PART THREE
Creating and Maintaining Well-Being in Mind, Body, and Spirit

CHAPTER 6:
CONNECTING THE MIND AND BODY THROUGH YOGA

In the last chapter, we discussed how to address difficult emotions and communicate love and forgiveness to others. Chapters 4 and 5 were designed to help us heal emotionally, enhance our well-being, and improve our interpersonal relationships. This chapter continues the theme of emotional healing. Since emotions are felt in the body and since yoga involves moving energy through the body, the physical practice of yoga can help us heal and connect these two seemingly separate aspects of ourselves. The mind and the body are not actually separate, and yoga heals all parts of us.

This section introduces the history of yoga, the science behind its benefits, and the various forms of yoga practiced today. It is designed to help readers considering yoga find the right practice and reap the many benefits of this unique form of moving meditation. Keep in mind that yoga is not really "exercise" per se. It is more about mind-body connection than simply moving the body. For this reason, I discuss it separately from other forms of "exercise," which are discussed in the chapters that follow.

The original reasons to practice yoga, to find peace and connect to the divine and to one's true nature, are as useful today as they were five thousand years ago. Yoga is far more than moving the body into shapes. Yoga philosophy is a tremendous teacher. It helps us learn to be kind both to ourselves and to others. After all, we are all connected. Yoga postures or *asanas*, meaning the physical practice of yoga, help us get in touch with our bodies, our feelings, and other people. Yoga practice can help us become better people, kinder people, and people who strive to bring more light to the world.

Yoga and Aging

Yoga has special benefits for us as we age. In *The Science of Yoga: The Risks and the Rewards*, William J. Broad chronicles every scientific study of the benefits of yoga from the early 1900s to 2012.[138] This science demonstrates that a regular yoga practice can result in fewer hospital visits, less reliance on prescription drugs, and fewer coronary events, including fewer heart attacks and deaths due to a sick heart.[139] Yoga also improves balance and thus results in fewer falls.[140] Additionally, yogis have healthier spines[141] and less depression and anxiety.[142]

Finally, yoga can literally increase our lifespans by lengthening our telomeres.[143] Telomeres lie at the tips of our chromosomes, the central repository of genetic information in the cells. Longer telomeres turn back the clock and result in longer lives. Remarkably, yoga can lengthen these telomeres even when you start the practice late in life.[144]

Introduction to Yoga: More than Just Pretzel Poses

Judging by the explosive growth in yoga in the Western world (including the United States), one would think yoga is relatively new. In fact, yoga is one of the oldest practices in history used to calm and clarify the mind. The longevity of the practice alone gives yoga credibility. Thousands of years ago, an Indian sage named Patanjali wrote the first yoga text, the *Yoga Sutras*. These sutras contain an eight-part philosophy of life and a self-improvement program that includes ethical principles, observances, yoga poses (asanas), breath control, withdrawal of the senses, focused concentration, meditation, and for those who keep at it, enlightenment.

The asanas or poses, which we tend to associate with all of yoga here in the West, were originally devised solely to prepare Indian devotees for meditation. The word yoga comes from a Sanskrit word meaning to bind, yoke, or join. In physiological terms, yoga means to join the body with the mind. In broader philosophical terms, yoga explicitly acknowledges our union with all other living beings and with the entire universe. According to yoga philosophy, yoga is not what joins us with all other living beings. Rather, we are already joined, already one, though we may not be conscious of this unity.

Yoga is about connecting with ourselves and others. While it is hard to document where and when he said it, Albert Einstein purportedly discovered this scientific principle in 1905, as he explains:

> A human being is a part of the whole, called by us "Universe," a part limited in time and space. He experiences himself, his thoughts and feelings as something separated from the rest—a kind of optical delusion of his consciousness. This delusion is a kind of prison for us, restricting us to our personal desires and to affection for a few persons nearest to us. Our task must be to free ourselves from this prison by widening our circle of compassion to embrace all living creatures and the whole of nature in its beauty.[145]

According to both the quotation attributed to Einstein and ancient yoga teachings, we exist only in relation to the world, including other people, so we have no separate existence in any real sense. We are completely and inseparably connected on a physical, mental, and emotional level with all other beings. This reality of connectedness explains why we feel terrible after we treat another person badly. The idea that we are all connected differs from the ideas behind many Western religious traditions, which often separate rather than join people together. Consider, for example, how many wars have been fought in the name of religion. Yoga, however, is not a religion at all. Yoga philosophy and asana can be practiced by people of all faiths or no faith at all.

Nevertheless, yoga philosophy suggests we refrain from harming other living beings; we act truthfully; we refrain from stealing, hoarding, and envy; and we live a purposeful life. These restraints or ethical principles are similar to those espoused by most major religions of the world, but in yoga there is no shame. We avoid these harmful practices because through connectedness, when we harm others, we harm ourselves at the same time.

History of Yoga in the West

While yoga first appeared in the West in the early nineteenth century, it wasn't until the 1960s that yoga really began to take off, after a few prominent Indian yogis moved to the West to share their teachings. Around that time, The Beatles met Swami Vishnu-Devananda, the founder of Sivananda Yoga. After that, George Harrison began studying yoga and Eastern religion and later, the whole band began practicing Transcendental Meditation. It was during this time that many of The Beatles' most iconic songs were written.

Ken Dychtwald, PhD—one of the world's foremost experts on aging and longevity and author of nineteen books, including *Bodymind*, *Healthy Aging*, and *Age Wave*—started practicing yoga in 1968 when he was just eighteen. Remarkably, it was yoga that brought him to his life passion, longevity and aging. After studying and working at the Esalen Institute in the 1970s, he moved to Berkeley, California, to cofound the renowned SAGE Project, where he taught yoga to older men and women. His interest in studying and speaking out as a change agent for aging grew from there, from yoga.

Ken shared with me a few things we might not know about yoga back in the day:

> Back in the early 1970s, there were very few serious practitioners of yoga in America. There were a handful of teachers and only a smattering of students in America. After the Beatles and Ram Dass—formerly Dr. Richard Alpert of Harvard—journeyed to India and began popularizing Eastern approaches to mindfulness and mind/body development, yoga began to come alive. Then, when B. K. S. Iyengar introduced his approach to yoga, and Bikram began attracting celebrities in Los Angeles, millions of Americans created a demand for a wide range of yoga programs and centers, a proliferation that still continues today.

Your Yoga Practice: Getting in Touch with Your Body

Most people in the West try yoga to feel better physically. I initially practiced yoga for the simplest of reasons. It made me feel great. Many of us live from the head up. Many of us overwork the mind and mostly ignore the body. What most of us need is to work the body harder and the mind less. We need to move around more while also clearing the mind. Clearing the mind calms it and makes it more efficient and effective at problem-solving. It improves concentration, focus, and creativity. It also feels good.

This is where asana or pose practice comes in. Regardless of the type of yoga class, a unique feeling of stillness comes over us at the end of an asana practice. If you try it, you will feel the stillness and calm set in. You will feel different from when you walked in, and not just from the workout. You will feel rested in a general way but energized at the same time. Unlike other group movement classes, there is no place to go or be, and no particular goal in yoga other than being present. Ideally, you are able to live in the present moment during the entire class and stay focused on your breath and the poses.

The practice restores rather than exhausts. We get an opportunity to experience our life in the present moment. Asana practice keeps the mind from racing and nudges us into calm. The mind feels rested because clearing the mind is part of all asana practice.

In a humorous *New Yorker* cartoon, the teacher asks the class to do the pose that "everyone but Ron can do." But there is no competition in yoga, which is why the tongue-in-cheek cartoon is funny. There is no yoga Olympics and no need to out-yoga anyone or do anything you don't want to do. Take what you like and leave the rest. If the class you attend does not feel this way, find a different one.

Paradoxically, when we do the asanas or poses, we are moving but also stopping the chatter. Stopping the mind's chatter while moving the body allows us to reset. This pause clarifies our thinking and makes us more efficient, not to mention more self-aware and empathetic. Asana is a form of moving meditation. Perhaps not surprisingly, then, asana is a frequent gateway to more contemplative practices such as seated meditation and chanting.

Choosing a Yoga Practice or Class

So how do people begin a yoga practice? Many of us start taking yoga at the gym. While I did this, and it sent me on the path of yoga, gyms can be odd places to practice yoga. The energy can be competitive and fitness focused. There will likely be few things said at the beginning about yoga philosophy and few heartfelt messages about personal growth. The classes are often just poses. The classes also may be taught by fitness instructors who specialize in other things, such as spinning or muscle conditioning or sculpt classes. Nevertheless, the gym is one place to start your practice.

Another place to start practicing asana is live or taped online classes. My husband Stewart and I did this for a long time. Back then we interspersed the DVDs (remember those?) with studio classes. This makes it possible to practice a bit every day without going to a studio every day. If you choose to practice with online courses, it is best to go to a studio once in a while to make sure your form is correct.

Studio classes are critical to developing a healthy practice. But how does one find a good studio? Word of mouth is one good way. Studios pop up all the time and they are of varying quality. Studios that have been in business for a long time are better for beginners than brand new studios. New studios are often filled with new teachers, and beginners need to practice with experienced teachers to avoid injury.

Regardless of the studio you try, ask about the experience of the teachers before you buy a class package. You need to feel comfortable and trust the studio and the teacher in order to get anything out of a yoga class. For example, I am sixty-three years old. I have been in classes with very new teachers who encouraged me to do things I knew would not be good for me. We know our own bodies better than anyone else.

When first taking studio classes, try to pick a restorative, beginners, fundamentals, basics, alignment, or Yoga 1 class. Sometimes these classes are also called hatha, gentle, or slow yoga. Restorative or yin classes involve mostly resting in various healing poses and although I often practice yoga in a more active way, I find these classes to be deeply healing and a wonderful place to experience yoga's power to bring us home to our integrated selves. In the beginning, avoid vinyasa, flow, mixed level, intermediate, Yoga 2 or 3, hot yoga, or power yoga.

Above all, listen to your body. Stretching and expanding are good; pain is not. Try a few different teachers, too. When you meet a teacher, think about your overall impressions of him or her. Also think about your own intention in taking the class. What is it that you hope to get out of it? Do you want to be pushed physically? Do you want significant interpersonal growth, which requires feedback on poses and other aspects of the practice? Or are you mostly looking for an encounter with a teacher with an open heart and an ability to help you develop self-acceptance?

In my own classes, my goal is to help everyone feel better about themselves during the class and to help each person learn something about themselves. I tend to appreciate this openhearted approach in the classes I take, rather than a "tough love" approach.

All classes aim to help you live in the present. Experiment and see what speaks to you. Finally, don't be surprised if emotions come up while you are practicing, even in a group setting. Sometimes people even shed a tear or two. This is a normal way to let emotions work their way through your body, but fear not, you don't need to cry to be a yogi.

I suppose it is obvious that I love yoga. While yoga doesn't cure every problem, it does make it easier to deal with life's challenges. For me, yoga makes for smoother sailing through a tumultuous life, and an ability to deal with life's hardships more easily and productively.

As you develop your yoga practice, if you do, try to stay open to whatever other challenges and growth opportunities your yoga practice brings you. You've heard about many of the physical and mental benefits of yoga, but the benefits of yoga don't end on the mat. We practice yoga to be calm, strong, and flexible, but yoga can also help us find the inner voice that points us toward our greater purpose. At first, the shifts yoga creates are subtle, but over time they can be momentous, assuming you are open to wherever your practice takes you.

CHAPTER 7:
COMING TO TERMS WITH THE OLDER BODY

No doubt, there are many inspiring things about aging and the benefits it brings. What happens to the physical body is not one of them. All of us, from professional athletes and dancers to desk ninjas, are going to see and feel our bodies change as we age. There are things we can do about this aging process, which is the subject of the next several chapters, but the body will still change. It helps to keep a positive mindset and to bring awareness to the process of aging. Here, we discuss the aging body and mindset, reference groups, and a few good resources on physical well-being.

Nonattachment to Yesterday's Strength and Youth

Nonattachment is a yoga principle and practice that helps us accept things we cannot change and encourages us to be attached to our effort but not to the result. Nonattachment is highly useful in helping us accept the things we cannot change about aging. To start, we can learn to accept that we can no longer do what we once could. This is a hard pill to swallow. I recall my late father looking at a picture of himself doing a somersault over a piano in his late teens and lamenting that his body still longed to do that somersault over the piano. He was seventy-eight. I was in my fifties at the time and a bit dismissive of his comment. What a difference a decade makes. Now in my sixties, I know exactly what he was saying. Even if we take care of our bodies, they still get older. It is a fact of life.

Loss of Strength

As alluded to above, most of us have lost some of our physical strength over the decades. It's no fun, but it is also a tradeoff. Recently, my best friend from high school remarked, "After doing yoga for so many years, you must be really great at yoga." The truth is, no, I am not. I used to be better at yoga. Like many sixty-something yogis, I have lost some of my poses. Not so fun.

Having said that, we all also know those rare people who don't lose much strength and fitness as they age. For example, a retirement community with which I have worked in Taos, New Mexico, counts among its residents eighty-year-olds who still ski. I should say eighty-year-olds who still ski Taos, one of the highest and steepest mountains in the United States. They're exceptionally fit at eighty and beyond.

Similarly, I recall a time in 2011 when my husband and his bestie were training for the Santa Fe Century, a bike ride. They were fifty at the time and had just ridden up a huge hill in the Sandia Mountains near Albuquerque. They stopped at the top, gasping and breathing hard from the effort. They turned around to find two seventy-somethings passing them on their bikes, asking one another, "Should we stop or keep going?" The septuagenarians kept going, leaving my husband and his friend in the dust.

Very high levels of fitness can be maintained into our seventies and beyond, but there is a cost, just as there is a cost to chasing a youthful appearance. As Chip Conley explains in *Learning to Love*

Midlife, it's all about priorities. He has a friend who is so obsessed with regaining his six-pack abs that he no longer enjoys food or drink and has become no fun.[146] For me, that would be too high a price to pay. And the price you pay, as Conley kindly explains, is the number of hours and the money spent on the endeavor. I would add, in addition to time, that we also expend a great deal of headspace (mental effort) maintaining that level of fitness.

Loss of Youthful Appearance

Acceptance that we lose our youthful appearance as we age is another lesson in nonattachment. It is also another hard pill to swallow. For decades I have been telling yoga students to love their bodies. I now know this is unrealistic. One of my favorite media hosts in mental well-being and self-care is Swiss podcaster Kristen Truempy As a self-described overweight person, she suggests that loving the body is asking too much. Perhaps just coming to terms with the aging body, with some acceptance of its limitations, is enough. For good or for bad, this is what living in an older body looks like.

Finally, a few words about beauty regimes designed to maintain youth. Wrinkles and sagging skin are another area in which to practice nonattachment. Conley shares a story about an actress who decided in her forties not to treat every wrinkle. She told Conley that the entire beauty industry is a conspiracy against women, a sentiment with which I agree.[147] I am willing to use face creams and occasionally get an injection here or there, but I don't want looking young to become my purpose in life. That would take up too much of my time and headspace. Still, it's hard, and as a woman, you notice when people no longer notice you. I suppose this happens to men as well.

I recall telling my husband not long ago that retinol, an anti-aging product I've used on and off since my forties, no longer works for me. The reality is not so much that it no longer works, but that I am asking much more of retinol in my sixties than I did in my forties. Bottom line, we are going to age. There's only so much we can do to try to stay and look young, and that striving is taking up valuable headspace, not to mention time and money.

Moreover, our headspace is more valuable than our time and money because (1) our time is limited, and (2) a positive mindset is the key to well-being. Surrounding ourselves with others who are not youth-obsessed helps too. Obsession with a youthful appearance can vary geographically (Southern California, for example, is very looks-obsessed), but wherever you live, you can change your reference group.

It also helps to focus on what the older body *can do* as opposed to what it looks like and what it cannot do. I recently broke my foot and the immobility impacted my mental health even more than my physical health. This experience tells us something about the importance of moving the body for mental health. It also demonstrates the intricate connection between the mind and the body. Being able to move is a huge gift, one for which I am immensely grateful now that I *can* move again.

Attachment to Physical Heath

While we can't maintain our old strength level or our youthful appearance forever, we can all get in or stay in good physical condition. We need to be unattached to eternal youth, but uber-attached to our physical well-being. Yes, the body ages and becomes less strong and agile, but it can still move and serve us well as we age.

In my neighborhood, located near a large natural recreation area, I see tons of older people running, biking, and walking every day. If you want to move your body, you just have to do it. A body in motion stays in motion, as they say. A gerontologist I interviewed expressed that sentiment in this way: "Older bodies are like older cars. They need regular lubrication. If you don't keep them moving and in service, they stop working."

Thus, when it comes to maintaining physical health, we don't need to fully accept the aging process. We can stay attached enough to the physical body to keep it as fit as possible. Attachment to good health is healthy, even if attachment to looking young is not. Without our physical health, we can't enjoy the other parts of our lives.

In his book, *Thinking Smarter: Seven Steps to Your Fulfilling Retirement and Life*, Shlomo Benartzi asks us to prioritize various goals in retirement, such as working on our own terms, staying in our homes, and staying physically healthy. I value working as a professor and teacher and assumed this, along with life with my husband Stewart, was my top goal. I assumed I would work until I was ninety just like my late mentor Fred Hart. When I had to do the work to prioritize my goals for retirement (a task we take on in chapter 11 of this book), staying fit enough to remain independent was my top goal. Why is this so surprising? Because I don't spend as much time as I could on this goal now.

A lot can be done to slow physical aging, as people like Tao Porchon-Lynch and Joseph Pilates demonstrate. Tao Porchon-Lynch was still teaching yoga in her nineties and lived to be 101. Joseph Pilates invented Pilates, one of the healthiest forms of rehabilitation and strength building. Pilates has become an incredibly popular method around the world for recovering from injuries and staying fit. Joseph Pilates's approach was designed to rehabilitate injured dancers and is now helping people ages fourteen to 104 stay muscular and strong, especially in the core. Joseph Pilates himself lived to be eighty-three, a ripe old age at the time, and was almost impossibly fit until his passing. And don't forget the Taos skiers or the Sandia Mountain bikers. Be fit for the sake of your health, not for your ego or your looks.

Without physical health, we fall into dependence, one of the three plagues of aging. Without good health, we can't enjoy the last decades of our lives. One of my interviewees, Kathleen, joined an exercise class when she realized that, due to her husband's health issues, their independence depended upon her keeping up her strength. She said that shortly after her husband was diagnosed with Parkinson's disease, she found group fitness and has gone religiously for over a decade. Kathleen knew that if she also began to fail physically, they would both become dependent.

While there is a wealth of information available on physical movement as we age, it is not that complicated. The first step is to keep moving and if you're not moving now, get moving. If this means slowly walking around the block for you right now, do that. If this means just doing a few pushups on your knees, do that. If this means light stretching, do that. All movement is beneficial. Ideally, your movement menu will include strength training, flexibility training, and cardiovascular movement, even if it is slow cardiovascular movement.

Resources on Physical Health

To get focused on physical health, I suggest putting together a small library of books on physical well-being. Three books I rely on regularly include *The Healthy Hedonist* by Janet Bridgers; *Lifestyle Medicine Handbook: An Introduction to the Power of Healthy Habits*, a medical textbook written by four doctors about healthy lifestyles; and *Younger Next Year* by Chris Crowley and Henry Lodge. I also highly recommend *Ageless Aging* by Maddy Dychtwald (with Kate Hanley).

The Healthy Hedonist is light and commonsensical but has changed my life through tiny changes that are enjoyable, things like setting out your exercise clothes the night before, walking a lot, shopping at farmers' markets, making healthy smoothies, and taking more enjoyable showers. There are lots of easy steps we can take to feel joyful and healthier. The author's premise is that we can enjoy life to the very fullest while simultaneously developing healthy lifelong habits. The byline on her back book cover is "When she was good, she was very very good, but when she was bad, she was more fun." This reflects her rejection of rigid health regimes and appeals to my rebellious don't-tell-me-what-to-do side.

Lifestyle Medicine Handbook: An Introduction to the Power of Healthy Habits is encyclopedic in length. Written by four medical doctors, this book is used regularly in their practices. It is a particularly great resource for future problems that may arise, including facing specific health issues. It is also deeply practical, suggesting for example that if you need to move more, get a dog.

Younger Next Year is an inspiring if not intimidating tome with step-by-step instructions for getting moving and staying moving. It also has advice on nutrition, keeping an active social life, and reducing stress. The authors describe in detail things you can do to stay fit. Yes, illnesses can interfere with this, but if you don't have a serious debilitating illness, these authors have no time for excuses. They urge us to not use aging as an excuse to be sedentary.[148]

The Washington Post described *Younger Next Year* as "brain-rattlingly, irresistible, hilarious. If you're up for it, [this book] could change your life."[149] Like I said, this one is serious about getting people healthier than they were last year. While I am not willing to do everything they recommend, this book speaks truth to the sedentary soul in each of us.

Ageless Aging contains exceptional chapters on mindset, fitness, food, sleep, health care, hormones, maintaining a healthy mind, and remaining purposeful, among others. It is my go-to book for aging women, but I recommend it for everyone. While *Ageless Aging* focuses primarily on maintaining a healthy body, my favorite feature of *Ageless Aging* is its discussion of the role of purpose in healthy aging. Because the mind and the body are connected, having purpose in life will keep you moving.

CHAPTER SEVEN

Health, Reference Group, and Mindset

If you are sedentary, physical health can be most easily improved by changing your reference group. Just like with financial reference groups, which keep us spending and treating our money like those around us, we can stay physically well by hanging out with other fit people. You can also turn sedentary activities into active ones. Interviewee Denise always suggests a walk or hike instead when someone asks her to lunch. You can also meditate while walking.

Having an exercise buddy is priceless. I have had the same exercise buddy for over twenty years, my pal Aliza. We used to take Muscle Hour classes together at the gym, a good impetus to get out of the law clinic by 4:15 p.m. on Mondays and Wednesdays. We still take dog walks together. She is also my current yoga student, and we take Pilates classes at the same studio.

If you have never really worked out, you are in for a treat because you'll be able to make a lot of progress quickly, assuming you develop a routine you can keep. Keeping up a routine requires you schedule your physical exercise before anything else in your appointment book and consider these times sacred.

Everyone over sixty-five can belong to a gym for a little or no cost under the Silver Sneakers program. You can use Google to find the nearest spots for you. I have found it easiest to begin exercising by doing group fitness classes rather than working out alone. After moving to New Mexico in 1998 and eating admittedly delicious but unfamiliar and fatty foods for a couple of years, I put on almost twenty pounds. To get rid of the extra weight and feel better, I took the class called Muscle Hour. It was a one-hour weightlifting class that helped me drop the weight and completely change my body. By the way, group classes are fairly inexpensive and a great way to meet others on their fitness journey. The camaraderie keeps many of us moving and lifting well beyond when we would stop if working out alone. If you prefer, you can also hire a personal trainer.

Staying physically well is a mindset and a lifestyle. Whatever you end up doing, you want to be able to picture yourself doing your chosen activities over the next decade. Of course, things will slow down, but you still want to be able to visualize doing your chosen activities over the long haul. This is what well-being looks like for you.

CHAPTER 8:
PHYSICAL MOVEMENT

Mantra: Movement Heals

In this chapter, we explore movement as an elixir to aging. It is a topic about which I feel passionate, but I am no health nut. I don't believe in exercise and eating right just because. I am simply trying to take care of my body, have lots of fun, and enjoy life in good health for as long as I can.

Before we start, let's be honest. It is not that easy to move the aging body, particularly one that has become sedentary. We get tired as we age and sometimes just don't want to move. I wish there was a pill that could be taken to make us want to move our bodies more. I would be the first one to take it, as I can be sedentary at times. Once in my head for long periods of time, I sometimes forget my body. Unfortunately, this is not something we can afford to do.

Because physical well-being isn't separate from mental well-being, we start with a brief discussion of stress and movement.

Stress and Movement

Stress robs us of good health. To keep stress at bay, I suggest breath work, meditation, and slowing down. I also see a therapist and try to meet with good friends a couple times a week, rain or shine. These activities help reduce stress. Yoga, discussed at length in chapter 6, can be a game-changer, especially if you don't consider it exercise but rather a way to keep the mind and the body connected and healthy.

While all of these practices reduce stress, nothing beats movement for lifting a foul mood or motivating us to do great things. Physical exercise reduces stress and literally reorders the cells in the brain. Reducing stress is one of the primary reasons to move your body. Moving the body can also improve our social lives and help us get good sleep. Socializing and good sleep further reduce stress. Thus, physical movement is a one-stop shop for improving peace of mind.

Movement as Medicine

Movement is the first pillar of healthy aging. A big reason why the body ages is not that it is older but because we become less active and the body atrophies. In retirement, we often have fewer obligations, so we move less. This does not have to happen. We can instead use our additional free time to move the body.

Despite all that I know about exercise, health, and aging, I am still surprised by how much of wellness and well-being relates back to the body and how deeply connected the mind and body are. I can be sluggish at times, but when I think about how deeply connected the mind and body are, and how incredibly important my mind is to me, it motivates me to move around more. Use this Purpose Practice to give your brain a little boost the next time you need one.

> ### PURPOSE PRACTICE 8.1
>
> Vigorous movement, even for two minutes or less, improves brain function. You can do this before an important presentation, meeting, or phone call, or whenever you need a brain boost. Next time you need a boost, try running in place or doing a set of squats or lunges for sixty to ninety seconds. Then breathe, and enjoy the energy and clarity of mind.

You'll also want longer bouts of exercise to become the norm for you. The number-one reason I consider movement the most critical piece of healthy aging is not because it will lengthen my life or help me look better or be fitter. It is because all exercise elevates mood. It literally makes us happier and healthier. Movement increases our enjoyment of life. Some studies show that exercise is as effective in treating mild depression and anxiety as prescription medicine. This is not to say you don't need your meds, but if physical activity is available to you, you can use it to make your life better.

Younger Next Year teaches that we can move more rather than less each year. There are of course limits, but even if you are very inactive right now, you can set aside more time for movement. Start slowly. Put your exercise schedule in your calendar and honor it like any appointment. Crowley and Lodge even say that you should make exercise your next job. You have time now, so why not? Not sure where to start? Start with walking. It is universally available to most of us and among the very best things we can do for our health.

Younger Next Year shares in painful detail the process by which our bodies are currently deteriorating every moment of every day. I will leave out most of the dismal science, but according to Crowley and Lodge, exercise is the only thing that can stop this deterioration. They describe this ongoing decay by explaining that

CHAPTER EIGHT

biologically, there is no such thing as retirement, and that various parts of our bodies are replaced every few months.

These rapidly decaying cells and muscles are designed to be replaced often, in case cells or muscles get sick. For example, older cells are more likely to get cancer so it is good to replace those cells. For another example, the spleen's job is to destroy blood cells and other mechanisms to purposefully dissolve our bones so we can grow new ones. We actually want this turnover of cells. It is critical to our health. For some other examples, the authors claim that our thigh muscles are completely replaced every four months, our blood cells every three months, and the blood platelets every ten days![150]

None of this healthy replacing happens automatically. We have to help the process along through exercise and movement. We stay healthy by allowing these systems to continue to replace themselves often. Old cells, bones, and muscles decay. When they are not replaced, they weaken and get sick. Like pruning a plant so new growth can replace the old growth, we can grow more of whatever the body is ridding itself of through exercise.

To get more precise about what to do and how often, Crowley and Lodge insist on four days of cardio and two days of weight training every week for the rest of your life. These authors are also militant about how long one needs to do this cardio exercise and weightlifting. I rail against this sort of rigidity but also want to share what I know in case it is useful to you. If you take one thing from this chapter, it should be that movement is the best thing for keeping your mind and body youthful.

The most common forms of exercise are cardiovascular movement, which fuels the heart, and weight or resistance training, which fuels the muscles. There is also flexibility exercise, which holistically heals the body.

Cardio Movement

Movement is a great elixir for the body, but cardiovascular exercise, also known as cardio, can be especially good for the heart, the mind, and the soul. Studies show that this form of exercise, which includes anything that gets the heart pumping, reduces mild depression and anxiety. Even slow walking for twenty to thirty minutes a day cuts the risk of heart disease and a large list of other ailments in half. If you already do this amount of cardio exercise, double your time for double protection or work up to more active movement like light jogging or fast walking. If you don't do anything right now, just start. A walk around the block is exponentially better than nothing.

Getting started with cardio movement doesn't need to feel like "exercise." Many people universally dislike the whole idea of exercise. My yoga teacher Dave Yoss had the funniest line. He said, "Just think, if we could fly and that was considered exercise, people wouldn't want to do it."

So don't "exercise," just move. To start, take a long (slow if need be) walk each morning and add more active cardio activity as the days pass. In *The Healthy Hedonist*, Janet Bridgers explains that she goes as many places as possible by foot as a key to staying healthy. She also says that for her, waking up, throwing on her exercise clothes, and heading right out eliminates double thinking. She is up and at it without a thought. What is she doing? Walking, which is great for the mind and great for the body.

You can also use your growth mindset to think about movement. Don't consider walking exercise. Consider it antidepressant activity, mindfulness, enjoyment of nature, or returning to your true self. Consider saying one of the mantras we have developed in this book while walking. Or listen to books or podcasts on your phone. Or look for birds. It's your choice what you do. Just assume it is going to be amazing and do it.

How you think about these issues will affect how you do them.

A study of housekeepers in a hotel chain showed that if you told them their work promoted fitness, they actually built more muscle and burned more calories on the job than those who just thought of their job as work. Their mindsets literally increased the benefit of their physical activity without them even knowing it.[151]

> **PURPOSE PRACTICE 8.2**
>
> Set a goal for movement. Perhaps use your phone to work up to ten thousand or fifteen thousand steps a day. If you already do that, add more steps. Start small and work your way up. Find a neighbor or a friend to join you for accountability. A goal is to do this every day and get to the point where it is simply habit to move your body.

My own advice is to start by moving more. Period. Turn on music and dance, garden, go for a bird walk. Just move. If you are seriously unfit right now, and I have been there, start with fifteen minutes of walking. Just keep adding minutes until you can get to forty-five minutes, and then begin doing something more active. Try to get that heart rate up for as long as you can.

While I might leave it at that with regard to your cardio journey, I don't want to deprive you of the information you need to really kick your body into action. For extra insurance against premature aging, Crowley and Lodge insist upon a heart rate monitor and say that we each need to work up to forty-five minutes of cardio exercise at 80 percent of maximum heart rate four times a week, rain or shine. They insist upon four cardio days a week, no ifs, ands, or buts.[152] This means four days of serious cardio such as jogging, using the elliptical and other gym cardio equipment, swimming, biking, tennis, skiing, hiking, or walking fast enough to get the heart rate up.

Don't discount a basketball or pickleball game with friends, water aerobics at the gym, gardening, doing chores around the house and garage, dancing, vigorous housecleaning, and so on. It all adds up, and if the heart is pumping, it is cardio.

Weight Training

The other ingredient in healthy aging besides cardio movement is weight training. If you are out of shape, just twice a week will do wonders to improve your health. In terms of how you do it, free weights are more effective than those big weight machines you see at the gym because with free weights, you will be working your core in every exercise. On the machines, the machine is holding you in place. Still, if you can only do the machines for some reason, do that to start. There is a little picture of how to do each exercise on the side of each machine.

If weight-lifting sounds foreign and scary, you can hire a personal trainer for a couple of sessions and have the trainer write down the exercises. They can look at your body to ensure that your form is correct. Doing fifty squats with poor form will help you less than ten good ones. Also, you can hurt yourself if your form is not correct.

Once you learn the moves, you might consider group weight-lifting classes at a gym. I have really loved these classes, which go by names like *muscle hour* or *body pump*. You do many reps with light weights. Group classes add the accountability of requiring many reps long after you would have stopped on your own. When I do my own workouts, I often don't work as hard as I should. Both personal trainers and group classes reduce the risk of stopping when it gets hard. Those extra reps are what build the muscle, which is what increases metabolism and keeps us from falling. Weight-lifting also makes the body look amazing. While cardio makes you *feel* great, weights make you *look* great whether you are forty or seventy.

CHAPTER EIGHT

Mobility Movement: Pilates and Yoga

Flexibility enhances every other form of exercise. In addition to weights and cardio, both Pilates and yoga enhance flexibility and mobility and improve overall well-being. For me, yoga and Pilates don't feel like exercise so are easier to keep up. If you think that stretching and flexibility are not so important, think again. My husband works out hard with weights and when he goes to a personal trainer, he is often told that he needs to stretch more to improve his physical strength, overall mobility, and health.

To get more specific about Pilates workouts, they are exercise sequences that elongate the body and strengthen muscles through stretching and resistance training. Pilates sequences are done either on specialized equipment, such as a bed-like reformer, on a wall of springs, or on the floor. The focus is on control of movement and muscular endurance, and particularly on strengthening the core. The benefits of Pilates include improved posture, improved flexibility, and increased muscle strength and tone, particularly in the abdominal muscles, low back, hips, and glutes.

Pilates exercises can be individualized and are as helpful to an eighty-year-old as an eighteen-year-old. For this reason, this form of exercise is especially useful for the aging body. After all, it was designed for those who have been injured in some way, and by the time we get to retirement age, most of us have all been injured in some way.

The long-strong muscles Pilates helps create keep us from falling and if we do fall, keep us from being injured from the fall. Pilates also has psychological benefits. By increasing abdominal strength and improving posture, Pilates allows us to stand up taller and use our bodies better in other activities and sports. Because it improves overall posture and appearance, Pilates makes us look leaner and stronger and can increase self-confidence.

People often ask how Pilates and yoga differ. Both improve balance and strength, but for me, they are very different. First,

Pilates focuses almost exclusively on the body while yoga connects the body to the mind through the flow of movement. Moreover, Pilates was born in the 1920s and yoga has been around for thousands of years. The breathing is also different. In yoga, you breathe into the belly and the breath relaxes you and helps you relieve stressed, tight areas of the body. In Pilates, you breathe into your chest or ribcage and use the breath to activate your core.

This difference in breathing reflects the focus of each practice. Pilates is about tightening things, like your abs or your ribcage to your spine or the back of your legs to the reformer or mat. Yoga is about opening the body rather than tightening it. Pilates is mostly about controlling muscles and yoga is mostly about releasing them. Using plants as an analogy, yoga is like an unfurling vine, flowing and flexible, and Pilates is like a tree trunk, strong, tight, and neat. Ideally, you try both and see what speaks to you. You don't have to pick. I like to practice both.

Movement and Digestion

We discuss digestion more in the next chapter on nutrition, but keeping the body in motion helps us digest our food and keeps our organs in good, clean shape. Because poor digestion is correlated with cognitive decline, good digestion is yet another reason to keep moving.

When the Body Falls Apart

All this talk of moving the body is well and good when it's possible to move the body. As we age though, the body may experience temporary or more permanent bouts of what I'll call "falling apart." Perhaps you have a side stitch and it takes your energy away even though it's a small thing. Maybe you drop something on your toe and it really saps you of energy. Or perhaps you have a chronic disease, break a bone, or sprain soft tissues or ligaments.

CHAPTER EIGHT

There are so many ways in which the body can fall apart, even if we do everything in our power to take good care of it. Knowing that these things can happen, can be disruptors or lifequakes in Feiler's terms, is part of coming to terms with the older body. I have a close family member, as well as a close friend, with multiple sclerosis. Watching them deal with these issues is heartbreaking but also inspiring. It is amazing how people can adapt and survive.

The purpose of bringing this up is to acknowledge that yes, we should move the body when we can. There will also be times when self-care and compassion will require us to just lie around and rest. As one of my favorite pieces of art proclaims, "Things I've learned from my dog: some days it's OK to just eat and sleep."

So how can you figure out whether you're just being lazy or whether you truly have a physical condition that will not permit you to move your body in a particular day or week or month? Obviously, this will vary from person to person, but if at all possible, it's good to be honest with yourself and ask, "Could I get up and do something, anything?" Being somewhat inert by nature, I know that sometimes I am just being lazy. Don't want to move? Put on your exercise clothes and go to the gym or outside. Give yourself credit for even that much!

Movement, Individual Bodies, and Mindset

Like all other aspects of life, it is important to have a positive mindset about movement. One mantra I love is the one that starts this chapter: movement heals. If you can keep that in mind, you can keep moving, even if you move slowly at first. It all adds up. If you really feel you can't move at all, try to connect with a yoga or Pilates teacher, a personal trainer, or a physical therapist. Many health insurance policies pay for physical therapy and this can be a great way to get started.

PHYSICAL MOVEMENT

The main thing is to not put up with your own excuses. Every day the body is decaying, but we can fight that decay by building muscles. This can be done through bodyweight exercises like push-ups, sit-ups, lunges, and squats; by going to the gym and weightlifting alone; by taking a weightlifting class; or through a vigorous Pilates or yoga session.

Also, don't forget the emotional benefits. If movement is at all possible, it should be done, especially when you feel sad, a time when you likely just want to lie around. Moving will help lift the sadness.

> **PURPOSE PRACTICE 8.3**
>
> Create a mantra that emphasizes your physical strength and repeat it for a set time, say ten minutes, every day. Call this your strong mantra.

Perhaps most importantly, see if you can have fun moving your body. I enjoy being outside, kayaking, watching birds, and foraging for mushrooms. I enjoy the strong feeling that lifting weights gives me. And yoga makes me feel alive in a way no other movement does. But everyone is different. And, while this is changing (take a moment to google the amazing Jessamyn Stanley), the yoga world has not always been kind to all body types. As Kristen Truempy says, yoga simply does not speak to her. Perhaps you love golf, gardening, biking, or mall walking. Whatever you love, just keep moving. In case you are thinking, "I am too old to start exercising," think again. You can begin exercising any time. It is never too late, as this case study shows.

Richard Morgan Case Study

Irishman Richard Morgan began exercising at age seventy-three when his grandson's rowing coach showed him a weight machine at the gym. He is now ninety-three and a four-time world champion in indoor rowing.[153] He has the aerobic conditioning of a healthy thirty- or forty-year-old and just 15 percent body-fat. As a point of reference, a typical percentage of body fat is between 25–30 percent in women and 18–23 percent in men. A large percentage of Americans fall well above even these levels.

In a time trial, Morgan's heart rate peaked at 153 beats per minute, well above the usual maximum heart rate for his age and among the highest peaks ever recorded for a nonagenarian. This maximum heart rate signals a very strong heart. Morgan reached this heart rate quickly, meaning his heart was able to rapidly supply his working muscles with oxygen and fuel, comparable to the heart health of a thirty- or forty-year-old. How did Morgan achieve this level of fitness?

Cardio

Morgan does cardio fitness exercise for forty minutes a day, but not that hard. About 70 percent of these workouts are easy, with Morgan hardly laboring. Another 20 percent are at a difficult but tolerable pace, and the final 10 percent are at an all-out, barely sustainable intensity.[154] I see this as twenty-eight minutes of easygoing ambling, eight minutes of heavy breathing, and just four minutes a day of work-as-hard-as-you-possibly-can cardio exercise.

Weightlifting

Morgan also lifts dumbbells two to three times a week. He does roughly three sets of lunges and curls, repeating each move until his muscles are too tired to continue. This is called lifting to failure. It's one thing we actually aim to fail at.

Moral of the Story

What made Morgan especially interesting to researchers was his late entry into fitness. He started working out just after retirement when he was "somewhat at loose ends then."[155] Could this be one of your purposes in retirement, staying healthy and alive as long as possible?

CHAPTER 9:
NUTRITION AND THE OLDER BODY

Food is truly one of life's greatest joys. It plays a huge role in my family's life and is among our greatest pleasures. As such, I eschew any practice that takes away from that joy. Calorie counting, carb counting, and rigid rules about what one should and should not eat can be real buzzkill. Eating, like physical movement, can be a highly holistic endeavor not to mention a delicious one, especially if we slow down and savor what we eat.

Mindful Eating

Eating can be almost a spiritual practice, if we slow down and savor our food. A slower eating practice can help us appreciate the food, encourage us to try new things, encourage us to eat more colorful food which is generally healthier than white and brown food, and encourage us to eat more slowly for deeper enjoyment. After all, if we love eating, wouldn't we love it more if we paid more attention to it and could do it for longer?

This practice below, adapted from Jon Kabat-Zinn's Mindfulness-Based Stress Reduction (MBSR) program, helps us connect with the joy and nutrition in our food.

PURPOSE PRACTICE 9.1

Take a tangerine or two or three berries or raisins and place them on a plate in front of you. Pick something you love. Very slowly observe them and all their traits: color, texture, and so on. Now pick one up and spend two or three full minutes examining everything about it. If you are using a tangerine, slowly peel it first. Once you have observed the food for a while, take a very tiny bite out of the first berry, raisin, or orange segment. Notice what you notice. Taste it very slowly and deeply. Note what you taste where on your mouth. Note the temperature, the texture, the sweetness or sourness. Continue with this until all the food is gone, paying as much attention to all the details as you can. This should take about ten minutes.

That was an exercise in mindful eating. While we don't need to eat that slowly at every meal, or even regularly, this exercise can help us learn to savor our food. While doing this exercise, did you notice how good the food tasted? Was it a bit like tasting that food for the first time? One benefit of a practice like this is to teach us how to get every drop of joy, every drop of pleasure, out of our food. Another is to help us learn the point at which we are full.

The exercise below helps us incorporate this mindful eating exercise into our meals.

PURPOSE PRACTICE 9.2

Next time you are eating, make it a point to slow down. Take each bite more slowly, and if it is fork food, put less on the fork, perhaps just one little veggie or piece of something at a time, rather than a whole forkful. Carefully look at the food before you eat it. Notice the colors and texture. Then proceed to eat as usual but more slowly. Chew slowly and pay attention to the food going down.

Try this again at your next meal and your next. See if you can begin to eat more slowly, more appreciatively as a matter of course.

Focus on Healthy Foods 80 Percent of the Time

Both *Younger Next Year* and *Lifestyle Medicine Handbook* discuss nutrition at length. I also really enjoy Dr. Joanna McMillan's podcast, *Mindfull*, which describes foods that are healthy for the brain. It turns out, the foods that are good for the brain are good for the entire body. Like movement, good nutrition need not be complicated.

Fruits and vegetables are the backbone of healthy eating. Fruits and vegetables contain live vitamins and enzymes that keep the cells of the body fed. As author and comedian Dick Gregory always said, "Live food for live bodies." Fruits and vegetables, eaten more or less in their natural unprocessed state, create quality fuel for our bodies. People who eat more of them look, act, and feel better. You can see their diets on their faces.

There are some fun benchmarks that make it easier to picture good nutrition. One is to make one half of your plate fruits and veggies in most meals. If this is unattainable, you can at least incorporate fruits and veggies into every meal, even if it is just a handful of something. Once you start, the body will begin to crave these foods if they are not provided, a happy cycle indeed.

I know some people don't like fruits and vegetables, but there are ways to work them in. Nutritionists insist that even a few bites of veggies, even with ranch dressing, provide unique nutrients that improve energy and overall health.

In *The Healthy Hedonist*, Janet Bridgers suggests smoothies. I love to start my day with a smoothie made in a bullet-style blender. The only requirement of my smoothie is that it be 3/4 spinach. The rest is whatever fruit is in the fridge, or unsweetened yogurt. It does not taste like spinach, and I relish it, plus I can be less pious with my choices throughout the rest of the day.

Another easy strategy is to shop the perimeter of the supermarket. That is where you find most of the fresh as opposed to processed foods.

Avoiding processed foods is something everyone says we should do but it is hard to get motivated. Everybody loves a good potato chip or Oreo cookie now and then, but check out this not-so-fun fact. Processed snacks made by big food companies like Frito-Lay and Nabisco were purposefully designed to get people addicted to the food and to make tons of money off those addictions. These foods have also been instrumental in this country's obesity problem. This has similarities to the opioid crisis. The Sackler family purposefully marketed and sold addictive opioids to Americans to line their own pockets.

Hearing about this purposeful addiction plan has helped me eat less junk food. I still eat potato chips, but I do it less often now, knowing I am withholding my support for an industry that prioritizes profits over the health of our nation. Remember that this is not an all-or-nothing proposition. You don't need to be perfect. I like the 80/20 rule. If you are eating heathy food for 80 percent of your diet, you can loosen up a bit on the other 20 percent.

Another way to incorporate healthy foods in your diet is to combine your nutrition goal with a social one. Get other people involved in making and sharing healthy meals. You might schedule one meal with a small group once a week or once every other week so that you can share healthy recipes and meals. Just like learning any new skill, hobby, exercise program, etc., it is easier to learn to cook if you do it with social support. It's also much more fun.

Ayurveda for Modern Times

Ayurveda, an ancient medical practice that has been used in India and Nepal for centuries, also provides a few eating tips that are obvious once you hear them.

For example, here in the West, we love to drink cold beverages with meals, but this slows digestion and can cause indigestion and other stomach discomfort. Your stomach is working hard to digest your food and pouring cold liquid on that process slows it down.

Second, the stomach is much smaller than we think, only about the size of a fist. When you imagine jamming a 1,300-calorie restaurant meal into such a small space, it's not hard to see why we feel bloated and lethargic afterward.

Third, it is recommended that we eat until we are about 75 percent full. I must admit I never do this. This is a someday goal as I just love food!

Don't despair if this sounds like no fun. No chilled wine with dinner? Touché! These are just guidelines, and no one follows them all the time. Again, I like the 80/20 rule. If you are following these guidelines and eat the right amount of food in the right quantities 80 percent of the time, that is 80 percent healthier than you may have been eating before. Food is joy, and we don't want to turn it into a chore.

Specific Foods for Physical Well-Being

In addition to eating a wide variety of fruits and vegetables, following the 80/20 rule, and not eating too much at a time, there are specific foods that are particularly healing and nutrious for older bodies.

Bone Health

It is no secret that bone weaknesses cause frailty in aging bodies. One place to look for advice on how to assist with this problem is, once again, Ayurveda. According to Ayurveda, these foods support bone health: organic milk, dairy products, and probiotic yogurt; dark, leafy green veggies (like kale and chard); sesame seeds; almonds; and figs.

CHAPTER NINE

Brain Health

In chapter 3, we discussed brain health as it relates to our thoughts and our mindset. Here, we focus on particular foods that can help us maintain a healthy brain and body as we age. The best foods nourish cells, increase blood flow to the brain, positively influence the structure of the brain, and enhance how cells in the brain communicate with one another. These foods help us stay mentally sharp and ward off Alzheimer's disease and other forms of dementia.

Before we discuss particularly beneficial foods, know that the brain benefits when we keep our blood sugar levels constant. Additionally, we need to eat fat, making fat-free diets unhealthy. The human brain is 60 percent fat, and while the body can make some of its own fat, eating fat helps us absorb other nutrients. Some fats, especially extra-virgin olive oil, are excellent for our health. Dr. McMillan suggests we substitute olive oil for almost all other oils because of its concentration of a type of fat we need but can't readily make, long-chain omega-3 fats. She is also a huge fan of fatty fish. These are two of her favorite foods and since learning about this, I have enjoyed upping my intake of olive oil, especially with sea salt on roasted vegetables.

Trans Fats

Dr. McMillan encourages us to use extra-virgin olive oil to reduce some saturated fats, though not all of them, and to eliminate the worst fats of all, trans fats. Her reference to trans fats reminded me that some years ago, San Francisco outlawed trans fats, causing my San Franciscan cousin to whisper to me, "Psst, anybody know where I can get a good trans fat sandwich?" His joke reinforces that when it comes to food, like exercise, we typically want to eat what we are told to avoid.

No need to do that when it comes to trans fats. They don't taste like anything, and replacing them with olive oil is a no-brainer.

Extra-virgin olive oil tastes amazing in and on everything, especially with a bit of salt in savory dishes or sugar in sweet ones.

So what is so bad about trans fat? These fats are used in store-bought junk food and bakery items to extend their shelf life. Extended shelf life is not a good thing. I recall a presentation by lifestyle medicine doctor Beth Frates in which she brought in years-old unrefrigerated hamburgers and fries from McDonald's that looked exactly the same as the day they were purchased. No kidding. It was alarming and reinforced what my grandfather once told me: if it does not spoil within a few days, you should not eat it as it has been laced (his word) with things that will not break down in your body and will never become real food. Michael Pollan agrees in *Food Rules: An Eater's Manual.* He says we should only eat food that will eventually rot.[156]

Pollan has a few more cheeky suggestions for eating well. First, it's not food if it's called the same name in every language (think *Big Mac, Cheetos,* or *Pringles*).[157] Second, real food does not arrive through a car window.[158] If only it did. That would be so handy.

There is more to dislike in trans fats. Even in moderation, they cancel out the many benefits of extra-virgin olive oil by upsetting the balance between the omega-3s in the olive oil and the harmful omega-6s in the trans fats. Trans fats are also hard to avoid if you eat out a lot. For example, some restaurants keep the deep fryer full of the same fat all day, serving up harmful trans fats. At the risk of sounding like no fun, it is probably best to order baked or grilled dishes in restaurants and eat at home when you can.

Just to review, here are some great omega-3 fatty foods to include in your diet:

- Fish and other seafood, especially cold-water fatty fish, such as salmon, mackerel, tuna, herring, and sardines
- Nuts and seeds, including flaxseed, chia seeds, and walnuts
- Plant oils, such as olive oil, flaxseed oil, soybean oil, and canola oil

- Fortified foods, such as certain brands of eggs, yogurt, juice, milk, and soy beverages

And, here are some trans-fat-laden foods to avoid:

- Commercial baked goods, such as cakes, cookies, and pies
- Shortening
- Microwave popcorn
- Frozen pizza
- Refrigerated dough, such as biscuits and rolls
- Fried foods, including french fries, doughnuts, and fried chicken
- Non-dairy coffee creamer
- Stick margarine
- Pre-prepared cake frostings
- Some pastries, donuts, and pies

Saturated Fats

Saturated fat is generally not great for us, but some of it is good, for example the saturated fat found in full-fat dairy products. Full-fat dairy products have been associated with healthy minds and reduced rates of dementia and Alzheimer's disease. We also benefit greatly from the fats contained in oily fish like sardines, mackerel, trout, herring, and salmon, as well as other seafood and caviar. For plant-based people, there is chia, almonds, walnuts, and avocados, as well as, of course, extra-virgin olive oil.

Fish Oil Supplements

There are also fish oil supplements. Krill oil is thought to be purer and to use better, more sustainable sourcing. All fish oils should be kept in a cool dark place to avoid oxidation, which will make the supplement ineffective and perhaps harmful.

Other Nutrients Worth Seeking Out

There is a series of other nutrients that fuel the brain, especially the B-group vitamins. The B vitamins improve glucose absorption and produce neurochemicals that make brain cells healthier. Conversely, low levels of B vitamins in the body correlate with depression, brain fog, cognitive decline, dementia, and various neurological problems.

In one study, one third of psychiatric patients were low in some B vitamins, including B12 and folate. Folate, B6, and B12 are particularly important for brain health, and low levels of those correlate with atrophy of the brain. As we age, some brain atrophy is inevitable, but staying high in folate, B6, and B12 can reduce the onset and extent of this atrophy. One Oxford University study showed that high levels of B6, B12, and folate slowed brain atrophy by 30 percent. While B-group vitamin supplements can sometimes be helpful, it is best to get these nutrients from food.

Here are some foods high in B-group vitamins, as well as Vitamins D and E, and a few other important nutrients. Seeing the list can be helpful in consciously and subconsciously directing us toward these healthy foods.

I do not eat meat, but have included meat here because science supports eating it. Of course, there are also alternatives, and you don't need to eat all of the things on the list:

1. Proteins
   - Seafood (especially shellfish, oysters, clams, mussels, squid, crab): riboflavin, iodine, iron, B12, zinc
   - Organ meats: thiamin, riboflavin, niacin, B6, biotin, folate, B12, iron
   - Beef: riboflavin, niacin, pantothenic acid, biotin, zinc
   - Chicken: thiamin, riboflavin, niacin, pantothenic acid, B6, biotin
   - Pork: riboflavin, niacin, biotin
   - Eggs: vitamins A, D, E, K, B1, B2, B5, B6, B9, and B12

CHAPTER NINE

- Dairy: riboflavin, B12, zinc
- Legumes: thiamin, folate
- Beans: niacin

2. Oils and Nuts
    - Extra-virgin olive oil: vitamin E
    - Whole grains: thiamin, pantothenic acid, niacin (though not as well absorbed as in meat)
    - Nuts and seeds: thiamin, B6, biotin, folate, magnesium, vitamin E
    - Peanut butter: B6

3. Fruits and Vegetables
    - Seaweed: folate, iodine
    - Dark leafy greens: folate, magnesium
    - Asparagus: riboflavin, folate
    - Broccoli: riboflavin, iron
    - Spinach: riboflavin, iron
    - Potatoes: pantothenic acid, B6
    - Sweet potatoes: biotin
    - Bananas: folate
    - Avocados: folate, vitamin E
    - Egg yolks: pantothenic acid, vitamin D
    - Tomatoes: pantothenic acid
    - Mushrooms: vitamin D
    - Dark chocolate with at least 70 percent cocoa: magnesium
    - Iodized or sea salt: iodine

Magnesium

Low levels of magnesium have been correlated with Alzheimer's disease while high magnesium levels correlate with high memory and brain function. Magnesium can be found in nuts, seeds, dark leafy greens, vegetables, and dark chocolate that has more than 70 percent cocoa.

Vitamin E

Vitamin E is one of the strongest antioxidants and is especially necessary for parts of the body high in fat, like the brain. High vitamin E levels, like high vitamin D levels, are associated with good memory. Good sources of vitamin E include nuts, seeds, avocado, and extra-virgin olive oil.

Sea Salt

Some iodized salt is good for many of us. I was surprised to learn that fancy pink Himalayan salt is not as good for us as sea salt because we need iodine. We should use all salt in moderation, but when we do use salt, sea salt or iodized salt is best.

Eating the Rainbow

Many studies show the benefits of eating a large variety of colorful fruits and veggies weekly. One study showed that people who ate one serving of leafy green vegetables a day had a slower rate of decline on tests of memory and thinking skills. Adopting this one habit resulted in the equivalent of being eleven years younger cognitively.[159] That is an incredible statistic. This is where my spinach smoothie comes in.

Eating more fruits and vegetables changes your gut microbiome so that your body begins to crave those healthy things. Dr. McMillan adores cruciferous veggies like broccoli, cauliflower, cabbage, and brussels sprouts for their microbiota. She insists upon at least two servings of fruit a day, especially apples and pears, which are released very slowly into the bloodstream as sugar.

She says not to worry too much about the sugar in these fruits as the skin contains enough fiber to more than make up for that sugar. She also suggests eating different types of fruit every day and eating some whole veggies and fruits every meal. Also, as alluded to above, the fiber is in the skin so we should eat the skin whenever we can. Dr. McMillan likes whole grains too for their nutrients and fiber and suggests legumes twice a week or more.

I know there are a million experts who can tell us what to eat. I consider the advice of Dr. McMillan more valuable than most because she is a scientist who runs randomized studies on which foods are best for optimal brain function. Because she studies brain health, her dietary suggestions are specifically designed to ward off dementia and other cognitive disorders.

Eating and Moving for Digestion

I saw a great sticker in a coffee shop that said, "Start a movement, eat prunes." As mentioned in the last chapter, good digestion is good for both the mind and the body, as constipation is correlated with cognitive decline. I hate counting either calories or carbs but make it a point to count grams of fiber. Some of my favorite high fiber foods are the following:

- garbanzo and other beans
- bulgar wheat
- berries
- greens like spinach and kale
- celery
- carrots
- apples
- cabbage
- wild rice
- very seedy bread

Embracing Your Inner Cook

When it comes to eating well, the very best tip is to eat at home most of the time. Eating at home has many advantages. First, it is much healthier. Restaurants use much more salt, fat, and sugar than you would at home, which might taste good at the time, but can make you feel bloated and sluggish later. Second, you can make exactly what you want. Third, you don't have to rely on other people to serve you, which could take longer than you like. Finally, it is much cheaper and there is no reason to waste money.

You might be thinking, I don't know how to cook, but that is one of the great benefits of retirement. Now you have time.

Parting Thoughts on Nutrition and the Older Body

This chapter contains a lot of detail on what to eat, as well as a few tips for eating well and getting maximum enjoyment from our food. Hopefully this level of detail does not take away from my main message. Food is both fuel and enjoyment. We are lucky to have so many healthy and delicious food options.

CHAPTER 10:
SLEEP, SOCIALIZING, STRESS, AND DEVISING YOUR INDIVIDUAL HEALTH PLAN

In this final chapter on health, we focus on sleep, socializing, and managing stress for better health. We also put all we have learned over the past four chapters into an individual health plan. We start with sleep, as every good day starts with a good night's sleep. Moreover, good sleep habits maintain a healthy brain.

Sleep

According to Maddy Dychtwald in *Ageless Aging*, quality sleep positively impacts appetite and metabolism, improves cognitive health and emotional regulation, boosts overall health, improves our appearance, and gives us energy to exercise and pursue the purposeful activities that bring meaning to our lives.[160] This is an incredible list of benefits, all from just getting good sleep.

This is not to say getting good sleep is easy. You may have heard that older people don't need as much sleep as young people, but it turns out that's incorrect. Everybody still benefits from eight

CHAPTER TEN

to nine hours a night. The reason this old person sleep adage is so popular is that it can be really hard to get a good night's sleep once you get to a certain age.

Why is that? First, when we really work our bodies, for example by going on a long hike or doing other intense exercise, or spend a lot of time outside, we sleep like babies. Not just any babies but babies who are really tired and don't wake up in the middle of the night. As we age, it's harder to get that kind of exercise.

Second, we tend to worry. Worry isn't more common among the elderly by any means, but there's something about our aging bodies that wakes us up in the middle of the night, namely *nature calling*. After getting up to use the bathroom, it can be difficult to get back to sleep when the mind wanders to our worries. For these times, it can be useful to have rituals for getting back to sleep after getting up in the middle of the night.

Mindfulness meditation apps can help. You can leave the phone by the bed and let it play for thirty minutes or so. You will likely fall asleep in the middle of the meditation and if you don't, you can run it again.

A positive mindset also helps neutralize worry. My mother and I used to buy books that were called "Happiness Is" that contain short phrases depicting surprising places to find happiness.[161] One of the phrases we loved most said, "Happiness is waking up in the middle of the night and falling right back to sleep." My husband and I have renamed this phenomenon our second night's sleep. And we tell ourselves, "Oh my goodness, I am so lucky. I woke up and now I get the chance to have not just one night's sleep but a second night's sleep too."

If you're thinking that just reframing these things in your mind will not make life easier, sorry, but that's not true. As we have discussed in many settings, although we are not our thoughts, we live our lives through them, and when our thoughts improve, so goes the rest of our lives. Mindset about sleep matters.

One last point on the importance of sleep: People who lack

sleep often look older than their years, but there is more than vanity at stake. Studies show that people who are sleep deprived have decreased cognition and motor skill functions, two things we want to preserve as we age.

Creating Sleep Rituals

Creating certain sleep rituals dramatically improves sleep. To share a few, according to experts, we should get up at the same time each day even if we get to sleep late the night before. Apparently, it is impossible to make up for lost sleep on weekends and holidays. Limit screen time during the last hour before bed. Go for a walk within a couple hours of sleep. Play relaxing music and do some yoga or meditate, some suggestions for which follow. Write down your thoughts or do a to-do list to get these thoughts out of your head. Buy an alarm clock and move your phone to another room.

Students in my mindfulness class did extensive research on sleep and came up with some ideas I had not heard. Getting up in time to see the sun rise is apparently wonderful at setting our natural sleep cycles.

You can also take a bath. When your skin cools off after being in hot water, your body moves into sleep mode. A tea ritual before bed can also be helpful, especially if you drink calming chamomile tea. Below are some yoga and mindfulness-based suggestions.

PURPOSE PRACTICE 10.1

Commit to a mantra for going to sleep. I use my regular Sanskrit mantra when I can't sleep. Find one you can remember to practice. It works!

It is important to have a good mattress. It is also important to be really relaxed and really tucked in, rather than still tense as you try to go to sleep. Sometimes I notice that even under the covers, I am mentally lying on top of the bed rather than relaxing *into* the bed. I am not fully relaxed, especially my head and neck.

To get the body to fully relax, you can go through each of your body parts in your mind asking each to relax, starting at the head or the feet. This is called a body scan. I have reproduced one version of the body scan in the Purpose Practice below. It is quite long, so if it does not interest you, just skip it. Just know that it definitely works to induce sleep.

> **PURPOSE PRACTICE 10.2**
>
> Body scans help us bring our attention to the present moment by feeling our bodies and the ground underneath us. We can experience life as it unfolds minute by minute and experience some much-needed space between our thoughts and feelings and our present moment experiences. Body scans calm the mind and relieve stress. When done at night, they can foster a great night's sleep.

When we do a body scan, we put aside our problems for a bit so we can rest and renew ourselves. When we are experiencing our bodies in detail and really noting all the sensations within our bodies, it is impossible to worry or think about anything else. This replenishes energy in the body and the mind.

The body scan meditation below can be read into the voice notes on your phone. You can then play it back and do the practice to your own voice. The practice takes about thirty minutes. There are also many body scan meditations available online and in the mindfulness apps. My own version is a bit unusual because it asks people to travel down a tunnel first before focusing on particular parts of the body. This separation of regular life and the body scan can help us drop into the practice.

Body Scan Meditation

Lie down on the floor on your back with a blanket over you and a pillow under your bent knees. Take the time to get very comfortable so you can lie still and move as little as possible.

Begin to focus on your breath. Don't try to change anything about it. Just breathe. Breathe in and out of the nose and then begin to lengthen both the inhale and the exhale, eventually allowing the exhale to become a little longer than the inhale.

Now imagine your very relaxed body just dropping closer and closer into the earth. Then imagine the body slowly moving down a very dark, very comfortable, cozy tunnel. The air in the tunnel is extremely calm. It smells beautiful, and it's very peaceful in there. You're traveling slowly down the tunnel and eventually landing in a very nice soft spot on the earth.

We'll begin by noting those places on your body where you can feel the earth underneath you. For example, your heels, the backs of your calves, the backs of your thighs, your glutes, your middle back, your upper back, your shoulders, and the back of your head. You might also feel your arms or your hands at your sides. Just notice the sensation of feeling the earth underneath you.

Continue that nice deep calming breath as you focus on those spots on the body where you can feel the earth underneath you.

Now, bring your attention to your left foot. Feel the energy around the left foot and see if you can identify any sensations in that left foot. Don't move the foot, just look for sensations like swirling or calming. Really feel that foot. Then, slowly and one at a time, bring the attention to the big toe, the first toe, the second toe, the third toe, and the pinky toe. Breathe energy into that foot. Allow yourself to feel that sensation just a little longer. Now simply let go of that sensation, relaxing that foot completely.

Now bring your attention to the left ankle. Feel the energy around that left ankle. Just allow your attention to rest on that ankle, and then very slowly move your attention up the back of the calf on that left leg and then the front of the shin, allowing the energy there to just be what it is. Very slowly, just feel that energy without moving anything and then, as you feel ready, slowly allow all of that energy to just fall away and relax into the earth.

Now bring your attention to the knee on the left leg. Notice any sensations and energy in and around that knee, back of the knee, front of the knee. Just let that energy flow. Then gently relax the knee and bring your attention up to the front of the thigh, that very large muscle. See if you can note any sensations there. Then bring your attention around to the back of the hamstring. Feel any energy that's there and then as you feel ready, simply allow that entire upper leg to also just fall away, slowly relaxing and releasing into the earth.

Notice any difference in the way the left leg and the right leg feel.

Now bring your attention to your right foot. Do the same practice with your right foot, then your right toes beginning at your big toe.

Move to your ankle, then to your right knee, just as you did with your left knee.

Then bring your attention to your right thigh and hamstring. Each time, feel any energy that's there, and then, simply allow that part of you to fall away, slowly relaxing and releasing into the earth.

Now bring your attention to the pelvic area. Really allow yourself to feel any sensations in that pelvic area and then slowly move the attention up to the stomach area. Really notice any sensations in the stomach here. There will be some, so take your time and really allow that energy in the pelvic area, hip area, as well as the stomach area, to just swirl and sway and be whatever it is. Breathe deeply into this entire area. Now slowly allow all of that energy to also drop down so both legs, the pelvic area, and the stomach area are all now very released and relaxed into the earth.

Now bring your attention up into the heart space. Allow yourself to feel the sensations in the heart and all the areas around the chest, really exploring that area, allowing the breath to deepen, noticing any other sensations such as the beating of your heart and anything else. Then, very slowly as you feel ready, allow that entire heart space and chest area to release and relax into the earth as well.

Now bring your attention to the left shoulder, noticing any sensations there, then slowly moving your attention down the arm, down the upper arm first, then to the elbow, then all the way down the lower arm, all the way to the wrist, and then slowly bringing the attention to each finger individually, first the pinky finger, then the ring finger, the middle finger, the index finger, and the thumb, allowing yourself to feel the sensations of that entire shoulder, arm, all the way down through the wrist and hand, and then slowly allowing that entire arm to relax and release.

Now move on to the right side and do the same.

Now moving your attention to your shoulders, allow yourself to feel whatever tension there is, whatever sensations there are, really allowing yourself to experience this often-tense area, breathing into the area and slowly exhaling out, and as you do, allowing all of that energy to just drop into the earth, allowing the shoulders to become very relaxed.

Now, bring your attention to the neck. Allow yourself to feel the sensations in the neck. Really experience that area, breathing into it as well, feeling anything that you feel, and slowly allowing the neck to release its tension and fully relax into the earth as well.

Finally, bring your attention up to the head. First, note the place on which the head is touching the earth. Focus on that area. Breathe into that area, allowing yourself to feel

CHAPTER TEN

any sensations there, then slowly bringing your attention to the front of the head, gently opening the mouth, bringing the attention up to the sinus area, and then up through the forehead and the sides of the eyes, and finally all the way to the top of the skull. Allow yourself to experience any sensations in that area, and then, as slowly as you can, roll the eyes back in their sockets and release and relax that entire head all the way down into the earth.

Breathe as you do this and now imagine that breath coming up through the top of the head. Imagine breathing in and out of the top of the skull. Continue here to be very relaxed, the entire body completely succumbing to the earth, relaxed and released into the earth.

Now, bring your attention above the body and imagine energy above the body moving slowly all the way from the head to the feet. That attention is cradling the body in this newfound relaxation. Take a few deep breaths and keep breathing deeply for a full minute or two, enjoying the support of the earth and this fully relaxed feeling here on the mat. Continue to enjoy this as you bring your attention back to the breath.

Now, we will slowly bring ourselves back up the tunnel. The tunnel is warm and cozy, very comforting, and we are slowly coming back up, allowing the breath to slow down even more and eventually coming all the way back up to where you started your practice in your present space.

Take a few more cleansing breaths and when you're ready, begin to bring a little bit of movement back into your fingers, and then a little bit of movement back into your toes. Lift your arms and stretch like a cat, moving in any way that feels comfortable, and getting ready to bring yourself back into your regular life, refreshed and renewed.

As you feel ready, open your eyes if they were closed, and roll over onto your right side. As you feel ready, very slowly return to a seated or standing position. Take your time.

Do this practice whenever you need to retreat to a nice calm place, in order to refresh your mind and body or get a good night's sleep.

Finally, consider doing a bit of yoga before bed. Here are two poses to try:

Insomnia Pose/Half Frog

Lie on your tummy on the floor or your bed. Bend your left arm at a right angle like a pillow above your head and rest your left cheek on it. Stick your right arm and right knee out to the side. Stick a pillow under the right knee and drop it toward the floor or bed. Relax and release. Set a timer for two to three minutes. Then do the same thing on the other side.

Legs Up the Wall

Sit next to a wall with your hip against the wall and your legs stretched out long along the wall. Pivot and lie the body down perpendicular to the wall while you swing your legs up the wall. It is OK if your hips are a few inches away from the wall. Leave your arms at your side and just drop into the pose. Set a timer for five to six minutes and focus on your breath. As thoughts arise, let them go like clouds passing in the sky, bringing your attention back to your breath. To come out, drop the legs back down to the side, move into a fetal position and rest there for a few long deep breaths. Take your time getting back up to a seated position.

You can also do a few other yoga poses in bed before you go to sleep. Any pose that can be done on your back can also be done in bed. You can also rub lavender oil into your feet.

Summarizing Good Sleep Tips

- Get up at the same time every day
- Get up to watch the sun rise
- Take a walk before bed

- Take a bath before bed
- Write down your thoughts or create a to-do list to clear your head
- Stop regular screen time (checking email, surfing the web) an hour before bed
- Store your phone in another room overnight
- Play relaxing music
- Do some yoga or meditate
- Drink calming tea
- Use a mindfulness app

Socializing

Socializing as we age is critical. Strong relationships fight all three of Atul Gawande's plagues: boredom, loneliness, and dependence.[162] Numerous studies show that people who maintain a few close relationships have better health outcomes, including longer lives. If you become isolated, it can be difficult to start socializing again, but it takes just one step to begin the process of spending more time with others.

Loneliness is dangerous for our health as it can elevate inflammation and increase blood pressure. According to Maddy Dychtwald, loneliness can even contribute to heart disease, depression, and early death.[163] People who are lonely are three to ten times more likely to get sick and die from all causes, compared to people who regularly experience love, connection, and community.[164] As Dychtwald notes, quoting Dr. Vivek Murthy after the pandemic:

> Our relationships are a source of healing and well-being hiding in plain sight. Given the significant health consequences of loneliness and isolation, we must prioritize building social connections the same way we have prioritized other critical health issues such as tobacco, obesity, and substance-use disorders.[165]

Our social relationships are the lubricants of our lives. When we are young, we often enjoy having a large group of acquaintances, but as we age, it is the quality of relationship that matters, not the quantity. According to the longest-running longitudinal study of happiness ever conducted, people who were most satisfied with their relationships at age fifty were also the happiest at age eighty.[166]

Intimate relationships protect us from the ups and downs of life and help us mitigate the physical and emotional pains of aging.[167] In *Learning to Love Midlife*, Chip Conley distinguishes between social isolation and loneliness. As he explains, social isolation can be a choice, but loneliness never is. If loneliness is an issue, Conley suggests some action steps that can help.

First, he suggests that you make a list of five to ten old friends with whom you have lost touch; then rank them by how much you would like to connect with them and start reaching out, one per week.

Second, Conley suggests you practice listening, which has become a lost art. As Conley shares, "Knowledge speaks, wisdom listens."[168] When you show interest in others, they gravitate toward you and find you fascinating.

Third, Conley invites us to find new communities by going places where you will meet like-minded people. Stay open and present and engage with people. Find your flock. You can start this process by hosting people in your home. During a rough personal challenge, Conley did this by hosting spiritual sanga dinners at his house for friends who followed varied spiritual paths. Stewart and I did something similar when we moved to New Mexico twenty-five years ago and had no friends. We hosted many parties for neighbors, and these people are still our best friends.

For a few more suggestions, consider going to a dog park if you have a dog. Studies show that people benefit as much from these experiences as dogs do. Or consider joining a yoga class, joining an exercise group, or taking a class at the gym. Another option that helps the brain and body in numerous ways is to take a class at your local college's continuing education program.

You can also attend a religious service or a neighborhood meeting, or even just go to a coffee shop and chat with the barista. Finally, it helps to actually schedule socializing well in advance. You might not want to go when the time comes, but you are likely to go anyway and enjoy yourself.

> **PURPOSE PRACTICE 10.3**
>
> Take one step this week to connect with an old friend or do one of the other activities listed above. Note the activity in your journal or on a calendar. Add more activities in the weeks that follow.

Take a Social Inventory

Think about and cultivate relationships with people upon whom you can rely. In *Build Your Village*, Florence Ann Romano asks, "Who is your emergency contact when you sign a medical form?"[169] Similarly, Michael Clinton asks, "If you were dying, which five people would you want at your side?"[170] In considering these questions, consider people who are alive or dead, and think about who shaped your worldview up to age twenty-one, then thereafter. Clinton then asks if you're still in touch with some of these people. If they are still alive, he suggests you reach out and find them.

Stress Reduction, Joy, and Self-Care

Returning to the subject of stress, besides movement, healthy food, sleep, and maintaining good relationships, managing stress plays a leading role in how we age. Chronic stress destroys the body, literally weakening the organs and breaking down the tissues. Many studies show that too much stress is like too much sitting. You might think that in older age you won't have as much stress, but it is likely that whatever you had before, you'll have similar levels of stress in older age. The stress we experience as we age will be different, but there will still be stress.

Useful techniques for keeping stress at bay are scattered throughout this book. Among other things, all forms of contemplative practice help reduce stress. And guess what else cuts stress? Physical exercise. All things come full circle here. Move that body!

There are also other ways to reduce stress. Music, particularly calming music like classical or yoga music, can soothe the soul. Or, if you are feeling low energy and stressed out about that, you can listen to upbeat, stimulating music. Music has been tied to good brain health. Recent studies, particularly by Harvard scientist Ellen Langer, show that listening to the music of your youth can even ward off or turn back the clock on dementia and other cognitive disorders.[171]

Getting out into nature is also a mood booster, especially when you don't really feel like it. Time spent outside is exponentially better for your mood than staying inside. Time outside also improves sleep.

When it comes to mindset about stress, remember that there will be times when hard things happen, when things are not quite right. If we keep this in mind, stressful events will not surprise us and may even become an accepted part of life. Embrace the knowledge that stressful things will happen. Despite these events, we can live with more comfort and even joy. We can even experience joy and sadness or disappointment simultaneously if we take time to care for ourselves. This is one of the blessings and challenges of life, to be able to experience joy when there's also anxiety, worry, sadness, or chaos. See if you can take the chaos in stride and search out happiness and joy.

I went through this process myself recently. In our friends' home in Bend, Oregon, while my husband was out camping, I realized how lucky we are. Everything externally seemed to be going wrong. My husband's back was killing him, which was hugely debilitating, his father was dying, and our seventeen-year-old dog (who is really a combination of my only child and the canine love of my life) was very sick. It was cold, wet, and uncomfortable, and everything was uncertain at best, yet there was still joy.

With a little effort and a bit of gratitude, we can focus on what we have rather than what we do not have. For us, we could still go on short, beautiful hikes, make yummy food, go out for happy hour, pet the dog, meet new people, and plan our next adventure, whether we ever went on the adventure or not. Daydreaming can be healing too. Sometimes all you need is something, anything, to look forward to.

This search for joy is both a blessing and a monumental challenge, but we can choose joy. We can develop a joyfulness practice and cultivate self-care, which can increase our lifespans and make life more enjoyable in the meantime. See if you can make joyful self-care part of your practice. Here are some self-care exercises to help reduce stress.

PURPOSE PRACTICE 10.4

Self-Massage

Use your own touch to relieve stress. Give yourself a healing massage. It is wonderful to be touched by others but as COVID-19 has taught us, it is just as important to touch ourselves. Smoothe coconut oil or similar all over your body, or just use your favorite lotion. Be sure to spend plenty of time on your neck and feet.

Do a Meditation for Your Heart

Because the body is where all emotions are felt, the term "broken heart" is descriptive. You can literally feel the heart hurt when you have been hurt. The heart is our touchpoint for love.

Many times throughout my day, I like to place my hands on my heart. This gesture is a way to connect with my body, remember that I have a body, and pay attention to what my heart truly wants. The meditation below helps us practice self-love. It teaches us to connect with our own hearts. It connects the mind and body, that body that we often forget we have. To get started, use your phone to record your own voice repeating the meditation below. Then play it back to yourself and do the practice. It takes just six to seven minutes and leaves you feeling refreshed and loved.

PURPOSE PRACTICE 10.5

Sit in a comfortable, dignified position with your back up nice and tall. Gently close your eyes, bring your hands to your lap, and sit as still as you can.

Begin to breathe deeply, watching the breath fill the lungs and then exhale slowly. Continue that breath for four or five more breaths.

Now, slowly begin to notice that the breath is entering the body and leaving the body.

Begin to notice that you have a body.

Now, bring both of your hands to your heart, one on top of the other. Begin to breathe very deeply into the heart as if the heart was like a big lung, filling those hands with cleansing beautiful air. Slowly repeat to yourself the words I love you. Slowly repeat these words again. I love you.

Begin to cultivate the habit of bringing the love that we pass to others every day back to ourselves.

Feel that breath coming in and out of those hands on the heart. You can switch hands if you like, putting the other one on top. Once again, repeat to yourself, I love you.

Now, slowly begin to think of things about yourself that you truly love. Perhaps it is that you are creative, brave, determined, and focused. Perhaps it is that you are kind, patient, considerate, and compassionate. Whatever resonates, take a few breaths to think of things that you truly appreciate about yourself.

Now, begin to think about the many ways in which you have loved and have been loved. Take a few breaths of gratitude for each of those opportunities.

After the tape stops, bring your attention back to the present and the space in which you inhabit. Stop and pause and open your eyes if they are closed. Then, move on with your day, but throughout that day, bring yourself back to these exercises in order to cultivate compassion and self-love.

Here, we have explored three ways, in addition to movement and a healthy diet, to improve our physical and mental well-being. These are good sleep, healthy relationships, and stress reduction. We can use this information to devise a personal health plan.

Devising Your Individual Health Plan

Below we provide tools for developing a plan to create better physical and mental health. We will list things we can do to move more, eat better, get better sleep, improve relationships, and reduce stress.

See if there are things you can do that hit more than one of these categories at once. For example, in our neighborhood, without planning, we often pile out into the street after dinner to enjoy the sunset and watch the birds. It is fun and serves three of the pillars of good health: stress relief, physical movement, and socialization.

PURPOSE PRACTICE 10.6

Take a piece of paper and use a pen to divide the paper into four quadrants. Now, using one quadrant for each category below, write down one or two things you can do to

- move more
- eat better
- sleep better
- socialize or improve relationships

Here are a few things that might appear in the squares:

Go for a walk once a day.
Make an exercise schedule and put it on your calendar.
Find one healthy recipe a week, and make it for friends.
Make a healthy-food grocery list.
Connect with an old friend.
Join a new group activity.
Send a gratitude note to a mentor.
Give yourself a massage.
Do yoga in bed.
Take a long bath.
Schedule a salon massage or pedicure with a friend.
Go to a dog park.
Watch birds.
Try a new group exercise class.
Sign up for a continuing education class.

Post your wellness plan ideas where you will see them throughout the day. Make a commitment to yourself to get started on the list, and add new things each week. Track your progress in your journal. Give yourself big kudos for whatever you do! You deserve it. Your body and mind, your whole self, will thank you.

PART FOUR

Creating the Inspired Retirement Life

CHAPTER 11:
DISCOVERING YOUR BROAD RETIREMENT LIFE OBJECTIVES

This next part of the book moves from physical well-being in retirement to setting broad retirement goals and maintaining a sense of purpose in retirement. To get you started, this short chapter helps you think about what you value or think you will value most in retirement. It provides opportunities to gain insight and self-knowledge that you can build upon in future chapters. Once you identify and prioritize your broad retirement values and goals, you can design a retirement life that achieves your unique objectives.

In *Thinking Smarter: Seven Steps to Your Fulfilling Retirement and Life*, behavioral economist Shlomo Benartzi provides a framework for setting broad retirement goals.[172] In this book, Benartzi shares what he calls his retirement goal-planning system or GPS, which helps us discover who we are, what we care about, and where we are trying to go. This chapter draws upon Benartzi's excellent research. Benartzi directs us to create a list of our own general retirement goals, to consider adding to our goals by reading other people's goals, and through the process, to create a comprehensive list of our unique retirement objectives. His process then helps us prioritize our most important goals.

CHAPTER ELEVEN

This entire chapter is one large, interactive Purpose Practice, so you will want to have your pen and notebook handy. In the first step, you identify your goals, the things that matter most to you right now, and those you think will continue to matter to you for the rest of your life.[173] Then you expand on that list, and finally, you prioritize your goals.

List Your Retirement Objectives

First, carefully list all the goals you have for your retirement life. Take your time.

Ask Others to Make a List, Share the Lists, and Consider Adding to Your List

Next, ask a few other people to create a similar list and share the lists, adding things to your list that seem important after reading other people's lists.

Consider Adding Other Goals from a List Prepared by Benartzi

Now, study your list carefully and read through the list below. See if you'd like to add any of the objectives below to your list as well. Don't add things that already appear on your list in different words, as your own words will be more meaningful to you than these. The goal of this first three-part step is to create an inclusive list before you prioritize the objectives on the list.

Because this book focuses primarily on non-financial goals, I have reordered Benartzi's list and placed purely financial goals at the end. It is still important to include these financial goals because if one of these goals is important but not yet achieved, you may need to work in paid positions longer than expected. This extra and longer work could conflict with other objectives.

Here is my paraphrased version of Benartzi's list:

- Health care: be able to get good health care in your community.[174]
- Housing: be able to choose where you want to live, for example in your own home.
- Travel and leisure: be able to take trips and engage in other leisure activities.
- Work and give back on your own terms: be able to choose to work part-time, begin a new career, volunteer for causes you care about, choose not to work at all, etc.[175]
- Self-improvement: be able to take classes and learn new skills.
- Social engagement: be able to enjoy family and friends and not feel lonely.
- Ending life with dignity: be able to live your last days on your own terms.
- Control: feel like you still drive your own life.
- Financial independence: know that you can meet your basic expenses.
- Lifestyle: be able to maintain your current lifestyle.
- Family bequests: be able to leave money to family as you like.
- Give to important causes: be able to contribute financially to causes you care about.

Peruse this list and add anything you care about that is missing from your current list.

Now that you have this comprehensive list of your retirement life objectives, drawn from your own ideas, those of others, and those provided by Benartzi, eliminate anything that is redundant.

CHAPTER ELEVEN

Prioritize Your Top Objectives: Whittle Down the List, Pick the Most and Least Important Objectives, Then Rank Them and Create Three Categories

Using Benartzi's system, you will now prioritize your top nine or ten goals using four steps:

1. Pick your top nine or ten objectives from the large list. This is hard but extremely important. We can't do everything. We need to choose. Go ahead and whittle down the list.

2. Once you have done this whittling, identify the most important goal and the least important goal. This will give you a "scale" or reference point for prioritizing the rest of the list.

3. With the most important goal and the least important goal in hand, rank the remaining goals in between the most important and the least important.

4. Place three or four of the nine or ten top goals in each of these categories or boxes:
   - most important
   - next-most important
   - less important but still in the top nine or ten

We know prioritizing is difficult, as all of the items on your list are your highest priorities. When Stewart and I did this prioritizing, following the instructions above, we first picked our most important and our least important goals. Then we ranked the rest, putting them in order, one, two, three, and so on. It was hard, and we often put items head to head to make our priority ranking. After doing the ranking, we created the three categories. You'll see that some of our goals are similar to Benartzi's but are stated in our own words. After several incarnations, here is what we came up with starting with Stewart:

Highest Priorities
Enjoy joint activities with Nathalie
Work on overall health and fitness
Volunteer, work when I want to, where I want to

Next Highest
Spend time with friends and family
Read
Have enough money

Lowest of the Highest
Help others access the outdoors
Get outside myself
Be a better person

And now for my list:

Highest Priorites
Be physically heathy enough to be independent
Live in the present moment with Stewart
Always have a dog

Next Highest
Live in my own home
Work on my own terms, including all sorts of teaching
Write and share my writing with interested audiences

Lowest of the Highest
Engage in self-improvement
Spend time with friends and family
Help other people find purpose

Prioritizing is the tough part, particularly when goals conflict, for example when financial independence conflicts with stopping work or working on your own terms. Your circumstances will determine your priorities. If money is not a big concern, financial independence will not likely top your list of goals.

Keep in mind that the further away you are from retirement,

the more likely it is that this list of goals will need to be modified. Things change over time. One example of this prioritizing in my own life is that I now know that being physically active is a very high priority. I could not have predicted this a decade ago because I had not yet experienced what it feels like to live in an older body.

Learn from Other Retirees

In addition to creating and prioritizing your retirement objectives using the steps above, Benartzi suggests talking to other retirees about what they have learned.[176] Just as young parents benefit from the experiences of others who have been through the experience of parenting, it helps to hear what others have learned in retirement. The stories I share in chapter 14 are designed with this purpose in mind, but you might also talk to people you know.

For Even Greater Insight, Write a Creative Story about You in Retirement

Our last exercise in this chapter involves visualizing and more journaling. So far, this chapter has proposed very structured exercises, but here we get a chance to be more creative.[177] Write down answers to these questions, which were also inspired by Benartzi and modified slightly:

> Take a few deep breaths. Now imagine a retirement life that is going well. What does that life look and feel like? What adjectives come to mind to describe that experience? Take time to describe that life fully in your own words. Let it be natural, just a stream-of-consciousness description of all the things that are going right, in whatever order they come to you. Don't think too hard about it. Just let it flow. Write it all down.

> Take a few more deep breaths. Now describe in your own words a retirement that goes badly. What does that life look and feel like? What adjectives come to mind to describe that experience? Take time to describe that life fully in your own words. Let it be natural, just a stream-of-consciousness description of all the things that are going wrong, in whatever order they come to you. Don't think too hard about it. Just let it flow. Write it all down.

Take a look at what you wrote, and in what order. In addition to the order, pay particular attention to adjectives and feelings that arose. These journal entries provide clues to your fears, goals, and priorities, and to internal experiences of which you may not even be aware.

Benartzi provides an example of some insights that arose in one of his interviewees. His interviewee described a good retirement as one in which she was giving back to society, living in good health in a pleasant environment, and seeing friends and family. The first few words of her vision of a bad retirement mentioned that she would be alone. This suggested that social engagement was more important to her than she realized. Again, being physically fit rose in my own list when I stopped to imagine a bad retirement outcome. This is not something I would have predicted, nor is it where I have spent my time preparing for my own retirement life. Go back and see if your own journal entry describing a bad retirement causes you to reprioritize your list. Keep your final (for now) list in a convenient place.

Hopefully, this short chapter has brought you awareness of what is most important to you in retirement. You may want to make a poster of these top retirement life goals. Using these goals as a starting point, we will get more specific in the next chapters, identifying times we have been in flow, activities we enjoy, and signature strengths, so that we can move beyond broad concepts and begin to plan our retirement lives. Keep in mind that you can redo the exercises in this chapter any time your circumstances change, and they will. Change is one of the things we can rely on no matter what.

CHAPTER 12: DISCOVERING YOUR SKILLS, VALUES, AND WHAT BRINGS YOU JOY

With our prioritized retirement objectives in hand, we now move into a discussion of work or avocation in the inspired retirement. This chapter is especially useful for people who have worked, will soon stop working, and are wondering what they'll do with their time in retirement.

Plenty of people wake up happy every day in retirement without much thought to what will bring them purpose in life. Others need direction on how best to use their newfound time. This chapter and the two that follow explore ways to find that direction.

According to happiness experts, unique joy and fulfillment is found at the confluence of our core values, our signature strengths, and those activities that bring us joy. This chapter explores these three attributes to help us find joy, purpose, and direction in retirement. We start with a general discussion of joy, and then get into the nitty gritty of what might inspire and challenge you in retirement.

CHAPTER TWELVE

The Paradox of Joy and Purpose

Despite common legend, joy is rarely derived from sitting on a yacht all day every day drinking martinis. For most of us, joy comes from feeling accomplished and solving life's problems, large and small. I have seen it again and again in my clients, colleagues, students, and of course, in my interviewees. Rising to a challenge is fulfilling because happiness requires some struggle. No challenge, no fulfillment.

Joy in retirement is no different. That too requires challenge. Retirement is both the end of something as well as the beginning of something else.[178] In *Hello, Goodbye: 75 Rituals for Times of Loss, Celebration, and Change,* Day Schildkret tells a story of a woman named Linda. Linda worked at a job she disliked as an insurance broker and finally made it to retirement. She had looked forward to this day forever. She even downloaded an app on her phone that allowed her to count down the days starting at 1,095 days until retirement. She was relieved when the day came, but suddenly realized that the real work began after she left. She had lived three decades of her life in a false professional persona, and in the process, had lost sight of who she really was. Her first goal in retirement was to shed her inauthentic skin and get herself back. As she explained, "When some people leave their job it's like their life ended. Mine began after I retired."[179]

Retirement is a relatively new phenomenon. In 1932, a mere 5 percent of elders received any public benefits upon retirement. As Schildkret notes, as a society, we haven't really figured out what this transition means or what it is asking of any of us. As he further explains, our culture sees retirement as "a time of deserved selfishness, and golf/mah-jongg dates, mixed in with an underlying dread of purposelessness, redundancy, and a fear of aging."[180]

To make his point, Schildkret describes a humorous foray into a greeting card aisle, where one retirement card featured a cartoon lady in a bathing suit, sipping a cocktail and saying, "I'm retired.

Do it yourself." Another had an image of a weekly retirement schedule checklist: Monday, brush teeth; Tuesday, shave; Wednesday, shower; etc. Along the same lines, I recall a humorous new "business" card sent by a friend upon her retirement. Here is what it said across the middle of the card:

> No job
> No office
> No appointments
> No commitments
> No hassles

While the side of the card did feature a picture of a person in a hammock, drinking a fancy cocktail, the message might as well have read "no purpose." Without a sense of purpose in our lives, we are not living the dream. Perhaps we are not really living at all.

As Alberto Villoldo explains in *The Heart of the Shaman*, many of our daydreams eventually become nightmares because what we think we want—ease—is not what we really want or need.[181] If there is no challenge in retirement, there will be little meaning. Think about it. If you have everything you want with little effort, no work, and no difficulty at all, what will you work toward? How will you gain satisfaction?

Much of happiness derives from times we have felt both challenged and fulfilled in our lives. As Schildkret explains, retirement requires us to ask big questions about our life as it changes, such as the following:

> How am I valued?
> What are my routines without work?
> Who am I without my job title?
> Is it OK not to achieve as much?[182]

As he acknowledges, these are not questions that can be answered immediately. Rather, they must be considered over time, and the answers will change. The idea of stepping back from work can evoke uncertainty, doubt, curiosity, and excitement. At the same

CHAPTER TWELVE

time, our culture expects that we can transition from work to retirement flawlessly.[183]

Visualizing retirement while still working is entirely different than actually living that retirement life. Too many retirees spend decades at school and work, only to feel disoriented and lost when that structure disappears. This can lead to depression or even despair.

Retirement and the Loss of Identity, Purpose, and People

Schildkret describes a woman named Judy, who had worked in Catholic ministry in a very fulfilling job. Upon her retirement, she felt completely untethered.[184] She didn't know who she was anymore. As Schildkret explains, the transition to retirement longs to be infused with purpose. Everyone comes into this world with a gift. Some people live their entire lives looking for theirs, wondering what to do next. Retirement can throw our purpose into question all over again.

In my interviews, I discovered that many people thought retirement would be easy but found it to be a challenge due to this lack of direction and purpose. For example, one person we'll call Sam said he went to a therapist after finding no real enjoyment in ticking things off his retirement bucket list. Travel in particular was not bringing the joy he anticipated. Sam said he got great advice from the therapist: "burn your bucket list." Apparently, he had been frantically working on ticking things off this list, but not stopping to savor the experiences. He now spends his time enjoying sunsets and long runs along the natural areas of his town. If he wants to go somewhere, he goes, but travel is not an obligation. It is up to him. For another example, a hospital administrator I interviewed retired abruptly during COVID. He found himself scouring the shelves of Barnes & Noble looking for a hobby as he had relied heavily on his work to find purpose in life.

Sharron, an Oregon State Park host, provides another example. Sharron was a physical therapist from Wisconsin who retired from the veteran's administration in 2016. She went back to work part-time as a physical therapist for a retirement community after five years off the job. She said working part-time was a win-win for her because she could choose her schedule and her shifts. When she is not doing that, she works as a park host in the Oregon State Park system.

Though Sharron eventually found her retirement sweet spot by combining part-time paid work with part-time volunteer work, she now feels she retired too early. She discovered after resigning that she loved her job and that in many ways, it was a cushy job, a fact she did not appreciate until she retired. She also missed the people with whom she worked. Once she had retired, there was no going back.

When asked why she retired when she did, she shared that in the federal government, you qualify for lifetime health care after a certain number of years regardless of your age. This gave her the freedom to retire whenever she wanted, which she did at age sixty-two. As she explained, "For some reason I had it in my head that I needed to retire once I was eligible. People look at retirement as this pot of gold at the end of the rainbow, but not much thought is given to what you'll do once you retire."

Sharron thought failing to plan one's time in retirement was a mistake. As she explained, "Just like they say, happiness is an inside job. You really need to think about what is going to make you feel happy and needed and purposeful. I found things that make me feel relevant, but it took time, and I could have saved myself some pain by thinking more about it before I retired."

According to Sharron, the thing she missed most about her job when she was retired was the structure of it. Many people I spoke with said the lack of structure left them unmoored, feeling unsure what to do with themselves. Sharron also missed the people. To address the social side of things, Sharron suggested building con-

CHAPTER TWELVE

nections in your desired retirement field before you actually leave your job, a theme that emerged in my interviews.

Similarly, Hannah worked for thirty-five years as an administrator in the county office of education in a small western town. Hannah retired at age fifty-six, also as soon as she was eligible. Her interview contained similar themes to Sharron's. Prior to retiring, she was even more excited to retire than Sharron. In her office, two years before her target retirement date, Hannah created a twenty-four-link retirement paper chain. At the end of every month, she would thrillingly and ceremoniously cut off one of the links. The ritual was invigorating and celebratory. She was working toward the goal of finishing up with great enthusiasm. She could not have been happier about her future retirement.

It surprised her to wake up shortly after she retired to a feeling of regret and hopelessness. She asked herself, "What have I done?" and "Now what?" Next came a deep depression. Her husband would come home from work and say, "Just be happy," but she could not seem to do that. When I found her two years later, she was working for the Oregon State Park system. In the intervening years, she volunteered with her service dog in hospice care but discovered that this work was too emotionally draining.

Hannah recalled a conversation with a grocery clerk after her retirement. He too quit too early and went back to work part-time to quell an unsettled feeling of anxiety over his retirement. Both really missed talking to people. In fact, Hannah discovered that she missed the social side of work most of all. Like many people who work at the same job for decades, she missed her seniority and status, as well as the regular human contact. She reported that weekends were OK, when others were off work too, but on Sunday nights she felt anxious and had difficulty sleeping. She tried to make a structure for her life, reading self-help books and exercising just as everyone advised. She even set out to knit one complex project a week, but none of this fulfilled her desire to feel needed and to connect with others.

A friend suggested antidepressants and her doctor said she would be a good candidate, but she didn't want to take drugs indefinitely. In telling her story, she explained that everybody needs purpose, work they can really get behind. Once she found her seasonal job for the Oregon Park system, she felt alive again. She described feeling good about preserving the land and historical monuments and being part of the wonderful system that is doing something good for society.

She also provided a very good lesson for educators worldwide. She explained that working for an educational institution or system is a highly positive experience. As she explained, "It's important to know that you're doing something for the future, for society. It is exceptionally powerful and rewarding to be part of such an important societal system."

We are all different. Hannah is goal oriented, and prior to retiring, she had few interests outside work. With her type-A personality, she loved and still loves to work toward a goal. If this is you, retiring won't change that aspect of your personality. It is important to plan for it.

Mindful Searching for Meaning in Retirement

In *Ageless Aging*, Maddy Dychtwald suggests anecdotes for what one of her friends calls "this empty wasteland called retirement."[185] She urges us to improve our *social fitness*, by making new friends, joining religious organizations, adopting a dog, and perhaps most critically, reigniting with purpose. As Dychtwald notes, those with a strong sense of purpose have less chances of Alzheimer's, cardiovascular problems, depression, stroke, and disability, as well as better overall health, greater cognitive function, greater life satisfaction, increased mobility, and longer lifespans.[186] She notes that we all have gifts and can all give back, which fuels our sense of purpose.[187]

One purpose of this chapter is to begin thinking about what makes you feel happy, purposeful, challenged, and mentally alive. For most of us, purpose, challenge, and mental stimulation come from engaging in some form of work, however broadly defined. Designing that retirement work life is the subject of the next chapter. That chapter also helps you design a life with the right *amount* of work. Not too little, not too much.

For now, we are conceptualizing what this meaningful work might be, keeping the options broad and thinking holistically. We all need purpose to get us up in the morning, to push us toward new challenges, and to motivate us to be active in our choices and lifestyle. Whatever we choose should be challenging but not impossible. Too little challenge and we are bored. Too much and we might decide to give up. We also want to feel that our work matters. In her book, *The Second Half of Life: Opening the Eight Gates of Wisdom*, Angeles Arrien poses helpful questions about finding meaning as we contemplate leaving traditional workplaces.[188] She asks us to quietly reflect on these questions:

> Where do you experience the spirit of fluency in your life and where are you willing to live "Like a river flows,/Carried by the surprise/Of its own unfolding"?
>
> What generates meaning, hope, inspiration, and curiosity for you?
>
> What private longings or callings have you repeatedly dismissed? What has prevented you from acting upon them?
>
> How do you regenerate yourself?[189]

In posing these questions, Arrien asks us to ponder our dreams, work, health, relationships, creativity, and heart's desire at this time of life. To prepare for the next chapter and the rest of your life, do the following Purpose Practice.

> **PURPOSE PRACTICE 12.1**
>
> Write a journal entry or make a chart or poster answering Arrien's questions.

What do your responses reveal? Many of us have spent decades working forty, fifty, or even sixty hours a week. What we care about now is likely different than what we cared about thirty years ago. We want to spend the rest of our time on things we care most about, rather than things on someone else's bucket list.

Before we focus on what brings us joy, we may need to unwind. As one high-level executive-turned-artist I interviewed said:

> I had no idea how high-strung I was until I slowed down enough to finally start to unwind. This took several months of just moving and breathing and questioning. It was scary and made me question a lot of the parts of my life, but in the end, I did not regret the past at all. I just knew I needed to do something new, something less time-consuming so I could focus on my new grandkid, and finally, on my kids. All the obligations that kept me from them suddenly became optional but that doesn't mean I knew what to do. I had no idea. In some ways I still don't, but I don't mind the searching and the questioning.

Perhaps you see that you may have been a bit trapped in your past life, and now have the freedom to make new choices. What a blessing it is to be able to choose how to spend your valuable time going forward.

Perhaps you would like to stay in the same field but accomplish more in less time. Thankfully, this is possible using the skills you have built throughout your life. Perhaps you would like to do something totally different with your time, based upon the activities you enjoy most. Ultimately the choice is yours.

CHAPTER TWELVE

Identifying Times You Have Been in Flow

As you picture your future life, see if you can find some flow in it. Modern psychologist Mihaly Csikszentmihalyi coined the term "flow" to describe past experiences during which you felt totally alive and engaged in what you were doing, a state in which time flew and you were fully engaged in whatever you were experiencing at the moment.[190]

Csikszentmihalyi studied flow in surgeons, artists, mountain climbers, and other high achievers, noting the relationship between effectiveness and this magical state of focused concentration. In studying flow, Csikszentmihalyi found that this state of mind can be so enjoyable that the mind becomes completely absorbed in the task.[191] He also found that flow could release otherwise dammed-up solutions into consciousness.

According to Csikszentmihalyi, flow is achievable only when we understand the ultimate goal involved, when the task is challenging but not beyond our skills or capacity to grow, and when we believe that the situation can be addressed through our actions.[192] Tedium, inability, and anxiety are buzzkill or "flow kill,"[193] as are external motivations that focus only upon pleasing others.[194] This alternative state of "antiflow" is found in any activity that is "meaningless, tedious [and] offers little challenge; is not intrinsically motivating; or creates a sense of lack of control."[195]

In this next exercise we will identify times when we have been in flow, felt most alive, and have literally lost ourselves in an activity or task, including losing all sense of time.

PURPOSE PRACTICE 12.2

Journal about a couple times in your life when you have felt fully alive while performing an activity or task, have fully lost yourself in a task and been in flow, and have been so engaged in the activity that you literally lost all sense of time.

Put your list somewhere handy and read it often. This will help you identify new flow experiences as you enter your next stage of life. To this list of flow experiences, we will now add our favorite activities, as well as our unique character traits, values, and skills.

Identifying Activities We Enjoy

In this section, we identify activities that we enjoy, first by making our own list and then by augmenting it with some other suggestions.

> **PURPOSE PRACTICE 12.3**
>
> Take out a big piece of paper and make a vertical list of twenty things you like or love to do.[196] Then create a few columns running across the top of the page, asking questions about the details of the activity. Try answering the questions below in the columns or make up your own questions. The idea is to find themes in your favorite activities.
>
> 1. When was the last time you did this activity?
> 2. If you have a partner, does your partner also like it?
> 3. Is it free or does it cost money?
> 4. Is this activity performed alone or with others?
>   - at home or while out?
>   - inside or outside?
>   - while sedentary or active?
>   - fast or slow?

Now look at the activities and the answers in the columns. Do you see any themes? Hang on to this list. We will come back to it.

Now pick from the list I made below and see if it creates other

CHAPTER TWELVE

ideas for enjoyable activities. This activity draws upon Shlomo Benartzi's notion that we all have blind spots when it comes to what is important to us, what our goals are, and what we want to do with our lives.[197] It helps to look at other people's lists.

PURPOSE PRACTICE 12.4

Mark the things on this list that you enjoy:

- Fixing something that's broken
- Playing the guitar with friends
- Attending a board meeting
- Helping new businesses write advertising
- Sitting on the beach
- Golfing
- Creating web content
- Bringing a friend a home-baked treat
- Helping someone else in need
- Making an object of beauty
- Helping someone find and buy a new home
- Attending sporting events
- Learning something new
- Watching wildlife
- Cooking
- Planning a vacation
- Writing a document for an organization
- Praying or meditating
- Attending a meeting with colleagues
- Reading or listening to a good book
- Giving a presentation
- Being with family
- Working out
- Having a beer or cocktail with friends
- Participating in community meetings
- Going for a walk

- Hiking or biking
- Public speaking
- Traveling to a new place
- Birdwatching
- Spending time with family
- Repairing a local hiking trail
- Hunting or fishing
- Doing yoga
- Shopping
- Teaching an exercise class
- Learning to fly a plane
- Learning your heritage and ancestry
- Meeting relatives you don't know
- Entertaining family or friends
- Taking care of grandchildren
- Creating the best lawn in the neighborhood
- Meeting friends for coffee
- Fixing friends' cars
- Working for a nonprofit
- Teaching
- Writing a letter for a friend challenging a charge or bill
- Writing a book
- Writing an article
- Creating a zine
- Working as an adjunct professor at a college
- Walking in the park
- Learning how to create pottery, paint, or engage in other artistic pursuits
- Learning photography
- Working with animals
- Mentoring others
- Playing with a pet

You now have a good idea of some activities you enjoy. See if you want to add anything from the list in Purpose Practice 12.4 to your list of twenty from Purpose Practice 12.3. Post the resulting list somewhere in your house. Next we will identify our unique character strengths.

Identifying Character Strengths

We all have unique strengths that relate to our character, who we are as human beings. Below I suggest an online test that helps each of us identify ours. The VIA character strengths test below was designed by the Happiness Project at the University of Pennsylvania to help people find meaningful work.[198] We can use it in retirement life planning to find meaningful work, hobbies, or volunteer opportunities.

The VIA character strengths test measures pervasive parts of ourselves that we can rely upon in good times and bad. The VIA Institute for Character explains the following on its website:

> VIA's work is about the core or essence of who we are as humans—our character strengths. These positive core characteristics of our personality are different from strengths of talent (innate abilities), strengths of interest (what we like to do), strengths of skill (proficiencies we develop), and strengths of resources (external supports).
>
> While each of these [other] areas of strength are important, it is character strengths that provide a pathway for developing each of these [other strengths].... For example, we use perseverance and self-regulation to pursue a talent in music or sport, hope in developing a new skill for work, curiosity as we explore our interest areas, and gratitude and kindness when we are tapping our resources. Also, it is our strengths of character that we ... turn to when we lose resources, talents, and skills, or when we lose interest in something.[199]

By using the test below to identify your character strengths, you can focus on and mindfully tap into these strengths throughout your pre-retirement planning and into retirement itself.

> ### PURPOSE PRACTICE 12.5
>
> To take the test, which requires about thirty minutes, go to the Authentic Happiness Questionnaire Center, University of Pennsylvania, available at https://www.authentichappiness.sas.upenn.edu/testcenter.
>
> You will need to create an account by entering a username and password.
>
> Then take the VIA character strengths test found at https://www.authentichappiness.sas.upenn.edu/questionnaires/survey-character-strengths, as well as one or two other self-awareness tests.

Record the results in your journal. Also take a screenshot of the results. Some interviewees reported having trouble finding their results after they took the test.

Spend some time looking at your results. Does anything surprise you? Go back to your top-twenty list of favorite activities, which may now list more than twenty. Which of these activities draw upon your VIA character strengths?

Identifying Forte Strengths: Merging Your Unique Skills with Unmet Need

Next, we explore your forte strengths or forte skills. These are strengths or skills that provide great value to others with little cost to you in effort or time. You have developed these forte strengths and skills through your years of experience, and can use them to vastly improve the lives of others if you choose. These activities may not be the most inspiring tasks, but they are meaningful because of the impact they have on others.

> **PURPOSE PRACTICE 12.6**
>
> Think of something or a couple of things that you can do easily but that would take most people hours if they could do the tasks at all.
>
> Try to think of things that you enjoy, or at least don't deeply dislike. Write these tasks down in your journal and then think about where you might provide these services in your community.

Perhaps doing a few of these things in your retirement will give you a deep sense of purpose, even though performing them may not feel like flow or bring joy in the doing. The joy comes from the significant impact of the work.

When I did Purpose Practice 12.6, I came up with four things I can do quickly and more easily than most people:

1. interpreting consumer contracts,
2. challenging a charge with a credit provider,
3. navigating end-of-life options like hospice, palliative care, and death with dignity, and
4. reading simple financial statements.

I learned through this exercise that even though I can, I don't want to spend much of my future time reading financial statements. Perhaps this is a good reason to not join too many nonprofit boards. I am willing to do the other tasks on the list but perhaps just for friends and family. Still, it is good to know that a little effort on my part can amount to a big help in someone else's life. Can you think of ways to use your forte strengths?

Becoming a Mentern, a Combination of an Intern and a Mentor

If working in a new field appeals to you, there could be unique opportunities hiding in plain view. For example, you might become a *mentern* in a field that has always appealed to you. In his book, *Wisdom at Work*, Chip Conley describes the process of becoming a mentern. A mentern accepts a job in a field in which they are a beginner, where they simultaneously learn a new trade, mentor colleagues, and share skills learned in a past career.[200]

Conley's mentern concept comes from his own experience as a mentern at the tech start-up, Airbnb. Conley ran the boutique hotel chain Joie de Vivre Hospitality for twenty-four years before being asked to join Airbnb as Head of Global Hospitality and Strategy. At Airbnb, he worked closely with CEO Brian Chesky as a mentor and helped connect the fledgling company with the travel and hotel industries. He also learned a great deal from his new colleagues about how a tech firm operates.

To become a mentern, you apply for and obtain an internship in a new field. While there, you mentor younger colleagues in interpersonal skills, emotional intelligence, intuition, decision-making, conflict resolution, and other soft skills gathered over a lifetime. This arrangement can be especially helpful for those who find traditional retirement unfulfilling. For example, Conley tells the story of Paul Critchlow who spent thirty years as an executive at Merrill Lynch and retired in 2015. Critchlow explained the following to Conley:

> The summer of 2016 loomed, for me, as uneventful. I'd retired a year earlier, and I was feeling a little bored, restless, and left out. My plans to do some personal writing of a memoir, some consulting, charitable work, and travel weren't quite cutting it. Then my neighbor, Sally Susman, the head of corporate affairs at Pfizer Inc. . . . took me to lunch. She was wondering whether I'd be open to being an intern for the summer. Why

> not!? Later, Sally confided her worries that I'd be insulted or our friendship somehow damaged. I confessed my fears that young people would reject me; the staff, resent me; or I might come off as an old out-of-touch know-it-all. We both turned out to be wrong.[201]

The mentornship worked out swimmingly and Critchlow was able to help younger colleagues reach their dreams.

Other skills you can share as a mentern include helping people learn office etiquette, self-management, personal productivity, leadership skills, conflict management, creativity, and technical skills in your area of expertise.[202] You can also give younger colleagues honest feedback in a safe environment, something that is both valuable and hard to get.[203] At the same time, your younger colleagues can teach you about technology, about the new industry you have joined, and many other skills.[204]

An arrangement like this is more likely to work if you go into it with curiosity and humility, a "humble mixture of teaching and learning."[205] For maximum success, adopt a beginner's mindset. Assume you have as much to learn from the younger people around you as they have to learn from you. No doubt this will be true. You will learn a lot.

You will also find yourself in the enviable position of working in an environment of intergenerational diversity.[206] Working with younger people keeps you young and keeps your ideas fresh. As interviewee Havens Levitt shares in chapter 14, you can learn so much about yourself and the world if you stay connected to people of all ages, including young people.

Volunteering

There are also endless opportunities to volunteer. The best way to find your niche is to follow your heart. Find causes that speak to you, things you enjoy. Draw on your character and other strengths, and your forte skills. Use these to find your ideal volunteer job. Any service you provide will help both you and the ones you serve. You can visit the elderly, be a grandparent to grandkids, help a neighbor, or volunteer for a religious organization, prison, school, or charity. Remain humble and remember that those you serve can teach you valuable lessons as well.

To get the creative juices flowing, consider the volunteer services in these real-life examples, provided by Connie Zweig in *The Inner Work of Age*:

- Work with firefighters and help them recover from trauma,
- Leave corporate life to teach environmental classes at a community college,
- Leave retired life to teach environmental classes in high school,
- Leave the insurance industry to become the president of a synagogue,
- Return to Liberia, where this particular volunteer was in the Peace Corps, to set up solar lights for business, homes, and hospitals,
- Teach meditation in prisons, where this volunteer reported learning as much from the prisoners and they did from him,
- Provide free temporary housing for families in need,
- Bring refugee children, separated from their families, clothes and toiletries,
- Sing protest songs at rallies, in support of social causes.[207]

Other high-impact volunteer opportunities include mentoring, tutoring, and spreading awareness about any issue that is important to you. Some terrific organizations with which to connect include Senior Corps, the National Park Service, Meals on Wheels, Feeding America, Canine Companions for Independence, Peace Corps, The Prem Rawat Foundation, Days for Girls, and Habitat for Humanity. If the outdoors speaks to you, also check out state park systems.

When doing volunteer work, don't be afraid to tackle problems that seem intractable, like homelessness or climate change. When working on large social issues like these, it can feel like our work doesn't matter, that it is trivial and won't actually make a difference. This is almost always untrue. Every little bit helps. The work matters, even if we don't solve a bigger problem. Just try not to be too attached to the result.[208]

Another idea to consider is teaching. Most people have strengths and skills they can pass to others. If this interests you, read on. Otherwise, skip to the conclusion of this chapter.

Considering Teaching

Some people teach their long-acquired skills in retirement. There are many settings in which to teach and good reasons why teaching and retirement are a good fit. For one, sharing your knowledge is a gift. For another, your brain is wired to teach even as you age.

According to British psychologist Raymond Cattell, we build two forms of intelligence over a lifetime: (1) *fluid intelligence*, or the ability to reason, think flexibly, and solve novel problems, and (2) *crystalized intelligence*, the ability to use a store of knowledge learned in the past, through our lifetime of acculturation and learning.[209] According to social scientist Arthur Brooks, who uses Cattell's work in his book *From Strength to Strength*, fluid intelligence starts to wane in our forties, but crystalized intelligence keeps increasing as we age.[210]

Brooks differentiates between the two by describing fluid intelligence as "innovation" and crystalized intelligence as "instruction."[211] The takeaway is that older people can continue to share crystalized knowledge gained over a lifetime, even if some fluid intelligence decreases as we age. Older teachers are often better teachers too. According to the *Chronicle of Higher Education*, older professors get better teaching evaluations than younger ones. This supports the notion that crystalized intelligence stays with us.[212]

Also, teaching can be a great way to give back. Brooks shares these two stories in his book. First, a fifty-eight-year-old male actuary said this:

> I am at the point in my career where I am looking forward to retirement, not as a chance to stop working but more as a chance to work on other things that I am finding have become very important to me. In addition to my day job I am teaching financial math one evening a week to graduate students. I find this very rewarding as I bring the insights of my long career to these young, aspiring minds. They have a thirst for learning and I enjoy meeting them and helping them see the insights beyond the textbooks.[213]

Similarly, a female television journalist told Brooks this:

> I feel lucky to be inside academia, which seems to value older people. I'm practically young compared to some of the faculty I work with and they are fascinating, brilliant folks. That's been one of the most wonderful differences between TV news and this. Adults are valued, hold leadership roles, and their knowledge is appreciated. Because TV news relies on innovation, this is not possible.[214]

While not everyone can teach at the university level, there are many opportunities to teach in continuing education programs, junior colleges, senior centers, small business education programs, camps, day care centers, religious centers, and more. Teaching may be a way to not only give back, but to also become more well-rounded and perhaps, happier. As Connie Zweig explains in *The Inner Work of Age*, as we age, we can expand out rather than just moving up.[215] For some people, teaching may also be less stressful than many other avocations and could allow you to enjoy life more.

If you do try teaching, try to think of yourself as a beginner even if you are a leader in your field. There is a difference between knowing a subject matter and teaching it well. Good teaching is interactive, which is why few people learn much from listening to a lecture. See if you can make your instruction a two-way street, one in which you learn from your students, and they learn from you. Get to know your students as people. Ask questions. Show interest. Have a conversation. Try to learn students' names, as well as something about them and where they came from. Welcoming the students where you find them builds trust and collegiality and improves learning.

Parting Thoughts on Your Skills, Values, and Joyful Activities in Retirement

You now have a wealth of information about what activities might bring you joy and purpose in retirement, in light of the activities that bring you joy and a sense of flow, that align with your values, and that capitalize on your unique strengths. You will use this information in the next chapter to plan the days of your inspired retirement, but for now, pause and reflect on what you have learned about your unique joys and strengths.

CHAPTER 13:
THE NUTS AND BOLTS OF THE INSPIRED RETIREMENT

This chapter helps us plan the nuts and bolts of retirement. It is particularly useful for those who have not yet retired, but also of use to those who have already taken the leap. In these pages, we first explore whether there is unfinished work to do before retiring. Next, we create an individual retirement plan. We help plan your time based on what you love and care most about.

There May Be More Day-to-Day Time Than You Think

Most people have more free time in retirement than they anticipate, a fact borne out by my interviews, as well as this recent news story. In it, a financial services company asks the question, "How will you spend your newfound freedom when you cut back on work?" The article explains the following:

> Don't let logistics cloud your vision for retirement. Before you clock out for the final time, it's also important to have an idea of what's ahead—after all, you'll soon have forty or more hours a week freed up. According to Kiplinger, frustrations

> at work or a bad boss aren't good reasons to retire—rather, "the reason to retire is because one has the burning desire to pursue other interests, goals, and lifestyle choices."
>
> "These new pursuits should be clearly defined and laid out," advised Kiplinger. Keep in mind that many leisure activities don't constitute "a full-time pursuit . . ." See if you can realistically envision what your day-to-day routine may look like once you're a retiree.[216]

In this chapter, we follow this advice and design our own unique retirement life schedule. This is a process and a journey as your choices about how to spend your time will change over time. You can switch up your schedule as much as you like. In this first section, we assume you are still working at your regular job, thinking about what's next.

Unfinished Business

If you are still working, are there any legacies you would like to leave at your current job? It is fine if you don't feel the need to make additional contributions, but asking this question avoids regret. My interviews included many stories of regret, including stories from people who wished they had waited to retire to protect a favorite assistant or colleague, stayed through a restructuring, stayed long enough to hire new key employees, or stayed long enough to see a legacy project through.[217] Some of these regrets could have been avoided with better planning.

In *The Second Half of Life*, when discussing how to make our final years of work more meaningful, Angeles Arrien asks these questions:

> Where are you being called in your work? What has heart and meaning for you in this job? What would you like to be doing? What specific actions can you take to support this call?

What are you searching for in your work? What satisfies you? What contributions do you want to make? What action can you take to support the search? What is important for you?

In what ways is your workplace struggling? Are you struggling within it? Do you see any patterns to the struggle? What can you do to disrupt these patterns and create a new dynamic?

What breakthrough do you want to create in your work that would lead to a major advance for the organization in the next three months? What plan of action would you generate to make this breakthrough happen?

The archetype of return is to come back to known experiences and harvest a different result. What do you want to return to that you have found effective in your work? How can you apply this effectiveness to the current issue you are tracking? What would it provide for the organization and your colleagues? What action can you take to implement an effective return?[218]

PURPOSE PRACTICE 13.1

You needn't answer all of the questions above, or even any of them, but do use them to observe what you enjoy most about your current work, what you struggle with, and how you might improve your workplace before you leave. Are there additional contributions you would like to make before retiring? Use the questions to think more broadly about anything else you might want to do before you walk out that door for the last time.

Do a journal entry or make a chart or poster answering these questions. Make a plan to take steps toward the goals you have identified.

In addition to making some final contributions in your last years or months at work, you might want to begin cutting back your hours at work. If cutting back is possible, this will give you time prior to retirement to learn about new things you might pursue and new social circles you might want to join.

For example, Daniel, an agricultural scientist in Mexico, featured in more detail in the next chapter, was forced to retire under his company's mandatory retirement policy. One year from his retirement date, his company transitioned most of his work to others in his organization, giving him time to consider what would come next for him. He and his wife traveled, and he took his time deciding whether to consult, how much to consult, how much to charge for his consulting, and so on. If this type of breathing room is available to you, it can make the transition much smoother.

It is especially important to think about the social circles you will inhabit once you retire. Some of my interviewees had already become part of their new retirement community before they left their job. Sherri Burr was both a law professor and an author for three decades. In the five or so years before she retired from law teaching, she became more and more involved in various local, national, and international writing organizations. By the time she retired from full-time teaching, she had already recreated her retirement community and her retirement contacts.

Do More in Less Time

Working fewer hours in the final year or years of your career can help you find your way to your next life. Many jobs allow you to gradually work less as you contemplate retirement, especially jobs for knowledge workers, whose primary work activity is thinking.[219] Science consistently shows that we can only do so much quality thinking in a day. Thus, working fewer hours does not mean you will accomplish less. At this point, you likely have so much domain knowledge that you can do much more in far less time than you could when you were younger.

As explained by Alex Soojung-Kim Pang in *Rest: Why You Get More Done When You Work Less,* many successful people throughout history have worked far fewer than eight hours a day. Studying history, he concludes that after four to five deeply concentrated hours of work per day, we are spending more time doing less quality work. We may even accomplish less in eight hours than we would in four very focused hours.[220]

It is mentally impossible to put in twelve, ten, or even eight hour days when thinking deeply and clearly. According to another expert, four hours of intense, high-quality work per day generates the most creative product:

> If you were to study some of the most admired creative thinkers, writers, and artists to have ever lived, you would find that all shared a passion for their work, an intense desire to succeed, and an almost superhuman capacity to focus. Yet, when you look closely at their daily lives, they only spent a few hours a day doing what we would recognize as their most profound work.
>
> The rest of the time, they were hiking mountains, taking naps, going on walks with friends, or sitting around thinking. In short, their creative productivity was not the result of endless hours of toil, as some may like to believe.[221]

There are many examples of these four-hour-a-day savants. German novelist Thomas Mann wrote numerous essays and novels and won the Nobel Prize for Literature in 1929. He worked from 9:00 a.m. to around noon. He reserved afternoons for reading, writing letters, walking, and napping. He resumed some light editing in the late afternoon or early evening for an hour or two.[222] Anthony Trollope, a great nineteenth century English novelist, wrote from five in the morning to just before eight a.m. and published forty-seven novels. He then left for his post office job. Charles Dickens wrote nineteen books, working from nine to two, with a break for lunch. After five hours, Dickens was done for the day.[223] Egyptian novelist Naguib Mahfouz worked as a civil servant during the earlier portion of the day. He dedicated his late afternoon (4:00 p.m. to 7:00 p.m.) to writing fiction. Canadian writer Alice Munro, who won the 2013 Nobel Prize in Literature, wrote from eight in the morning to just before noon. After that she was also done for the day. From this work, she supported herself.

Without breaks, no one can think straight, resulting in fewer results with more effort.[224] Work too little, and you probably won't ever be at the top of your game. Work too much and you may become drained and burned out.[225] This is good news as we age. Our priorities may be shifting toward relaxation, fitness, relationships, and matters of the heart such as fulfilling life goals. By cutting back on hours at work, we can ease into retirement and shift our time toward future prospects. But how does one do this? Here are a few ideas.

- Chunking: It is more productive to work in smaller chunks of fifty to seventy minutes with breaks in between.
- Toggling: We can improve brain efficiency by switching from tough mental tasks to more mundane ones throughout the day.
- Sleeping and Napping: While we all know people who sleep less and do just fine, sleeping more usually leads to better productivity. Dickens, Mahfouz, Munro, and Poincaré all took an afternoon nap and prioritized sleep.
- Meditating: Many studies show that a regular meditation practice can improve focus and make us more productive. Time spent meditating is returned to us many times over. I am often able to do hours of work in just forty-five minutes to an hour, first thing in the morning, right after my morning meditation practice. I can also solve seemingly intractable problems at this time when the mind is clear.

Imagining Doing Something Different

At the end of our careers, we are at the top of our technical knowledge. We know a tremendous amount about what we do. Yes, our brains may be slowing a bit, and we may forget things, but we know a lot. Think about what you now know. Could it be that you know enough about that? Is it time to learn something else, to pursue something that you have always wanted to do but have not yet had a chance? Explore these questions in Purpose Practice 13.2.

PURPOSE PRACTICE 13.2

If you were not in your current job, what would you do? If money were no object, how would you spend your valuable time?

If you could reinvent yourself right now, what would you become? Put another way, if you died tomorrow, what would you miss not being able to do or accomplish?

Journal about these prompts.

Staying Flexible

Former Unitarian Universalist Reverend Christine Robinson, also featured in the next chapter, noted that if you're fortunate, you'll have an opportunity to start thinking about what you want your retirement to look like several years before it happens.

As we have been discussing, a little planning can be immensely helpful in preparing for your retirement. It is important, though, to balance that planning with a light touch. As Reverend Robinson explains, things will change. You might end up not liking the activity you've chosen, your health might deteriorate, or you may need to care for grandchildren or a parent. She suggests staying flexible but still having a plan.

One of my interviewees had a great line about that, saying, "The first rule about retirement is that initially it's in the future. And the future is often not what we expected."

Reverend Robinson also talked about Retirement One and Retirement Two. In Retirement One, there are plenty of activities, and perhaps quite a bit of work as well. But by the time Retirement Two comes along, the body has started to change, and there could be many hours spent at doctor's appointments and otherwise caring for the aging body. This doesn't mean you are washed up. It just means life changes as we change.

Creating Mindful Transitions

Reverend Robinson's church has a rule that retired reverends cannot attend the church they led for one year after retirement. This allows the congregation to get used to new leadership. As Reverend Robinson explained, a leader who is stepping down still has implicit power but is no longer in the top leadership role. Without some separation process, some people in the community may continue to rely on the former leader, even though there's a new leader in place. The Unitarian Universalist church, like many other denominations, has worked hard to make sure this doesn't happen and that these implicit powers do not undermine or underhandedly affect the new leader's capacity to lead. Eventually, the prior leader can return to the community and work on less powerful projects. This process keeps parishioners from using the former leaders' relational power to continue impacting the organization in an oversized way. Other organizations could learn from this approach. If you are a leader stepping down, you can also create your own barrier to implicit power.

Creating Your Day-to-Day Retirement Life

Successful retirement life planning is easier if you can picture the nuts and bolts of your retirement life before you leap into it. If you have already taken the leap, don't worry. You can still create an inspired retirement.

While not everyone needs a highly detailed vision of their life in retirement, many find it useful to create a schedule at least at first. With this goal in mind, now we plan our time using a modified system created by Mitch Anthony, author, adviser, and consultant to the financial services community. Anthony has helped many companies make their approach to financial planning more holistic and life-centered, as opposed to strictly money-centered.

In his book, *The New Retirementality*, Anthony suggests we create a portfolio of our hours each week, in addition to our financial portfolio. To do so, we compare how we spend our time now to how we would like to spend it, splitting up our 168 hours a week into time spent with

1. family and friends,
2. work/career,
3. downtime (surfing the web, listening to music),
4. sleep,
5. health and fitness, and
6. personal growth (hobbies, learning a new skill).

Anthony calls the way we spend our time now our *current life portfolio* and how we would like to spend our time, our *desired life portfolio*.[226] With these two concepts in mind, *current life portfolio* and *desired life portfolio*, Anthony suggests an exercise to help visualize your present life compared to your desired retirement life. I have done this exercise several times and found it very useful. I also added three categories, one for contemplative practice both formal and informal, one for meals including preparation, and one for personal grooming.

Below is Anthony's exercise with my three additional categories added. For each category, both today and in your desired-life portfolio, figure out the hours you spend or will spend. Then calculate the percentages of time spent or that you would like to spend on each category.

PURPOSE PRACTICE 13.3: OPTION 1

Use the categories below to create your own current portfolio. Record how you spend your 168 hours a week now. You can use Excel, or just type or write it in your journal.

CURRENT LIFE PORTFOLIO	hours per week (168 total)	percentage of hours per week
Family and friends		
Work/volunteering		
Downtime like TV, the internet, and movies		
Sleep		
Health and fitness		
Personal growth		
Contemplative practices, like sitting, meditating, praying, thinking, petting a dog		
Meals including prep		
Personal grooming		

Now, rebalance your portfolio by writing down how many hours per week you would like to spend on these things.

DESIRED LIFE PORTFOLIO	hours per week (168 total)	percentage of hours per week
Family and friends		
Work/volunteering		
Downtime like TV, the internet, and movies		
Sleep		
Health and fitness		
Personal growth		
Contemplative practices, like sitting, meditating, praying, thinking, petting a dog		
Meals including prep		
Personal grooming		

I learned so much from this exercise, and just for fun, have reproduced my own numbers below.

CURRENT LIFE PORTFOLIO	hours per week (168 total)	percentage of hours per week
Family and friends	10	6%
Work/volunteering	55	32.5%
Downtime like TV, the internet, and movies	5	3%
Sleep	63	37.5%
Health and fitness	10	6%
Personal growth	6	3.5%
Contemplative practices, like sitting, meditating, praying, thinking, petting a dog	5	3%
Meals including prep	10	6%
Personal grooming	4	2.5%

Now create that same chart for your rebalanced or desired life portfolio.

DESIRED LIFE PORTFOLIO	hours per week (168 total)	percentage of hours per week
Family and friends	15	9%
Work/volunteering	30	18%
Downtime like TV, the internet, and movies	5	3%
Sleep	55	32.5%
Health and fitness	20	12%
Personal growth	19	11%
Contemplative practices, like sitting, meditating, praying, thinking, petting a dog	10	6%
Meals including prep	10	6%
Personal grooming	4	2.5%

From this I learned that I want to work twenty-five to thirty hours a week in retirement. I also learned that between my two jobs now, I have been working fifty to fifty-five hours a week, much more than I predicted. I also learned that I spend more time sleeping than anything else.

If this past exercise seems too complex, there is a simpler way of looking at the situation, that assumes you will keep your non-work activities more or less the same in retirement but will redirect some or all of your work hours.

PURPOSE PRACTICE 13.3: OPTION 2

Figure out how many hours you currently work and commute each week. Then figure out your ideal desired number of hours working/volunteering and commuting each week. Subtract the ideal hours from the current hours. This is your newfound time. Redistribute that newfound time in the categories below. If you like, add some of your own categories as well.

For example, let's say you spend fifty hours working and commuting. Now, deduct the number of hours you expect to work for pay or as a volunteer in retirement. Let's assume that this results in twenty-five fewer work and commuting hours. You now have twenty-five hours to distribute among the categories below. Pick your own number of ideal work/volunteer hours and have at it. Split up that newfound time as you see fit.

Redistribute your newfound time here:

REDISTRIBUTE WORK HOURS	hours per week spent working/ commuting (___ hours total)
Family and friends	
Work/volunteering	
Downtime like TV, the internet, and movies	
Sleep	
Health and fitness	
Personal growth	
Contemplative practices, like sitting, meditating, praying, thinking, petting a dog	
Meals including prep	
Personal grooming	

Also feel free to be more specific, listing things like exercise, particular work or volunteering, a regular date night or appointment with friends, whatever you like.

Parting Words on Creating Your Own Retirement Journey

To make time to figure out what to do next, it helps to spend less time working during the transition. It also helps to acknowledge

CHAPTER THIRTEEN

that there will likely be some work after retirement. It may just be different work. With the right preparation, it will also be meaningful work. As an analogy, think of your life like a meal. You can compare this pre-retirement reduction in work to enjoying a great meal, but one in which you eat a bit less. Less is sometimes just as delicious, but only if there is something substantial on that plate.

Leisure alone will not provide purpose for most of us. Leisure is fabulous but so much sweeter after accomplishing something meaningful. Meaning is different for everyone, so take time to figure out what brings you meaning and how much you would work and at what, if you had a choice. This work need not be in any particular field, nor must it be paid work. But it must be meaningful to you.

Any kind of challenge can help us find purpose and meaning, even if the recipients are mostly ourselves and our circles. Doing more of what we want to do is more fulfilling than doing what others want us to do, but how can we tell the difference? By figuring out what we want and what makes us happy. Hopefully this chapter and the last one help you answer these questions.

CHAPTER 14:
REINVENTION STORIES

Here, I share more detailed stories from about a third of my interviewees. They are stories from a representative sample of people from different fields, age groups, genders, ethnicities, sexual orientations, and worldviews.

Many of these people struggled to find the right balance between work and play in retirement, and most have found that balance, at least for now. Remember that purpose and meaning change with time and there is never just one purpose in life. We have flexibility and freedom to grow and to change as we age.

Most people in this chapter and those that preceded it are unidentified. However, some interviewees have asked to be named in order to highlight a particular project on which they are working or service to a particular community. In sharing these stories, I aim to tell you not just what these people chose to do, but also how they transitioned into their inspired retirement lives.

Some people were happy to be very unstructured about this transition. Others sought to replicate the type of hours and life they had while working full-time. These stories may provide clues for what might work best for you.

CHAPTER FOURTEEN

Mindful Transition Logistics

The first stories in this chapter describe some of the logistics of retirement. As I was interviewing people, these three related transition themes emerged. First, not surprisingly, involuntary retirement is harder than voluntary retirement. Second, spending time preparing for retirement makes the transition smoother and happier. Third, working part-time in the same field before retiring has helped many people.

A Scientist in Thoughtful Transition

For decades, Daniel was a scientist with an international agricultural nonprofit that brought emerging technologies to smallholder farmers in the developing world. He had a lot of time to prepare for retirement since his organization had a mandatory retirement at age sixty-five. Retiring was hard for Daniel because he absolutely loved his job. He helped entire communities use modern and sustainable agricultural practices and worked not just with those communities but also with some of the leading scientists in the world.

One year from his retirement date, his nonprofit asked Daniel to begin transferring his projects to younger scientists in the organization. He found this hard and explained that it is very difficult when you work in a profession for a long time not to identify with your job, for example, no longer to be "a scientist."

In retrospect, Daniel found the handoff process advantageous. It gave him time to accept his situation and to adapt to change, to begin to let things go a bit. He said that if you work for a very long time in the same discipline, especially for the same institution, and you love your work, you become very focused on what you're doing and can overlook the other things in life.

The fact that Daniel had a full year to think about his retirement was a big blessing. While still employed, he worked a bit less and had time to consider other opportunities in life. His wife suggested they travel a bit during that transition year, and they did. Daniel had a little less work to do and was grieving the loss of the job. The travel helped, as did the transition to having less responsibility at work.

When asked if he had advice for new retirees, Daniel shared something his own mentors shared with him: "If asked to consult, wait six months or a year. Give yourself time to consider if this is what you want to continue doing." He had already been asked to consult and was pondering how to set his hourly rate. He was also considering how much to work. As we discussed this, he shared his relief at no longer having to write grants and create budgets for himself and up to fifteen other employees. He did not miss this part of the job and was still working on finding his place in retirement.

Daniel said that he and his wife refer to these first years of retirement as the *go go years*. They plan to move around and travel. Daniel was aware that there would be another phase in his life, during which they would slow down.

From Full-Time to Part-Time Reverend

Christine Robinson retired from being the senior reverend of a Unitarian Universalist Church in Albuquerque, where she had worked since 1988. She was the only reverend until around 9/11, when the church grew significantly and hired a second reverend.

Reverend Robinson left her senior reverend job at a time when her parents needed extra care. She retired earlier than anticipated, as the associate reverend was able to step in. Reverend Robinson took six to eight months to transition to retirement. This was very intentional. During this time, she stopped exerting significant influence over the church's long term planning and focused on what she called "nostalgia work." She preached on grief and the difficulties and joys of change. She and other church leaders told the story of her ministry, which encompassed more than half of the congregation's life. She got past church leaders together to process what they had experienced together . . . the good and the bad. She tied up loose ends, left notes for her successor, helped the congregation understand why they wouldn't see her for a while, and turned over many duties to those who would soon have them while they could still ask questions.

After retirement, Reverend Robinson worked part-time for about five years. At first, she worked as a part-time consultant to other churches going through transitions. When the pandemic occurred, many churches went through a tremendous transition moving onto Zoom. This changed the ministry and made it possible for senior reverends like Reverend Robinson, who had retired, to work part-time on Zoom for churches in other parts of the country.

Mindfully Opting for Employee Off-Ramp Offerings

Willis began working at IBM in the early 1980s and retired at age fifty-six, after working there for thirty-two years. At the time, IBM had a transition-to-retirement program that made it possible to reduce employees without laying people off. Under the terms of the program, for one and a half years, employees could work three days a week, get paid for four days, and keep their health insurance and other benefits.

Tired of some of the red tape and enticed by the transition-to-retirement program, Willis signed up for the program. He found the transition very helpful. During the year and a half, he relaxed a little and once he fully retired, he tackled long overdue home projects, biked a lot, and pursued hobbies like lamp building. This was the point at which Willis discovered that even in retirement, there are rarely enough hours in the day.

Despite this lack of time in the day, Willis ultimately decided to return to part-time work. A few years after retirement, he was contacted by a smaller computer company with a great mission, namely providing computer services with a negative carbon footprint and thus a less negative impact on the climate. At the time, the stock market was down and he was paying dearly for health insurance. He also felt his brain could use more stimuli. He loves the work, the company's mission, and his boss.

Self-Reflection, Planning, and Mindful Transitions

Throughout this book, we have talked about how to use mindfulness to plan a safe landing and a happy retirement. These next three stories demonstrate how pre-planning for retirement can help.

From College President to Law Professor and Interim Director of the JCC

Aaron was a university president when the pandemic hit. The school needed a new strategic plan, and Aaron knew the planning process should be led by someone who would be there to implement the plan. After fifteen years as president, he did not want to commit to another five years, and thus decided to retire. The job was all consuming and much of his social life also revolved around his colleagues at work. He was leaving his job for good reason at a good time, but it was still a big transition. Obviously, his departure left a big void in his daily life.

I spoke to Aaron right after he retired, as well as a few years later. When asked what advice he had for new retirees, Aaron said if he had to do it over, he would devote more thought in advance to what he might do in the next phase. He knew he would not be content doing nothing but didn't fully consider the options to stay engaged. The process was complicated by the fact that he retired just as the pandemic hit, a time of isolation for many of us.

CHAPTER FOURTEEN

The first six months were dull but since then, Aaron has made meaningful choices about how to spend his time. He returned to teaching through an online Juris Doctor program, which he loves, and has been active on various nonprofit boards. And most recently, Aaron accepted a position as the interim director of his local Jewish community center.

He and his wife spend time in the winter in Florida, with both old friends and many new ones. Finally, and most importantly, he is able to spend a great deal of time with his three beautiful granddaughters. He said the following:

> A friend said I "suck at retirement," but in retrospect the past four "retirement" years have been extraordinarily fulfilling.
>
> My general advice to those considering retirement may seem obvious. First, the decision requires self-awareness, a real understanding of the kind of activities and engagements that will be fulfilling. To be sure, that understanding is very personal and will differ from individual to individual.
>
> I believe, however, that it is a prerequisite to a successful retirement. Second, it requires planning and affirmative steps to implement those plans.

Besides its lessons on the importance of self-reflection, Aaron's story also captures two often-overlooked silver linings: the chance to spend more time with family, and the opportunity to use one's remaining years doing something new. These themes recur in many of the stories that follow.

Transition from Army Colonel to Swim Coach

Kyle was in the army as an infantry officer for over twenty-five years, rising to colonel and culminating with command of a special mission unit. At age forty-nine, he retired from the army using a Department of Defense career transition program. Through this program, combined with volunteering, he became a high school teacher and swim coach. He chose this path through purposeful reflection. After working in and supervising direct combat for almost three decades, he longed to help young people learn about civics, compassion, and compromise. He explained the following:

> I spent my career dealing with world problems after they erupted, as both a soldier and as a high-level official. I longed to get in front of these problems through teaching and coaching, so I became a history teacher and a swim coach. I was a collegiate swimmer myself and saw the benefit of early athletics on a person's work ethic. I also know that athletes are often seen as not civic minded and caring mostly about themselves. Athletics can also be misogynistic. I consider my new position an honor and use it to teach civics, community values, respect for others, anti-misogyny, and basic human respect and dignity.

Kyle is deeply passionate about his new work, just as he was about his old career. His advice? Explore your passions while you are still working in whatever amount you can fit into your life. Also, become a committed member of your desired community long before you retire. Kyle volunteered as a swim coach at the school in which he later became a teacher. The school ultimately hired him full-time after his volunteer work and his internship. They could see his passion for the position and had witnessed his commitment firsthand.

During his transition to military retirement, Kyle was recruited for government executive leadership positions and various corporate jobs with salary potential of $200–400K on top of his retirement pension. He was adamant about not wanting to chase money or work in these jobs. Even though he was just fifty when he retired, he valued the time he could now spend with students more than the money he could earn elsewhere. While his former colleagues insisted that he would miss the excitement of the army, miss the money, and have a hard time with the kids, the job has fulfilled his expectations and been extremely rewarding.

Kyle values the feeling of giving back, which he had watched his own father do. He suggests asking yourself, "What could I give society based on my unique experience?" Kyle adds that "making an impact on someone else's life makes us better people, more human, and it feels good."

In Chip Conley parlance, Kyle was also a mentern. The head swim coach at the school was quite a bit younger than Kyle. While Kyle learned coaching from his younger boss, Kyle taught life lessons to his younger colleague in return. In order for this to work, however, Kyle said you need to give up some control. I might add that this too makes us better people, more human.

From Army Platoon Leader to Sherriff

When he first retired, R.J., an army platoon leader, did what many high-level retirees in the military do. He worked in a management role. The pay for these jobs can be very high, but R.J. did not find it inspiring. He had never wanted a desk job and while he had the skills to manage staffs, budgets, etc., he chose to take a lower paying job instead. This is another example of someone who chose passion over profit.

R.J. was a tank platoon leader, then special forces officer for the army for twenty years. When he retired at age forty-two, he first formed his own small consulting business performing business analysis and commercial project management, and then became a defense contractor. When managing contractors during the pandemic, R.J. realized he wanted to do something more meaningful, to make a more significant contribution. He had always wanted to work in law enforcement, so he applied for a volunteer position as a reserve deputy sheriff in his community. This required a six-month academy, three nights a week, to prepare. He worked in this capacity for several years, before signing on as a full-time sworn deputy, and completing another training academy at the age of forty-seven. The new job fit perfectly with his military skill set and desire to serve his community.

When asked if he had any advice for new retirees, R.J. started with humility, describing the need to be willing to start at the bottom of the career ladder, even if you are highly skilled. He said you also need to be willing to take undesirable shifts and learn from others, a form of beginner's mind. That said, R.J. mentioned keeping current in professional certifications so you can go back to your old line of work if you need to.

Regarding interviewing, R.J. recommends rehearsing your interview answers to likely questions so you can be prepared to sell yourself and your skills. R.J. said that he, as well as those he hired as contractors, usually fell back on the typical panel Q&A prep—situation, action, result. While those are, no doubt, a key part of the conversation, it was not until his sixth interview (out of twelve screening calls and thirty-six applications) that R.J. actually delivered an impact statement and took control of the interview, rather than merely waiting for others' questions. In other words, although highly skilled and successful, R.J. had to relearn how to job hunt and interview, something many of us will not have done for decades.

R.J. said one of the benefits of a career change is that you can finally shift your attention to family and relationships with others—you're not working twelve hours a day to put out fires at work. Working nights has allowed him to spend afternoons with his teenage son and attend his activities, things he could not do while on active duty or as a manager of personnel across multiple time zones.

R.J. also had great retirement advice regarding relocation. Since military personnel typically relocate often, R.J. had lots of experience watching successful and unsuccessful relocations. He suggested figuring out what your family needs and will need, now and in the future, before committing to a new job in a different city. Once you know where you want to be, based on these needs, then it's time to look for work or volunteer opportunities in your chosen community.

CHAPTER FOURTEEN

Capitalizing on Unique Career Skills

Another theme that arose from my interviews was the inspiring ways in which retirees used the skills they built in their long careers in other contexts, often for the benefit of others.

From Telecom IT Expert to Volunteer for Black Churches and Financial Literacy Communities

David and Sheila Gipson worked for a large telecommunications firm in the computer programming division. David spent four decades designing computer software for his firm, and Sheila worked there on and off while raising their two children. They were also very involved in their faith community and in the Black community as a whole. After raising their kids, Sheila resigned from the telecom job and became an associate pastor.

After moving from New Jersey to Florida, David began working part-time for an independent contractor of his old employer, as well as for three nonprofits. One is a New Jersey church with six to seven thousand members, and another a Texas church with around two thousand members. His work involves setting up software systems to help organize requests for pastoral care made by parishioners. He also provides mentorship for the clergypersons in these churches. Through his work, David provides tech solutions to keep the needs of pastors and their members from falling through the cracks. The third organization he works for is a nonprofit that helps people become debt-free. For this organization, David developed an app that helps people reduce debt.

This nonprofit work speaks to two of David's heartfelt retirement goals, supporting faith communities and helping people reduce debt and become more financially literate. David's story demonstrates the magical combination of passion and skills. David is uniquely qualified to design, distribute, and support software systems and apps. While he could have chosen other ways to support the communities he loves, he uses his skills, honed over decades of professional life, to provide services that he alone can provide.

For all he has accomplished, David is a laid back guy who says he has no need for a rigid schedule. He doesn't give much thought to what he will do all day and takes life as it comes. He enjoys travel, hanging out with family and friends, and researching and cooking new meals. He specifically chose to keep his paid work limited to twenty hours or less a month so he can enjoy his time doing other things, something that was not possible while working full-time. David has created a life that involves some work, some goal setting, and some time simply taking life as it comes. Whatever he is doing, he is learning new things and enjoying life.

From Big City Physician to Border Doctor

Ellen was a physician in New York City for forty years. Between the ages of seventeen and sixty-seven, she never lived a single day of unscheduled life. When she retired in 2020, she spent the next three years living the same type of highly scheduled life. She scheduled her exercise, she scheduled her volunteer work, and she created a life with the same amount of structure and work hours as she had known for five decades.

After three years in retirement, Ellen loosened up a bit. When I interviewed her, she and her husband (also a physician) had just spent four months doing volunteer medical work at the Mexican border. Ellen was feeling a bit exhausted and, perhaps for the first time ever, fluid about what would happen next. She discussed how her sister, a speech pathologist in the public schools, had taken a gap year and sort of floated for a while before taking up painting in retirement. Ellen laughed and said she could never have done that. She absolutely needed to slide into retirement by working a lot rather than a little, even as a volunteer. Ellen's story shows that you have to know yourself. You are not likely to change your entire personality just because you retired.

CHAPTER FOURTEEN

From Commercial Litigator to Advocate for the Homeless and for Clean and Safe City Streets

Bill Keleher, a commercial litigator and real estate attorney for thirty years, was sixty when I interviewed him. In 2014, Bill downsized from a large law firm to a smaller one in pursuit of a better work-life balance. In 2023, he started downsizing his practice so he could pursue other projects and interests.

When I caught up with Bill, he was almost fully retired, reporting that he worked for pay just four to five hours per week for a few clients. He was just finishing his term as board president of Saranam, which provides a two-year program for families experiencing homelessness. The program provides housing, food, education, life-skills training, and community support to families. Saranam's goal is that families leave Saranam with the skills and education to maintain a solid and stable home and work life. Bill is inspired by the work of Saranam, and the ways in which it helps families improve their lives. He is extremely proud to have served on Saranam's board.

One of Bill's other projects involves helping to promote and organize a business improvement district for downtown Albuquerque. The goal is to use this new district to create a cleaner, safer, and more appealing downtown. The project involves building sufficient consensus among at least 51 percent of the real estate owners in the target area to support improvement plans. Once enough owners support the project, they will petition the city council to legally create the new district. The district will then collect and spend resources to improve downtown Albuquerque. Bill believes a strong downtown will improve all of Albuquerque and finds heartfelt satisfaction in using the skills and relationships he developed as an attorney in this organizing and nonprofit work.

Creating Meaning Person to Person

Sometimes one's primary retirement purpose is to help those around them, especially friends and family who really need it. Helping individuals in need can be as meaningful as working for or starting a nonprofit, especially when that help truly changes the lives of those we love.

Career Waitress Finds Purpose Helping Her Inner Circle

Delia worked for thirty years as waitress at one of Albuquerque's top restaurants. She felt loved and appreciated by her regular clientele, one of whom gave her a $250 tip on her last night. When speaking with me, Delia noted how her true friends from work are still her friends. Those who were more like acquaintances are no longer in touch, but she thinks that is fine, noting that work was all they had in common.

In retirement, Delia spends her newfound time helping her friends with childcare and transportation. She feels honored and fortunate to be able to provide these services to those she loves. She acknowledged that for some people, just helping friends and family might not be enough, but for her, surrounded by so many people in need, it is an honor to serve in this role. She literally changes the lives of those around her in big and small ways, a sign of true affluence and meaning for her.

Delia noted that she had been fortunate enough to buy her own small home and to be able to set aside money to create an annuity that, along with social security, matches her pre-retirement income. She noted that many people she knows, perhaps most people, cannot retire for financial reasons. She added that, compared to people who have a lot of assets in the market, she has very little anxiety around money issues. She believes she has sufficient assets to meet her needs and finds that to be enough.

CHAPTER FOURTEEN

Fitness and Self-Reflection as Avocation

Sometimes taking care of ourselves or our immediate family is enough to provide purpose, particularly if we or a loved one has suffered trauma or other serious illness. Here is an example of what that might look like.

Police Officer Dives Deep into Self-Reflection

Police officer Denise knew the day she entered the force that she would retire as soon as it was available to her, exactly twenty-five years from her start date. She literally counted the years, then the days. Her employer had a pension that, when combined with her social security, allowed her to maintain her same income and standard of living post-retirement. She was only fifty when she retired, and I caught up with her eight years later.

Denise said she spent much of her life fantasizing and dreaming about what it would be like to be retired. Those fantasies and dreams did not go to waste. They taught her how much she loved travel and pointed to other things that would provide purpose after retirement.

Despite her pre-planning, Denise met with some bumps in the road. First, Denise and her wife divorced after eighteen years of marriage. The split broke open old wounds incurred in childhood and in law enforcement. Although it was heartbreaking at the time, the divorce helped Denise in the end and allowed her to explore parts of herself she didn't know.

She spent much of her newfound time engaging in physical activity and deep self-exploration. A sufferer of complex PTSD, she practiced inner child work with her therapist and learned to face some of her unhelpful ideas and shadow selves. Denise embraced yoga and mindfulness activities and looked forward to trying somatic dance in a safe environment. Denise found that getting to know herself and working out some of her childhood issues, as well as those from her life in law-enforcement, kept her engaged. Her focus now is on self-exploration and self-care.

Denise is an example of someone who planned well for retirement and stayed open to where life took her. Her life journey took her inside herself and allowed her to see a bright future. Her story shows that purpose in retirement does not have to mean serving others directly. Sometimes becoming more internal and at peace with oneself is more than enough.

Becoming Part of the Community You Want to Join

A common piece of advice shared by interviewees is to become a member of the community in which you hope to be a part well before retiring. Here are two examples of how that process might manifest.

From School Teacher to LGBTQ+ Leader and Activist

I interviewed community leader Havens Levitt at a local restaurant in Albuquerque. Our interview was peppered with interruptions from other patrons stopping by to say hello to Havens, a seventy-year-old lesbian and retired schoolteacher who has been active in the LGBTQ+ community since she came out nearly fifty years ago.

Havens retired from full-time teaching in 2012 and spent the next two years advocating for marriage equality in New Mexico, a goal accomplished in 2014.

In 2016, Havens became the program director of Older Rainbow Community Albuquerque (ORCA—formerly a chapter of SAGE), a nonprofit advocacy and support group for older LGBTQ+ New Mexicans. In this role, Havens was the face and top leader of the organization. In 2021, she scaled back her hours

CHAPTER FOURTEEN

at ORCA to become a trainer and mentor, working about fifteen hours per month. As a mentor, she acts in a role similar to Chip Conley's role at Airbnb. She is a behind-the-scenes adviser to other leaders and employees.

In addition to her current work for ORCA, Havens also acts as a volunteer trainer for GLSEN, a nonprofit that helps create LGBTQ+-inclusive classrooms and provides other support to LGBTQ+ youth in schools. Her work at GLSEN is particularly synergistic with her long career as a teacher and her long-time interest in LGBTQ+ advocacy.

All of these post-retirement roles were a natural fit for Havens. She was already part of the community in which she hoped to work post-retirement. Moreover, due to her knowledge and connections, she was able to move adeptly into new roles on issues about which she feels passionate. When asked what advice she had for others either in or transitioning toward retirement, she said this:

> Take on projects that connect you with younger people. Part of what was so enjoyable about working on marriage equality was that many of the people involved were young. I learn so much from young people. Being with them keeps me from getting stuck in place or being attached to outdated ideas. The LGBTQ+ community has changed so much in the past fifty years. I want to stay relevant in all aspects of life, including the growth occurring within the LGBTQ+ community. Also, I can pass on my learning in my training sessions. It is a win-win.

There are at least two helpful lessons from Havens's story. First, it helps to be involved in the community you want to be part of before you retire. Second, being around younger people keeps us young and helps us understand the world from a perspective different from our own. Staying adept at societal changes also keeps us young.

In terms of process, Havens said she has great boundaries and was flexible in creating her post-teaching, retirement career. She has been relatively busy the entire time but did not set out to work a certain number of hours in retirement. She let the spirit move her from opportunity to opportunity, relying on old contacts, but also new friends and serendipity to guide her.

From Professor and Author to Full-Time Author and Small Business Owner

Sherri Burr is the author of thirty-two books, the twenty-seventh of which, *Complicated Lives: Free Blacks in Virginia*, was nominated for a Pulitzer Prize in history. A graduate of Mount Holyoke College, Princeton University, and Yale Law School, she enjoyed a long academic career. While teaching law, Sherri was writing her books as she was also caring for her aging mom and disabled brother.

Before leaving her academic job at age fifty-seven to write full-time, she spent a decade connecting with various national and international writers' groups and nonprofits. These contacts did more than give her a place to land in retirement. They led her to useful information. Through her research, Sherri learned that her family had kept a secret from her and her brother, namely that they were descendants of Vice President Aaron Burr's family of color.

Two years into retirement from academia, and then again two years after that, Sherri reported being very satisfied with her life. A large key to her successful transition is the time she spent building connections within writing communities nationwide and internationally.

Returning to a Prior Vocation

A few of my interviewees said they wished to return to a career they had abandoned years earlier, including one psychology professor who wanted to return to being a social worker, her first profession. Below is another such story, that also instructs us on balance in retirement. For many people, even though there is more time after retirement, there may still not be enough for everything you want to do.

From Bankruptcy Judge to Child Advocate

After being a federal bankruptcy judge for fourteen years, Jim Starzynski was able to spend a few more months with his beloved career law clerk James Burke, completing all his cases. Shortly after 8:00 in the evening of December 31, 2012, having just filed the last item on his pending case list, they turned out the lights and left the courthouse, satisfied to have left a clean slate for his successor.

Jim's rough retirement plan was to have more leisure time to raise his youngest child, who was not yet four, and to spend time refereeing soccer matches, reading, and returning to a prior lawyering role, working part-time representing children in neglect and abuse cases filed by the New Mexico Children, Youth, and Families Department (CYFD).

When it came time to implement this plan, there were a few surprises. First, Jim reported that taking care of a toddler at his age was more tiring than it looked. Then, the family adopted horses and donkeys from the Nevada Bureau of Land Management rescue pens, and he learned taking care of the animals also takes a lot of time. Jim has refereed soccer and read, though eleven years into his retirement, he reports that the reading has largely devolved into listening to NPR and podcasts.

The real surprise for Jim was that the part-time legal work was not always part-time. The work has periodically approached full-time work. It ebbs and flows with community need and is deeply impactful. As he explained,

> I worked as a *guardian at litem*, a person appointed by the court to protect the rights of children in contentious cases.
>
> When the state files a legal action to remove a child from the home because of abuse or neglect, that child is entitled to an attorney, just like the Children, Youth, and Families Department (CYFD), and the parents each have their own attorneys.
>
> The child's attorney ensures that CYFD is doing what it is supposed to do to protect and help the child, and that the parents improve their parenting enough to keep the child at home. Leveling the playing field for the most defenseless in an often uncaring adversary system is a mark of our civilization and a deeply worthy undertaking.

It is easy to see how Jim might work more than part-time, even at age seventy-eight, on this worthy work.

Creating Opportunities for Other Retirees

Given the growth in aging populations and the likelihood that millions will retire in the next decade, there are endless opportunities to serve older populations in meaningful ways. No one exemplifies this capacity better than Paula Getz, who serves other retirees in her own retirement.

Paula Getz Gets Serious about Older Adult Job Opportunities

Paula, founder of and adviser to the NM-NEW program, was born and raised in Santa Fe and graduated from the University of New Mexico Anderson School of Management. After that, she worked in Colorado and California consulting and selling and supporting computer equipment for decades. She worked in Silicon Valley during the dotcom boom, a unique opportunity at a unique moment in history.

CHAPTER FOURTEEN

She moved home in 2005 to support her parents. At the time, she worked virtually as a global vice president of Oracle, a multinational computer technology company. She loved this job, which allowed her to supervise people all over the world. During the years right before she left Oracle, she became the volunteer co-chair of the Oracle Pride Employee Network (OPEN), a diversity program supporting LGBTQ+ employees. She called this her "gay job," which she did in addition to her "day job."

During these last years at Oracle, she thought about what her off-ramp would be. She knew she wanted to do something new and decided to help others move from profit to purpose as they transitioned in midlife. She saw many opportunities for retirees or semi-retirees to transfer valuable skills learned in their careers to nonprofits, municipalities, start-ups, small businesses, and others in need of these skills.

While thinking about how to help in this way, Paula joined various nonprofit boards. She soon saw how many career skills acquired as a project manager transferred to her board work. She could easily help nonprofits put on events and tackle other complex tasks by breaking things into manageable, project-based parts.

While doing this board work, it occurred to her that no one should have to make this transition from profit to purpose alone. From there, Paula conceptualized a nonprofit to help people transition from career into other purposeful work, either as a paid employee or a volunteer. From this idea, NM-New Elder World, or NM-NEW, was born.

NM-NEW connects businesses, nonprofits, and civic organizations with new elders who can share wisdom, skills, and expertise with those in society who need them. NM-NEW also helps new elders identify their purpose or purposes in life and find meaning. In addition to connecting new elders with organizations that need their skills, NM-NEW also provides training in new fields and skills, and helps new elders engage in other meaningful ways.

REINVENTION STORIES

Paula explained that her work is driven by harsh economic and demographic realities. First, 25 percent of Americans will retire into poverty, making part-time work a necessity.[227] Second, one third of the US population is already over fifty and by 2030, almost 30 percent will be over sixty-five. Finally, as we have discussed elsewhere, staying purposeful keeps people happy and healthy. According to Paula, failing to do so creates a tremendous tax on our health-care system and the overall economy. As such, keeping new elders engaged is not just nice. It is an economic imperative. It also keeps people from dying prematurely.

NM-NEW also does advocacy work. It actively takes on ageism by partnering with organizations that want the benefits of an older workforce, which include a workforce that wants to work part-time, on a project-to-project basis, or as a replacement for high-level employees who need to exit the workforce temporarily for medical or other reasons.

Paula eventually partnered with a local community college that already had the infrastructure to house her project. She partnered with Community College of New Mexico (CNM), which has been a wonderful partner. CNM already has a job placement system, a sophisticated website, and physical locations to hold classes, interviews, and workshops. This community college partnership model can be used by other similar organizations nationwide, for great societal and individual rewards. Paula is a role model for those who seek to identity need in their community and then move actively to fill that need. Thousands of people of all income levels will benefit from this work, which can be used as a model for other communities.

PURPOSE PRACTICE 14.1

Make a short list of things you could relate to in the stories above. What did you learn about your own path from these stories?

CHAPTER FOURTEEN

Parting Thoughts on Inspiring Retirement Stories

There are as many ways to live an inspired retirement as there are people on this earth. Hopefully, these examples provide insights into what will inspire you. Enjoy the search because as always, getting there is half the fun.

CHAPTER 15:
THE RELOCATION EQUATION

Two of my favorite authors have published books with virtually the same name—Carl Franz, whose book is about travel in Mexico, and Jon Kabat-Zinn, whose book is about meditation. In both cases, the books are called *Wherever You Go, There You Are*.[228] Wherever you are, you are still just you, doing what you do best.

Nevertheless, location matters. We have many choices in this world when it comes to location but also many things to consider. The right geography can enhance our lives in multiple ways. In this chapter, we think about where we want to live, imagining that we have a lot of choices, just for the sake of examining what would make us most happy. We must live somewhere so we might as well live where we can live our best retirement life.

This chapter assumes you have the money to relocate. It also assumes you might be interested in relocating. If either of those statements is not true of you, feel free to move on to the next chapter.

For many people and for many reasons, where they already are is perfect. They have a support system. They know where to shop and go to the doctor or hospital. Family is perhaps close by. It is also easier to stay put. Still, freedom and daydreaming can be fun.

CHAPTER FIFTEEN

In this chapter, we pretend we are moving, or if you do not need that thought experiment either, feel free to move on to chapter 16.

There are hundreds of wonderful places to live in the United States and around the world. Where to move or even whether to move is highly individual. These first two exercises help us move toward some viable options, but you don't have to move. It is fun to ask, "If I did, where would I go?" This first exercise takes a while but sets the groundwork for the rest of this chapter.

PURPOSE PRACTICE 15.1

Assume you have moved to a lovely place that you chose because you like it. You don't need to picture an actual place, just picture your life.

1. Now picture an ideal day at home in that new location. What do you do hour by hour with your days?

2. Now picture traveling for friends, fun, family. How will you get to these places? Ideally, how long will it take from this new location?

3. Now picture the weather. How does that help you live your dream life?

4. Finally, imagine you need emergency medical care or specialized medical care. How available will that be and how far away?

We do the ideal day exercise in our new unidentified locale to see what is the best case scenario in terms of activities, weather, and distance from an airport and health care. Now we will get more concrete. Looking over the ideal day answers above, pick some possible retirement locations for our geographical retirement experiment.

> **PURPOSE PRACTICE 15.2**
>
> Picture a few places you have heard about or visited that you might consider for a new retirement life. This is a quick off-the-cuff exercise. No need to overthink it. Write down four or five places that sound appealing and if you can, narrow it down to a town or region. Now, next to each, write down a word or two about why you might choose it.

Keep those notes handy as we discuss some relocation considerations. This is fun and equally rewarding whether you decide to move or stay put. It affirms what might work for you and your family.

Prioritizing What Is Important in a New Location

We are big travelers and always a little bit geographically restless. We took a year off before marrying and went to thirty countries around the world. We then relocated from Philadelphia to Albuquerque when we were about forty. It is hard for me to believe we have lived in the same home for twenty-six years. We have kept our home but also lived elsewhere during those twenty-six years. We have been on sabbatical or worked summers abroad in three European countries, as well as Mexico, South America, and six US towns outside New Mexico. Wherever we move, we do what we can to see what it would be like to really live in the place, not just be tourists or travelers.

We've experienced many of the different ways we can live in a city or remote location and we know there's a lot of variety. Throughout all of this, we have experienced some truly lovely places and also some unanticipated impediments to our happiness. I also talked to many relocating retirees and share some of their relocation lessons in this chapter.

Relocation in retirement is very common. The Motley Fool estimates that 40 percent of current workers plan to relocate upon retirement.[229] That is a huge number of relocators. While financial reasons like lower cost of living and taxes motivate much of this movement, there are other factors as well. Many city people want to escape the crowds and traffic and move to the country and many suburban people want to move back to the city so they don't have to drive. As a society, we are experiencing an enormous generational migration to and from cities, towns, wilderness, foreign countries, etc. The options are so plentiful it is surprising people can choose at all. Of those 40 percent of US retirees who plan to relocate in retirement, one third of those (13 percent of the overall retirees) plan to do so abroad. Some popular places outside the United States to retire include Portugal, Costa Rica, Mexico, Colombia, Panama, Belize, and various parts of the Caribbean.

As you picture your life in a different place, keep in mind that things happen in life that can disrupt our lives. People get sick, we need a certain type of health care, things that Lifestorian Bruce Feiler calls *Lifequakes*. This is why it is critical to truly picture yourself and your life in these places, hour by hour, activity and Lifequake by activity and Lifequake. It is also important to imagine full-time life in a place you usually associate with vacation. There could be some surprises.

In our own lives, Stewart and I like our solitude. We love wildlife, so we are always drawn to natural locations for vacation. But vacation is different from full-time life. For example, on vacation we look for food we can't make at home. We gravitate toward unique foods and foodie places. We have learned, especially after being in a foodie town for longer than just a vacation, we don't need fancy food in our regular life. Heck, we don't want it. Too rich, too fussy, too many pinecone infused raviolis, etc.

And, though we love being away from it all, we learned that it is not practical to live too far from an airport. Even though our parents are deceased and we don't have kids, there are still family events to attend. In fact, family can be a reason not to relocate at all.

To relocate or not to relocate, that is the question. Considering options can help answer the question. Money is part of the decision to stay or go but other things may matter more, things like community, family, health care, transportation, the view you see when you wake up, how easy it is to get outside, the location of the gym if you use one, the housing available, and so on.

A Few Retirement Relocation Stories

As far as where you want to live and in what type of retirement locale, it's hard to get it perfectly right the first time and you don't need to. You can move again if you want to and maybe that is good. I've talked to many people who have relocated in their retirement, some more than once. We all change and so do our needs.

Relocation is particularly popular with people who want to live well in a cheaper area such as the Caribbean, Mexico, or Central America. Also popular is moving to the mountains or to a small town near nature with lots of outdoor activities or moving from a big suburban home to an urban condo or townhouse. Also, there seem to be a lot of Californians moving up the coast to Oregon (and other places) to escape the cars and the people.

Some of these moves have worked out swimmingly. For example, one busy northeastern academic and his wife moved to Tucson, and he became a park ranger. He still works in his academic field, writing scholarship and teaching as an adjunct professor, and they both have an active volunteer life, as well as good friends. They live adjacent to the National Forest in which he works, which creates an instant community of like-minded folks. They love the milder weather compared to the Northeast and he loves his new job. It is literally perfect.

CHAPTER FIFTEEN

Daniel, a Mexican scientist featured more prominently in the last chapter, and his wife are trying to sort out where to live. They have been moving back and forth from a town in Mexico to a town in the United States, both of which are quite hot in the summer. They are looking for a cooler place to live in the summer and are considering many options. They don't want to get too far away from their children and have been considering Ajijic, San Miguel de Allende, and other places in Mexico. The latest place they tried was a beach town not too far from where they currently live in Mexico.

Another relocation story comes from David and Sheila, who were also featured in the last chapter. David and Sheila moved from New Jersey to Florida after living in New Jersey for forty years, where they both worked in the computer programming field. They did research and decided to move to one of three locations: Albuquerque, where their daughter lives; Arizona, where they had lived in the past; and Bradenton, Florida, where David's nephew lives. The nephew loved Bradenton, they got to know the community a bit, and they eventually chose Bradenton, for two main reasons. One, it had a much larger and more vibrant Black community than Albuquerque or Phoenix, and two, Florida has no state income tax.

To make the transition, they sold their New Jersey home and bought a home in Bradenton, Florida, with the proceeds. They moved into an apartment in New Jersey and kept the home in Florida as a vacation home for ten years. The timing of the move was driven by economics. David wanted to work as long as he could, but ultimately decided to quit at age sixty-six because it no longer made sense to stay in New Jersey and maintain two houses. They were ready to move. The thought David and Sheila put into their choice made it a good one.

Quite a few other people I spoke with moved to locations and later found that they weren't ideal. For example, one southern California couple decided they wanted to spend their retirement hiking and hanging out with their dogs. They built a house on the top of a private mountain in Colorado and discovered that although this did bring them very close to outdoor activities, they missed the convenience of being able to go to a store or restaurant, both of which were now thirty minutes away. Also, it was very windy on the top of that mountain and the road was always bad but was particularly treacherous in the winter. They hadn't thought about how much they would enjoy the location as they aged, and it soon became more work than they wanted to do. In the beginning of their retirement when they were fairly young, it was fine, but as they aged, the location was no longer practical. It also didn't offer the health care they needed. Ultimately, they sold that home and moved to the outskirts of Bend, Oregon.

Bend is an it-town for outdoorsy retirees right now. It is particularly popular with wealthy retirees who want to be close to nature but live downtown where they can walk to restaurants, yoga studios, etc. We know many Bend folks who poo-poo outlying areas and say they would only live right in town. However, due to the influx of new residents and short-term rentals like Vrbos and Airbnbs, downtown homes now cost $1,000,000 or more.

The couple I describe above had no need to live that close to town. From their house on the outskirts, which cost well under $200,000, they could go into Bend in twenty minutes, could go to grocery stores and restaurants less than a half mile away, and could get into the wilderness in ten minutes. For them, this was the ideal spot.

A successful approach to finding a good retirement location is to go to a place where you have vacationed a lot, perhaps in a second home or time-share, and spend more and more time there. Florida is a popular example for East-Coasters. Try experimenting with what life would be like there if you did not return to your primary residence. Does this location have what you need to be happy on a permanent basis? I have seen many situations in which people bought or built their retirement home well before retirement and worked their way into their new community. Many people have done this in Santa Fe, not too far from our home.

This approach can be very successful, but there are also pitfalls. Vacation homes are special in part because they are an escape from day-to-day life. You don't pay the bills there or return phone calls or do day-to-day repairs. If you have a second home, will it still feel special if you have to do the fun parts and the not-so-fun parts from this locale? Also think about the weather. Florida is not as fun in the summer, as we learned when my snowbird father-in-law got stuck there due to poor health for five years straight. Also, some areas in Florida have serious hurricanes, something not experienced during popular vacation months and not featured in real estate brochures.

Low Maintenance Living

One of the downsides to our home in Albuquerque is also one of its best attributes. It is located on almost an acre of land. When we were younger it was a blast to plan, plant, and cultivate. Now we need to hire people to do this.

If you are moving, you have an opportunity to realistically consider how much effort you want to put into maintaining your home, particularly the outside. David and Sheila, the New Jersey to Florida transplants discussed above, prioritized buying a home with category-5 hurricane windows so they could avoid manually putting up wood shutters and then taking them down.

What Kind of Community Are You Looking For?

Some of the places we have visited are known for having vibrant retirement communities. Some of these are lovely all around. Some are nice but expensive. Some are precious, a bit too full of themselves, focused on keeping the community looking beautiful but full of rules about garbage and parking and lawns, what you are allowed to do with your own property, and so on. We even know of one community that would not allow visible solar panels. While pretty communities are nice, we also value our freedom and would not want to live under so many edicts.

This journey is individual. There is no substitute for going and living in your chosen spot for at least a week or two but preferably a month or two. We call this the "virtual" move. If you are part of a couple, perhaps one can retire earlier and go scouting. Or you can go for a long vacation. However long you are there, go to community events and see if you like the people you meet. Talk to people about what they do for recreation. Go to community centers and religious institutions. Attend classes on topics you care about. Try to figure out who comes and goes and who is there to stay. More on that later.

Community Case Study: Yachats, Oregon

Some towns attract the crowd you want to be part of. Again, everybody is different, but one that stood out for us was Yachats, Oregon, on the Central Coast. There is an incredible sense of community. Virtually everyone in town volunteers in some fashion or another. For example, on one rainy Saturday, twenty-two people showed up to maintain one of the trails above the town. When they were done, they received a free lunch at the iconic Drift Inn.

Then there is the Yachats Commons, a community center offering fantastic fitness and other classes for which you pay just two dollars. The instructors don't get paid; rather, the money goes to keep the community center going. I especially love the 10:00 a.m. fitness classes with Kevin, and there is yoga too. While the mostly senior crowd works out, the kids in the free daycare in the same building occasionally run by and say hi. It is a great intergenerational environment and you get the overall feeling that if someone was in need, they would get what they needed.

CHAPTER FIFTEEN

Neighborhoods without Neighbors

When you think about relocating, also think about whether you are looking to become part of a community and if so, what kind of community. Many popular tourist towns in the United States have been decimated by short-term rentals like Vrbo and Airbnb. In order to keep up with high prices of homes and mortgages, owners in ski and other tourist towns have turned their homes into short-term rentals. Investors have also bought homes in these markets and turned them into short-term housing because the practice generates exponentially higher revenues than long-term leasing.

These short-term rental neighborhoods have no real neighbors. During the busy seasons, the neighbors are transient and not part of the community. They don't volunteer to maintain local trails or help out in the local library or community center. The houses are occupied but not by community members. In the off-season, there are empty houses everywhere, neighborhoods without neighbors. Either way, the communities are not vibrant ones. I would not want to own a home in one of these neighborhoods, at least not one that I planned to live in full-time in retirement.

Also, watch out for neighborhoods full of second homes or vacation homes with few permanent residents. In one community in which we lived, there were twenty-four homes in our development and only four housed permanent residents. We were staying for a couple of months in the cold, rainy fall. During the week it was literally just us and those four occupied homes. The weekends brought a few residents from surrounding cities, but it was still mostly a ghost community, great if you need parking, but otherwise a bit eerie. There was no real community. We loved it because we sought solitude, but this would not be a good place for us to retire.

On both coasts and in the inland town of Bend, Oregon, we saw examples of this "neighborhoods without neighbors" phenomenon. We also saw some wonderful, vibrant communities in the areas nearby, so go and check it out before you move. Ask questions. Be prepared to challenge your assumptions before making the big leap. Try not to fall for a house until you know what the community is like.

Other Relocation Factors: Cost of Living, Health Care, Family, and Social Support

Forbes and Kiplinger regularly publish issues on the best US towns in which to retire. These focus on things like the average cost of housing, health-care systems, community activities (which are often more plentiful in university towns), crime rates, public transportation, and a good economy if you want a part-time job. Here, I focus on a few of these factors, as well as proximity to family and social support.

Cost of Living

If cost of living is a consideration, it helps to look back on your ideal day exercise in Purpose Practice 15.1, to see what your ideal day costs in the new location. Fully picture your life in this new place in order to figure out if it is affordable. Hiking is cheaper than golfing or skiing. Also, if you are moving away from family, will you need to pay for travel for you or for your family to visit you? I never assume that if I move away, it is other people's burden to pay to get to me. I know I may need to pay their way. We discuss taxes below, but keep in mind that some of the places that impose extra taxes also have a low cost of living. You need to balance all of this if finances are a driving force in your relocation.

There are three types of taxes to consider: sales tax, tax on social security, and overall income tax. These states have no sales tax: Alaska, Delaware, Montana, New Hampshire, and Oregon. Cities can impose sales tax though. Regarding taxing social security, the federal government taxes social security and these eleven states also tax social security: Colorado, Connecticut, Kansas, Minnesota, Missouri, Montana, Nebraska, New Mexico, Rhode Island, Utah, and Vermont. These taxes vary by state and some states don't start taxing social security unless you make $100,000 or more per year. Do your own research. As for income taxes, as of 2024, Alaska, Florida, Nevada, New Hampshire, South Dakota, Tennessee, Texas, Washington, and Wyoming are the only states that *do not* levy a state income tax.

Health Care: The Big Unknown

When considering a new location, look at the costs of health care and the infrastructure and geography of health care. Will health care costs be higher? Will there even be good health care? I won't assume cost is your main concern in relocating but feel safe assuming good health care will always be a priority. Look at both how *close* you will be to good health care and whether it will indeed *be* good health care. First, consider the quality of the health care. Health care quality has decreased in many parts of the country, especially after the pandemic when many health care workers retired or switched fields. Insurance costs, labor shortages, and other factors have also made it harder to get good health care. Do research in your specialty if you already have a disease or condition that requires a specialist. You can ask your current provider for referrals too.

Next, calculate how long it will take to get to a good hospital or physician. At our New Mexico mountain house, it is forty-five minutes, which is at the outer edge of our comfort zone. As we age, this outer edge will decrease.

Distance to Family

One hilarious blog had a byline on relocating titled "Family: Too Close or Too Far." I say bravo to this sentiment. Some people love hanging out with their kids and grandkids 24/7 and plan to do much more of this in retirement. If this is you, have you talked this over with them? Next door could be too close for you or them.

Also, what are the expectations? Providing childcare once a week, or every workday for five days a week? How might this affect existing relationships and your own mental health? On the other hand, moving ten hours away by plane provides a different kind of strain and will be costly in both time and money. We learned this moving from the East Coast to New Mexico. This is not to say it was not worth it, but distance to family is part of the equation for many of us.

Social Support

This brings me to a final issue to think about: social networks and support. For us, it is probably not practical to relocate. We don't have children and even if we did, we wouldn't want to move somewhere where we didn't know anyone. We have a wonderful social network in New Mexico and we hope to stay here. The health care can be horrendous and the poverty depressing, but everything is a tradeoff. As one friend once said, "It is hard to put a price tag on sunny skies, a diverse population, great food, and wonderful friends and neighbors." These are some of the things that are important to us. Our existing social network is a high priority, and while we were able to build a new one at age forty, we'd rather not do it again at sixty-five or seventy.

Quirky Differences between You and Everybody Else

Finally, there are considerations I have not been able to come up with, things you must have in your life that limit your options. Here is one example. We have always been drawn to living in other cultures. After we got married, we quit our jobs and spent a year traveling the world. We still love to live abroad but we simply cannot live without dogs. Dogs are generally not practical in many foreign places so we have to figure out new ways to scratch this particular international itch. Working abroad part-time is our solution, but we don't think we could do it full-time. Is there something unique about you or your needs that narrows the search for you, something I have not come up with?

There's No Place Like Home

As we close this discussion of geographic location in retirement, keep in mind that whatever you choose is fine. Wherever you go, there you are. No decision is irreversible. Even relocation gurus Bob and Melinda Blanchard eventually missed their home state of Vermont and returned. This unconventional couple moved from the United States to the island of Anguilla on a whim and opened the world-renowned Blanchard's Restaurant. They called Anguilla home for decades and loved most everything about it.

Their books are valuable resources for people following their dreams through relocation, especially *Live What You Love* and *A Trip to the Beach*.[230] These books describe how the Blanchards followed their dreams of living in the Caribbean. The Blanchards eventually returned to Vermont, but not because the move to Anguilla was a failure. It was perfect for their lives in those times. They eventually wanted a change. That change was to return to where they came from. Sometimes, there is no place like home, even if it is also true that "wherever you go, there you are."

We close with one more exercise to make the decision to move or not a bit more concrete.

> ### PURPOSE PRACTICE 15.3
>
> Pick a couple of your favorite places from your relocation possibilities, and revisit Purpose Practice 15.1 in each place. Now

imagine that you suddenly have a pain in your chest. What will you do next? Where will you go?

Now picture that someone in your family is ill or passing away. How will you get to them? How long will it take? Maybe you're thinking this doesn't matter anymore because you're the one who's likely to pass away next, but seriously, compost happens. How will you get from where you are now to where you need to be?

Now picture your social circle. You know how you will spend your time but who will you spend it with? Also, let's say you need an emergency pet sitter or a drive to the hospital. How would you build relationships so that you had someone to call?

Compare the results in these different locations. Look at activities, health care, travel, and social circles. It is abstract and imperfect, I know. Just do your best.

As we move through the next few chapters, keep these journal entries in mind. If you are considering moving, make plans to visit some of the relocation options. On the other hand, if you know where you live now is perfect for now, this is one less thing to think about.

PART FIVE

Your Money and Your Inspired Retirement

CHAPTER 16:
A MINDFUL MONEY MINDSET PART I: STAYING INSPIRED WHEN MONEY IS TIGHT

Money is a touchy subject. Studies show that people would rather talk about sex or almost any topic other than their financial condition. There is shame, there is embarrassment, and there is guilt regardless of what you have, a little or a lot.

For decades, I have taught money management skills to young adults. No matter what, there are tears. Money is such an emotional topic that there is now a special kind of counseling that combines behavioral therapy and financial coaching to help people improve their thoughts, feelings, and behaviors around money. This specialty, known as financial therapy, was created in 2010 to address the many emotions people have around the money they have and the money they don't have.

This book contains two chapters about money. This one is written primarily for middle class people who suspect they might not have enough money. The next chapter is addressed primarily to those who feel they have enough money. We get more philosophical about money in the next chapter, but here we focus on the nuts and bolts of finances and retirement.

CHAPTER SIXTEEN

If you are on solid footing financially and feel confident that your retirement income will comfortably meet your needs, consider skipping to chapter 17 now.

Income, Wealth, and Information Gaps

Not having enough money rarely results solely from poor lifestyle choices. Most of us who are of retirement age have roughly the same income as our parents, adjusted for time. Lately though, it has been become harder for children to maintain the standard of living of their parents because the middle class is shrinking.

Being poor or underpaid in the United States is an epidemic as we live in a world of vast income and wealth inequality. As of 2021, US income and wealth distribution were both more unequal than in any Western country in the world, and more unequal than at any other time in history.[231] The US income gap is greater than that of India, the land of the caste system and the untouchables. Compared to the *income gap*, the US *wealth gap* is exponentially larger.[232]

Income gaps reflect the percentage difference between the highest-paid person in a society or private company compared to the lowest-paid person. Income gaps also refer to how much, on average, a white male makes compared to a woman or person of color in the same job doing the same work. On average, women make 70 percent of what men make for the same work and men of color make about 67 percent of what white men make for the same work.[233]

While these *income* gaps are huge, *wealth* gaps, meaning the amount of money people amass over a lifetime, are enormous by comparison. For example, as of 2020, the average Black family had saved $50,000, whereas the average white one had saved $500,000, a 1,000 percent wealth difference compared to a 20–30 percent income difference. The wealth gap reflects the effects of a lifetime of earning and saving less.[234]

Retirement is when the wealth gap really takes its toll. After working for decades in lower-paying jobs that don't provide pensions or 401(k)s, many people, particularly many people of color, must rely solely on social security in retirement. Even these benefits are often lower due to lower wages over a lifetime and other factors.[235]

I bring up these income and wealth gaps for three reasons. First, if you don't have much saved, you're not alone. Second, if you don't have much saved, you need not feel guilty or ashamed as it is likely not your fault. Third, if you don't have much saved, there are things you can do to address the situation on an individual basis. The general societal problem of vast income inequality is a different story. Until these income and wealth gaps are addressed on a societal level, they will persist on a societal level.

Returning to the subject of you and your family, information can be powerful. Besides these income and wealth gaps, there are vast personal finance information gaps. In other words, the gap between what individual people in our society have been taught about personal finance is as wide as the income and wealth gaps. Some people's parents taught them a lot about money, like my husband's parents. My parents knew nothing and had no knowledge to pass on. Some people learned early in school, at home, or from friends. Others didn't learn from anyone. This gap in general knowledge about personal finance makes this chapter particularly tricky to write. It is hard to generalize given the vast differences in what people know and have.

My Mistaken Assumptions about Money Attitudes and Retirement

The purpose of this book is to prepare people for the non-monetary aspects of retirement, yet it has been next to impossible to keep people off the subject of money when discussing retirement.

CHAPTER SIXTEEN

The vast majority of people, even those who have been assured that they have enough money, fear there won't be enough, perhaps because we can't predict markets or the cost of health care or a few other wild cards. This means anxiety about money still exists at virtually all levels of wealth. As a result, this chapter was born. Here we will explore steps we can take to ease that anxiety, namely how we can manage our money more purposefully and thoughtfully, and how we can reduce expenses when needed. This chapter covers the fundamentals of personal finance and offers some ideas for keeping your financial life balanced.

Money and Mindset

As with everything else, we get to choose what to think about and how to frame the issue of money in our own minds. As with mindful eating, thinking about our money more purposefully can bring insight and equanimity on the subject. Money serves no purpose in and of itself but is a means to an end, to something else we want or value. To start, it is useful to see if our money is serving us well or being mindlessly wasted. We get to choose how to use our money in society, what to buy and spend, and what to save or forego. Yet much modern spending is the opposite of mindful. We may not even want what we spend money on and simply spend out of habit. The exercises in this chapter will help you slow down and think about your money habits.

Your Money Background Story

I was taught absolutely nothing about money management as a kid. I learned what I know from my husband, who was raised quite differently. I also learned at work as I was a business lawyer. My husband and I have always worked in the fields of business transactions, lending, bankruptcy, and insolvency. We did this work in the context of business finance in our private legal practices. When I became a law professor, I eventually shifted my focus from business finance and business law to personal finance and consumer law. What about you? What is your money background story? What do you know about money and where did you learn these things?

Formulas for Success and Your Personal Balance Sheet

At its most basic, household finance is just math and it is the same math for multi-billion dollar companies as for middle-class households. To be healthy financially, you need to spend no more than you make, to be able to cover your regular and unexpected expenses without relying on credit and still have some money left over. This is sometimes described as living within one's means.

The idea of living within one's means sounds quaint in our credit-drenched world, but it is so much easier and more pleasant to live without debt. The peace of mind that comes with low monthly expenses is hard to put a price on, which makes being debt free, well, freeing. A mound of consumer credit is dangerous for everyone but particularly for retired people, who have less capacity to increase their net worth. Advertising be damned, there is a sweet smugness that comes with not buying into American consumerism, to that mantra that insists we buy tons of worthless garbage.

Basic Formula Repeated: Spend No More Than You Make

For many older people like you and me, it is comforting to live within our means. For younger people, like kids and grandkids, experts advise living below your means, meaning spending less

CHAPTER SIXTEEN

than you make so you can build wealth. This idea can put some people off. For example, one of my financial literacy students who grew up poor lamented how, when his family finally saved enough money to visit New York City, the twin towers were hit by the planes before they arrived. He felt his visit was too late and the experience had a lasting impact. He vowed to always live, in his words, "above his means." In class, I try to get students to pay themselves first by saving, so this was the opposite of what I was trying to impart. Still, I see where my student was coming from. Most people who grow up poor hope they will eventually have more.

As a point of reference about poverty, in 2024, the federal poverty guidelines were $15,060 for a family of one, $20,440 for a family of two, $25,820 for a family of three, and $31,200 for a family of four. Without question, it is hard for people who do not make a living wage to spend less than they make. Policy changes are needed to fix this problem, but in the meantime, we will do our best here to suggest some ways to help you spend less than you make or at least not more than you make. Of course, one size does not fit all, so pick and choose what speaks to you and find your own ways to cut back on expenses.

While it is difficult to make ends meet when one makes very low wages, you may have the same problem even with higher income. This is especially true if you don't give much thought to where your money goes. Slowing down and spending mindfully can improve your bottom line and your sense of financial freedom.

To understand your money, you will consider two elements, income and expenses. The starting point for all conversations about making ends meet is your net income. This is not what you get paid in your contract, or your stated "salary," but what you actually take home in income, after your employer takes out taxes, social security, health benefits, etc. Or, if you are on social security, it is what gets deposited into your bank account, minus what you need to set aside each month for taxes.

Figure out your net monthly income now, using your checking account statement. If it varies each month, add up all the income for a year and divide it by twelve to get a monthly figure. There is more math ahead.

A More Detailed Personal Finance Formula

With your net monthly income in hand, we'll shift our focus to expenses. Here is a more detailed formula, besides simply spending less than you make. It is from one of my favorite personal finance books, *All Your Worth* by Elizabeth Warren and Amelia Tyagi.[236] For people who are still working and not retired, these authors suggest spending 50 percent of your net income on "needs" or "must pay" expenses, 20 percent on savings or paying down debts, and the remaining 30 percent on whatever you like. Perhaps this formula works better for your kids or grandkids because you may no longer be saving or paying off debt. Just in case it is useful, I explain it in more detail below.

The key to using this formula is getting your basic, non-negotiable (sometimes called fixed) expenses within 50 percent of your net income. Warren and Tyagi describe these as the expenses you would pay if you were unemployed. In other words, these are the expenses you would pay just to survive, without any extras. Those are your "must haves" and include rent or mortgage, utility bills, a cheap phone, car payments, gas, car maintenance, car insurance, medical insurance, and basic groceries, but not specialty or gourmet groceries, meals out, gifts for family and friends, cable TV, XM radio, dog grooming, clothes, and so on and so forth.

Warren and Tyagi are not saying you can't have any of those other things. Rather, for the formula, these non-essential items will go into your "wants" category, which will consume 30 percent of your net income, and which you can spend exactly as you like. This category covers special food treats, meals and coffee out, cable television, books, movies and shows, travel, gifts for friends and family, and so on.

CHAPTER SIXTEEN

In Warren and Tyagi's formula, the other 20 percent of net income goes to pay off debts or save for retirement, a down payment, etc. While this formula has been criticized for being too flexible and not creating tangible financial goals, it seems to work well for middle income people who are still working.

Once you get to retirement and stop saving for retirement, the formula will change. On the one hand, you will no longer be saving for retirement, so there is more freedom. On the other hand, you won't be working for pay so you may feel your assets are not going to last. If you still have debt, you can follow the formula as is, paying 20 percent toward the debt. If not, you can either save 20 percent for unmet health-care or other needs, or spend that on discretionary items, making the split an easy 50/50 needs vs. wants. Or, if you need more for "needs," you can move that 20 percent to needs, making the split 70 percent for needs and 30 percent for wants.

This formula can be useful when talking to your kids and grandkids. What I like about it is that it encourages people to buy less expensive houses and cars so they will have some money left to spend on discretionary things. Banks encourage people to have the biggest mortgage they qualify for (often 45 percent of net income), because banks earn more fees on larger loans. Add a car payment, utilities, insurance and so on, and many people are left with almost no disposable income.

Back in the day, Stewart and I knew law firms that encouraged their young lawyers to buy expensive houses so the young lawyers could not quit working at the firm, even if they wanted to. We used to call this the "golden handcuffs." Living simply and keeping the debt low is comforting both in retirement and long before that.

Most of us are unaware of where much of our money goes. We have vague ideas about where it goes, but not the detailed data needed to direct our money to its best use. In the coming pages, you will learn more about where your money goes. In the first exercise below, you will compare your assets and your liabilities and create a personal balance sheet. Then you will follow your money so you can redirect it to what you most appreciate in life. After that, you will think about small steps that could save you significant money each month.

Creating Your Personal Balance Sheet

> **PURPOSE PRACTICE 16.1**
>
> Pull out a piece of paper. On the right side of that piece of paper, list all your assets (other than the house you plan to continue living in) and place a value on each.
>
> When you set the value, imagine you are selling those items now. Furniture and clothes are worth very little so don't bother listing those unless you could actually sell them. Even then, these items should be valued at garage-sale prices.
>
> Mostly, what will go on this list is bank account, stocks and other investments, real estate other than your primary residence, cars, recreational vehicles, jewelry, and so on.
>
> Add up the value of the items in the right-hand column.
>
> On the left side of the same piece of paper, list your debts, starting with your secured debts (mortgages, car and furniture loans, etc.). Now list all your credit card debts and other debts and loans. Include financed dental work and health care.
>
> Add up the debts in the left column.

This piece of paper contains your personal financial balance statement. Compare the two numbers. Debt uses up your future income and limits your flexibility. If you have assets that you could use to pay off debts, consider selling some of your belongings to get some debt paid off. This will create extra household cash equal

CHAPTER SIXTEEN

to the payments on those debts. You can spend that newfound cash flow on anything you like or save it. This is like giving yourself a raise.

Figuring Out How You Spend Your Money Now

If that was a personal balance sheet, what follows in the next few exercises is a personal cash flow statement, a comparison of the monthly net income you calculated above with your expenses. We will calculate the expenses, add them up, and then deduct them from the net income.

In this exercise, you calculate your current monthly expenses. You may find ways to cut these, but for now, we will just find out what these expenses are. We will split the process into two steps, something akin to the Warren and Tyagi formula, but modified. Rather than strictly wants and needs, I suggest you break down your expenses into recurring monthly expenses and discretionary expenses.

PURPOSE PRACTICE 16.2

Calculating Your Monthly Expenses

Step One: Make a list of your recurring monthly expenses, along with the amounts for these items. If some are annual expenses, divide the amount by twelve and add those to the monthly list. If the expense varies monthly, just estimate or get into your bank account and calculate to the penny. I know the amounts for these things are not all fixed, but they are recurring because we do have to pay the utilities, etc. every single month, even if the amount varies. The idea is to figure out what your regular (every month) recurring expenses are and deduct that total from your net income for the same period. You can also include an amount for monthly food. After that we will deduct more discretionary things like eating out, entertainment, etc.

I do this exercise fairly often. In my financial literacy class, the students and I do this before the class starts, so we can work with the data. While writing this chapter, I did the exercise again. For my monthlies, Step One above, I included many more things than you might want to, just because it helps my brain think about things I pay every month, rain or shine, home or abroad, etc. My Step One category is far broader than Warren and Tyagi's "needs" or "must spends."

These Step One things for me include my mortgage (with taxes and insurance), pharmacy and doctor copays, each bill for cell phones, landline, internet, XM Radio, Apple music, Audible, other tech costs, and all utilities (meaning gas, electric, water, and so on). I also include any payments I make to people to clean my house or work in my garden, our gym memberships, and anything else I spend money on every single month. I even add in amounts for our dog's vet bills, grooming, and special food; money to get my hair cut and colored; and dry cleaning bills. I also include all recurring car expenses including insurance, maintenance, and gas.

I put a lot of expenses into this Step One portion that are not necessities because I pay them even when we are out of town for extended periods. If I were suddenly unemployed, I would not include them, but for now, these are my regular monthly expenses.

For my Step One, I do not add in entertainment or restaurants as I consider these to be things we can, and very often do, cut way back on when we want to. We will figure out those expenses below in Step Two.

Step Two: After listing all your regular monthly expenses, come up with a list of other things you spend money on, and provide a monthly amount for each. This will include all the discretionary spending. My list includes donations to charity, restaurants,

CHAPTER SIXTEEN

> coffees out, gifts, movies and other entertainment, magazines, books, music, clothes, cosmetics, vacations and other travel, and massages and facials. If you are like most people, you will not really know how much you're spending on these things, but to find out, get into your credit card statements and bank accounts and look. You can also estimate, but if you do, just know that the estimate will be low. We always spend much more than we think we spend unless we track every dollar.

Looking at Step One, there are likely some things you can cut back on, for example, insurance, which we discuss below. You can also cut back on services at your home, beauty treatments, or gas, but most of the cutting back or redirecting of funds happens in Step Two.

Now look at your Step Two expenses. Here, there could be a lot to cut back on. You can even make a game of it. The pandemic taught us that we could cut our restaurant spending by more than half and not even miss the restaurants. We could have four friends over for what it would cost us to go out alone, and if that is reciprocated, you get three meals for the price of one, eat healthier, and enjoy lots of healing social time. We also save on groceries by putting a bit more effort into the shopping list, using coupons, watching sales, and not shopping when we are hungry. On the entertainment front, Stewart joined a movie club where he gets one or two movies and 20 percent off all concessions for ten dollars a month. He also got us a better deal on XM radio by cutting back to just one radio for his truck, and he created a family Audible account.

See what you can learn looking at your expenses. Are there any surprises there? Are you spending some money on discretionary things that don't seem worth it, money you could either save for future fun or redirect to another current expense? Are you spending your money the way you really want to?

This next exercise is where things get interesting. By tracking your expenses, you will find out where all the little expenses are and can redirect your money to what matters most to you. We track all our expenses from time to time, especially while teaching abroad on a set-expense account.

Tracking every little thing helps us decide what is worth it and what is not. Go ahead and spend, just spend money on what you enjoy most.

PURPOSE PRACTICE 16.3

Tracking Your Expenses

Get a little notebook or use your journal to write down everything you spend throughout your day. You can do this as you go, or do it at the end of the day. Write down every coffee, every grocery run, every parking meter, every dollar you've handed to an unhoused person . . . everything you spend, all of it. Do this for a week or two. Now, take a close look at that list. What was worth it, and what wasn't?

Mentally redirect funds to things you care about.

Tracking expenses also has the subconscious effect of reducing spending, so we won't have to write it down. The process reminds me somewhat of those food diaries people keep when they are trying to lose weight. Like the food journal, you might spend less in order to avoid writing it down. Tracking expenses can also be habit forming, in a good way. When you decide not to spend money on something that is not worth it, you can keep track of what you *don't spend*, and spend that money on something that is more worthwhile.

Here are some things I noticed on my expense tracking list the week I wrote this chapter. I spent almost $300 at REI when

CHAPTER SIXTEEN

my intent was just to stop by and repair my doggie jogger. Was it worth it? Probably not. I got a YETI cooler for one third off, which I thought was an amazing deal. I am not sure we need it but do think we will use it. Then I bought snow pants because I had put on weight and the old ones were tight. In that case, it might have been better to wait and see if the weight comes off.

As Stewart and I looked over our expenses this month, we noticed some trends. We do waste some food. Most people do. We're almost always happy with our meals out because we limit them. Stewart says he buys books, reads them once, and then gives them away when he could use the library. He also buys event tickets way in advance for concerts and jazz and film festivals, and often we cannot go. For me, I love to shop, a tendency I explain in the next chapter. This means I sometimes buy clothes and cosmetics I do not need and never use. I hate to admit this, but sometimes I'll clean out the back of my trunk and find an item that I purchased months before. It's usually something I don't remember buying and certainly never missed. If it is not too late, I return it.

These next three exercises could save you money. The adult students in my financial literacy class often save money through these small steps and over time, these savings add up.

PURPOSE PRACTICE 16.4

Eliminating Mystery Auto-Pays

Go into each of your credit card statements and closely examine each automatic payment on each bill. You will know them because there will be a phone number after each. See if you can figure out what each is for. For those you don't recognize, call them and find out what the expense is for. Cancel the service if you no longer want it. You can also call back and cancel later if you want to think about it. Chances are, you're using less than half of these things you're paying for each month.

By the way, companies that process auto-pays, like Apple (the source of many of our mystery auto-pays), are required by law to provide a phone number on the bill for the precise reason that people forget they have signed up and need a way to cancel them.

Not sure whether to keep it or cancel it? The default rule should be that you're going to cancel them all. Once you cancel, they will likely call and offer you a better rate just to get you roped back in.

By canceling unwanted things, you give yourself another raise.

PURPOSE PRACTICE 16.5

Shopping for Home and Car Insurance

To shop your insurance, you first need to call your existing insurer and ask for the details of your home and car insurance policies. You need to know your liability limits so you can share those with the other companies you will call. Then call around and see if you can get your home and car insurance for less. Get new quotes by comparing what your coverage is now with what the new companies can offer. Use these other offers to call your existing insurer and see if they will drop their rates. If they won't match your lowest quote, change insurer.

We saved $1,000 a year doing this by switching to AARP insurance once we became old enough to qualify at age fifty-five. Our existing company could not match the rate, but came back a year later, tail between its legs, and undercut the AARP rate we were paying. We were annoyed, but we returned to them anyway to save the money. We are about to switch back to AARP because of what I call premium-creep, a rate increase of just a few percentages every year, which results in high premiums once again.

Hopefully the money raised through Purpose Practices 16.4 and 16.5 have produced savings for you. You're giving yourself more raises.

Now we will move on to paying off debt, particularly credit card debt. Credit card debt is incredibly expensive. As my colleague Fred Hart used to say, people buy a sweater on sale for forty dollars, and then pay another twenty dollars in interest on it by putting it on a credit card. Credit card interest in 2024 typically runs 22–30 percent. Paying this interest is a huge waste of money. If you could save that money, you would be the one earning interest on it.

PURPOSE PRACTICE 16.6

Tamping Down Credit Card Debt

Put away all your credit cards except for one and when using that last one, don't charge more than you can pay off that month. Pay off whatever debt you can, perhaps by selling things. If you pay down the credit card debt and only charge what you can pay in full each month, your available income will grow.

This will give you another raise of sorts. Here are a few more tips for reducing expenses:

Saving Up for Splurges

Sometimes we like to save up for big purchases by making it a game. For example, the pantry game. We each get a small amount of money to buy groceries to augment things already in our own pantry and freezer. Whatever we save in new groceries or meals out we put toward something special.

Last year, we bought a fancy espresso maker, a Nespresso, and it amortized its full price within about seven months in coffee shop savings. The Nespresso makes better coffee than we can get out and was a great investment. Our Soda Stream is another example. It makes soda much cheaper than the cost to buy cans. In addition, it helps the environment by saving all those cans.

Saving on Entertainment

You can save money on entertainment and still have fun. For example, have a couple of friends over and stream a movie rather than going to a theater. Join a movie club. Join a pickleball or tennis club. Also, cooking for friends can be a blast. We enjoy going to shows and festivals but try to balance those with free activities like hiking, enjoying a book on tape, going for long drives, and so on. PublicLibrary.org has free books on tape.

Saving on Clothes

Another place to save money is on clothes. Many people don't need to spend as much on clothes once they retire. Even now, when I am still working, I love thrift stores and high-end consignment stores. Shopping for used clothes has two benefits: (1) it's usually cheaper, and (2) it's much better for the environment. It is a way to get really nice clothes inexpensively without relying on child labor, fast fashion, or any production that results in fuller landfills.

Saving on Travel

When it comes to travel, something many retired people want to do, not having work obligations saves money. You can go places in the off-season or during the week when destinations are typically much cheaper. Sites like Travelzoo or TripAdvisor are wonderful for identifying inexpensive travel opportunities, many of which are offered at times when other people can't take advantage of them.

We also try to spend less before a trip or vacation. For example, we paid several thousand dollars to rent a house in Oregon this fall while I was writing this book. Since we knew we would be spending that, plus eating out a lot, we decided not to buy clothes, sporting goods, or really anything except a few books during the months leading up to the trip. We spent our pre-trip time reading, talking, and planning.

In many ways, we live to travel. Being frugal on the lead-up, and sometimes on the trip too, makes more travel possible. It's amazing how much we spend when not in this "save up" frame of mind. When we're home, we can spend hundreds of dollars a week filling the house with food, dry goods, paper products, cosmetics, new (to us) clothes, and I am not sure what else. I just know it can be hundreds of dollars a week. In this way, being in a remote location, without stores or restaurants, can save money.

When Stewart was recovering from back surgery recently, we went on an inexpensive cruise, which we had never done before. We cut back pre-trip and paid around $2,500 total for the cruise and the transportation there for six days and five nights. We didn't buy anything on board, so it was almost a money-maker. No gas, no coffees out, no huge Costco runs, no Walgreens, no Home Depot, no restaurant and bar bills, and the list goes on. We were amazed to find out how much we spend without thinking when we stay home and how much we can cut out when away. It is also remarkable how much we can save by having a mindful hiatus on spending before a big splurge or trip.

Saving on Electronics and Other Miscellaneous

There are a few other things we do to keep costs down. We absolutely know that these would not be for everyone. We know for many people, cable TV is a real lifesaver, as well as a money saver. But for us, we don't have cable TV, we only buy XM radio services on sale, and we use Netflix, but only the basic services. We like to drive older cars and try never to replace our phones. In fact, we try to repair and replace everything rather than buying new things.

If you are feeling the need, based on advertising and social pressure, to get new phones, computers, appliances, etc., remember that our natural world is fragile and will do better with fewer discarded electronics. I was mad as a hornet to learn that new appliances do use less water, yes, but also have a useful life of less than half of older appliances. There is more about planned obsolescence in the next chapter, but you can feel good about trying not to buy new things when the old ones work perfectly well. You are doing yourself and our environment a favor.

Saving on Mystery Charges and Fees on Credit Cards and Bank Accounts

Stewart and I have worked in the financial services industry for a combined fifty years and are sticklers for fees. We look for hidden or "mistaken" fees on our credit card statements and our bank accounts. Trust us, they are far more common than you think. If we find a mistake, we call and ask to have it removed. If we accidentally miss a credit card payment deadline, we call and request that the credit card company remove the interest and late fees, or we threaten to cancel the card. We have never been denied. We try not to pay annual fees on credit cards or bank accounts. We also try not to use out-of-network ATMs.

Saving on Utilities

I keep an excel spreadsheet of our utility costs by utility and month. I like to keep the heat down in winter and keep the lights out when not in use. I like to try to beat last year's utility usage for a particular month. It sounds strange but I enjoy it. I also think about the environment. Reducing the use of electricity, fossil fuels, and natural resources will not only save money over time, but also help with climate change. If we all did it, it would help a lot, but every person's effort matters.

Saving on Food

Did I mention I love shopping? Part of this love is getting things on sale, including food. Today you could get spaghetti sauce for $1.99 instead of $2.99 if you bought five. I use coupons and buy in bulk, which is cheaper and cuts down on packaging. At the holidays, many restaurants will give you a twenty-dollar gift card if you buy one hundred dollars in gift cards. I use restaurant coupons and reward programs too.

When it comes to food, the best budget-friendly tip is to eat at home most of the time. Doing this has many advantages. First, it is much cheaper. Second, it is much healthier. Third, once you learn to cook, your cooking is better than what you can get in most restaurants, and you can make exactly what you want. Fourth, you don't have to rely on other people to serve you, which could take longer than you like.

A good friend edited this book for me and had this great thought on this topic: "I'd rather learn to cook at home than get a part-time job just so I can go out to eat." You might be thinking, I don't know how to cook, but you now have time to learn. Start small and work your way up.

Saving on Services

One place we spend more than many other people is on services. We hire people to help around the house, including to clean up inside and to help with the yard. This is a double mitzvah or blessing. These others get paid a fair wage, and we don't have to do these tasks. We try to use local companies, like a local pest control company rather than Orkin or other national companies.

Tips for People Who Love Shopping

Shopping creates an adrenaline and dopamine rush that can be addictive, which scientists study through brain scans. Since I have the shopping bug, I have used my mindfulness practices to pin down particular times when this shopping urge occurs, which is mostly when I'm feeling stressed out, bored, or deserving of a treat. Sometimes just shopping for groceries or household items is enough to scratch this itch.

If you love shopping for higher end items, go ahead and shop, online or in person, but just don't buy the item. Just wait. You'll get the rush from picking out the items even without purchasing them. Later, you can buy the items, but by then, the thrill may have passed. This approach sounds crazy, but it works.

Know You Can Change Your Habits If You Want To

You might find all this detail tedious and also just assume it is too late to change, but it is not. We can all improve our money habits at any age. My own habits have changed completely since my midtwenties. When Stewart and I first started dating, I owed $3,000 in credit card debt. He agreed to pay it off if I paid him back $300 a month. We love to say that this is how he "got the girl." In any case, prior to paying this off, I was paying the minimum balance and perfectly happy doing so. The idea that I was unnecessarily paying high interest never crossed my mind. I had no idea how to manage or even think about money or personal finance. I recall buying clothes at TJ Maxx, having my card declined, and thinking nothing of it.

I heard a similar story from an interviewee, David, about love and money but the roles are reversed. David had a full ride to a master's program in computer science at Purdue, provided by his employer, a telecom company giant. One of his checks from his employer bounced and he was broke. A woman in his program offered to lend him $300 to make ends meet and he took it. Once he was back in the black, he offered to pay her back by check. She said, "No thank you, I'll take cash." We laughed so hard in his interview, as he explained that this woman later became his wife. One of the things he liked about her was her sophistication around money.

Stewart was raised to never use credit except for a house. His family had no cars loans ever. They did not use credit cards, or if they did, they paid off the balance each month. This is why he was alarmed by my credit card balance. He just thought it was a waste to give that money (the interest) to a bank when it could be used or saved by us.

When Stewart started working as an attorney in 1987, his gross starting salary was $36,000. Of that, which was likely something like $22,000 in net income, he saved $10,000. I was making $56,000 and spending more than I made. I was putting the additional expenses on my credit cards, the payments for which reduced my future income.

When we bought our first house, our interest rate was higher than it should've been because of my poor credit. Over thirty years, if we had kept that mortgage, it would have resulted in almost $100,000 in extra interest payments. Thankfully, now my credit is good and we have a 3.5 percent mortgage.

The point is that we can all improve. Once we learn these rules, we can all make positive changes that don't feel like sacrifices. They just feel like mindful, purposeful choices.

Giving Up Money for Time

Time is worth a lot, sometimes more than money. We have voluntarily reduced our income twice since our marriage. One time was when we moved to New Mexico for a better, more relaxed lifestyle. We were lawyers in Philadelphia and became New Mexico educators. It was 100 percent worth it. We love it and are grateful for our lives. We are especially grateful that we never bought the expensive houses and cars our peers bought. We could never have left.

When we moved to New Mexico, however, our income dropped to 35 percent of our prior level, meaning less than half of what we were making. Our accountant was astounded. Unfortunately, we did not think to change our spending and soon half of our sizable savings was gone. We eventually figured out the problem and adjusted our lifestyle. We also started taking on summer work. We did not make much money from this work, but we got to live in Europe, expense free, and the work kept us busy and out of trouble. The point of all of this is that small changes matter, as does watching the dollars more closely.

We had given up money for time once before, back in 1988. We decided to get married and had this fantasy of taking a year off and traveling the globe on a budget ticket, mostly backpacking. We then decided to make a money pact or challenge and try to save $20,000 to fund a yearlong trip. We moved from a fashionable part of Boston to Lynn, a very unfashionable one, which dropped our rent from $1,400 a month to $560 a month. We didn't buy clothes or anything else, and in seven months, only ate one meal out, a lobster roll from a stand.

The apartment was sort of gross, especially the kitchen, but we stayed focused on our goal, spent our free time walking around town with travel packs on our backs, and planned our trip. With our goal in mind, it was much easier to get our expenses way down.

Spending after Retirement

Before we move into income in retirement, know that in retirement we may spend money differently. In retirement, some expenses will go down automatically, and others can be reduced without too much pain. Also, since retirement changes our goals, values, and how we want to spend our valuable remaining time, it can also change our spending priorities. It is a luxury to slow down and think about how retirement might change your views on money.

Our non-monetary needs also change in retirement. For example, a busy young person who is still working may find making coffee at home to be more delicious, less expensive, and a big timesaver compared to a coffee shop. A retired person on the other hand may receive incalculable social benefits from spending money at a coffee shop, where he or she interacts with others. Socializing is critical as we age, as we have discussed, so money spent on social events and interactions is worth more when other social opportunities may have dwindled.

Mindset Regarding Income after Retirement: Pensions, Social Security, and Private Savings

The rest of this chapter focuses on income in retirement. Like with a business cash flow statement, every household has money coming in and money going out. Once we hit retirement, regular income might dry up, and we may be watching our savings dip.

> **PURPOSE PRACTICE 16.7**
>
> If you are already retired, recall how you felt when you stopped getting paychecks and began drawing from retirement accounts. Did this change your perspective or your practices?

Spending Rather Than Saving

For many people I have interviewed, watching one's net worth drop causes anxiety. Keep in mind if you have saved money for retirement, you can spend the money. That is what it is for. Recalling how it feels to spend what you have saved is still helpful, as it may motivate you to prioritize what is important to you. We still want to live comfortably within our means even in retirement.

Remember, too, that there are two ways to make ends meet. One is to carefully examine expenses and reduce some of those, as we have described above. The other is to increase income, perhaps by working. Refer back to earlier chapters and consider if there is a place you might work part-time, consistent with what you love and how you can make a difference.

The benefits of working part-time in retirement are compounded by the social benefits of working. In 2024, there were many more jobs than people to fill them, including jobs for older people. This story from an interviewee is instructive as it describes both anxiety over retirement income and a decision to work part-time.

Russ, a high-level manager in the tech industry, decided to retire because the job had become stressful and also because the budget of his organization was getting tighter. He was a highly paid manager and wanted to ease that burden for his organization. I am always surprised at the number of people who quit for that reason. It feels so altruistic, particularly coming from businesspeople.

In any case, Russ reported that he retired a bit too early, not emotionally, but financially. He was one of the people who kept bringing the conversation back to money in our interview. His financial adviser had informed him that he had enough money, but he still doubted that and fretted over changes in the market. One reason he was uncertain about his financial adviser's conclusion was that he was not paying much attention to his retirement accounts until the several months leading up to his retirement. Watching these accounts was just not part of his practice. This story shows that it is important to understand and follow the ebbs and flows of your financial resources well before retirement so you can feel assured and get acclimated to changes in the market.

I interviewed Russ just two weeks after he retired. Within those two weeks, Russ decided to work part-time as a consultant in his field until he could gain comfort with his financial condition. This part-time work would allow him to take his pension but forego social security until he was older. He was sixty-three when I spoke to him and was planning to take social security at age sixty-seven, his full retirement age. In the meantime, he planned to work part-time.

The Three-Legged Financial Stool of Retirement Income

Speaking of pensions and social security, retirement funds are often referred to as a three-legged stool, comprised of pensions, social security, and private savings held in retirement accounts. Fewer and fewer Americans have pensions these days, leaving most Americans with a two-legged stool. The image is provocative in its unsteadiness. Private retirement savings and social security are more common than pensions, but some people may have just social security to rely upon, in that case a one-legged stool. Many of those people cannot retire or must work part-time.

Due to the income and the wealth gaps described above, people of color are much more likely to rely solely on the one-legged stool of social security in retirement. This results from a confluence of factors, including lower-paying jobs that rarely provide pensions or 401(k) plans. Even these social security benefits are often lower due to lower wages over a lifetime, health conditions that disrupt work participation, and inequitable access to education, which limits access to higher paying jobs.[237]

In your retirement, you will live off whichever of these sources is available. Each is discussed below.

When to Take Social Security

Everyone becomes eligible for social security at age sixty-two, though the benefits are much lower at that age. I have known many people who have needed to begin drawing social security at sixty-two, primarily because of health problems or in some cases, unemployment and overall poverty. If you need to take social security at age sixty-two, you know what you have to do.

For most of us, it is beneficial to wait until we are at least sixty-seven, or ideally, seventy, to draw social security. The benefits go way up at this point, so if you have other assets you can spend to make it to one of those later ages, you'll have much more security in the end. For example, if you were born between 1943 and 1954, your full retirement age is sixty-six. There are increments in between as well, but if you were born in 1960 or after, your full retirement age is sixty-seven. This chart explains the benefits of waiting if you can.

AGE OF RETIREMENT COLLECTION	PERCENTAGE OF SOCIAL SECURITY RETIREMENT BENEFITS
62	70%
63	75%
64	80%
65	86.7%
66	93.3%
67	100%
68	108%
69	116%
70	128%

According to the Social Security website, an invaluable resource, if you were born in 1960 and claim reduced social security benefits *before* your full retirement age, you may still work and earn up to $19,560 per year (as of 2024) without further affecting the amount of social security benefits you will receive. Earning more than that amount will decrease the size of your social security check.

If you wait until your full retirement age, you can work as much as you like and earn as much as you like, and nothing will be deducted from your social security award.

When to Take Your Pension

For people who have pensions, mostly local, state, and government employees, but also a few private companies, there is often a benefit to waiting to retire. However, this is not always the case as some plans are capped for higher-income employees. It is essential to go to your HR department and find out what you get for waiting.

Also, for both social security and pensions, if you die sooner rather than later, it is best to take the money sooner. You will be collecting over a shorter time frame.

Spending Private Retirement Savings

For money in 401(k)s, 403(b)s, IRAs, and other market-based retirement funds, you can access as much of these funds as you like, once you reach age fifty-nine-and-a-half. While you will often hear the advice that you should live off your interest and not spend the principal in these accounts, this is not a hard-and-fast rule. Many retirees spend the money in their retirement accounts and die with few assets. As far as I am concerned, that can work well, especially for people who still own a home. If worse comes to worst, you could always sell that home.

If you want to use the conventional wisdom and not spend the principal, experts suggest withdrawing 5 percent or less of the portfolio each year.

Example of the 5 Percent Rule

If you have $1 million saved, you can spend $50,000 a year under the 5 percent rule. If you have $2 million, you can spend $100,000 a year. If you have $500,000 you can spend $25,000 a year, and so on. Hopefully this is augmented by your social security and perhaps a pension.

Preserving the principal may not be possible for you and may not even be desirable if you have other plans for your money (such as using retirement funds to buy a second home that can be sold later), but a 5 percent withdrawal annually is thought to preserve your principal if that is your goal. In other words, the formula keeps you living off your portfolio's growth. Of course, the market ebbs and flows so there is always a bit of fluctuation in how much 5 percent amounts to.

The 5 percent rule was originally known as the 4 percent rule, a suggestion to withdraw just 4 percent a year for the best results. The original 4 percent rule is attributed to Bill Bengen, a financial adviser in Southern California who created it in the mid-nineties. Bengen now says that his rule has been oversimplified. He now suggests that withdrawing 5 percent a year is safe for most of us. Bengen created the 4 percent rule using historical data on stock and bond returns over the fifty-year period from 1926 to 1976. He relied heavily on the severe market downturns of the 1930s and early 1970s in coming up with the 4 percent rule. Bengen now says that even in bad markets, there has been no time in history in which a 4 percent annual withdrawal exhausted a retirement portfolio in fewer than thirty-three years.

How much you withdraw is deeply personal. We have no children and own some valuable real estate, not all of which we plan to keep. I have no desire to die with my full portfolio. You may not either.

There is also the question of how to hold your portfolio, in riskier stocks, safer bonds, targeted mutual funds, and so on. This is complex and we will not go into it much here. Read a book or two to learn more. Go see a financial adviser. However, it is wise to move part of your portfolio to safer investments as you age, such as money market accounts and certificates of deposit. After all, how much money do you really need? At some point, following the market dips and living with those consequences becomes tedious.

Medicare Planning

Picking the right Medicare plan is incredibly complicated, and also critical to financial success. The best book I have found on this complex topic is *Maximize Your Medicare: 2024–2025 Edition: Qualify for Benefits, Protect Your Health, and Minimize Your Costs* by Jae Oh, a leading national Medicare expert.[238] This book helps readers understand how and what to choose when deciding on Medicare options, including how to enroll in Medicare, avoid penalties, compare Medigap to Medicare Advantage plans, learn the differences between Medicare Parts A, B, and D, increase benefits every year, deal with special circumstances, and get the most from this critical benefit.

Some Final Thoughts on the Three-Legged Stool

Not everyone has three legs on their financial retirement stool nor does everyone need to. A great example is a friend who worked for the Connecticut Office of Engineering for thirty years. His state pension and his social security equal his ending salary. He doesn't have much money saved in private retirement funds nor does he need much. This is why websites that say we each need a certain amount saved by retirement are not helpful. Each of us is different.

What we need also depends on things like the amount of debt we carry and our future health care costs. Getting rid of as much debt as possible is always helpful when planning for retirement, and I generally recommend paying off all debt, even mortgages. However, in 2020–2021, fixed-rate thirty-year mortgages dropped to a historic low of between 2 and 3 percent. By 2023, rates were above 7 percent. If I had a 2.5 percent mortgage, I might not pay it off as I could do better things with my money in the stock market. In any case, we all have different needs, so it is hard to generalize, even about debt.

Parting Thoughts on Mindful Money When Money Is Tight

I have done my best in this chapter to generalize about topics that are hard to generalize and deeply personal. In the next chapter, we start from a different vantage point, one in which we assume we have enough and just need to figure out how best to use our money to our and society's best advantage.

CHAPTER 17:
A MINDFUL MONEY MINDSET PART II: THE SYMBOLIC ROLE OF MATERIAL WEALTH IN OUR LIVES

"Right. Money isn't everything—what's the other thing again?"

In this chapter, we further explore how we spend our money, what our choices tell us about our priorities, and how to connect our physical resources to our hopes, dreams, and values. This chapter is more philosophical than the last one, and more focused on societal needs than individual wealth. We discuss the accumulation of material possessions and the ways money both frees and binds us. We discuss the process of divesting ourselves of material possessions and financial stories we no longer need and explore how to use our time and money to enjoy our lives and to make the world a better place. Finally, we explore how money can give us real joy and happiness.

The word *wealth* has its roots in well-being. The word denotes not just monetary wealth, but other forms of well-being too.[239] Most of us don't realize this because of the outsized role money plays in our lives. As author, fundraiser, and philanthropist Lynne Twist explains in *The Soul of Money*, nearly everything about our society is driven by money, sometimes exclusively and detrimentally so.[240] Yet, we have the power to give money less influence in our lives and to align our money with our individual values and goals.

Unseating the "Not Enough" Money Myth

If you are like most people, your retirement plan has focused mostly, if not exclusively, on money. You likely have been asking yourself questions like *Will I have enough money? What will I actually need? Did I save enough? Did I do my calculations correctly? What will health care cost? What if I don't have enough? What if I have too much? What should I do with my money?*

These are important questions, but they address a mere fraction of what we need to consider when we plan for retirement. These money questions cannot be ignored but they are not the only questions or even the most important ones.

Let's assume that you *have* acquired enough money to comfortably retire. Despite having saved enough, you are likely to continue to ask yourself these questions because they reinforce one of the unfortunate money myths or mantras we repeat daily, namely that there is not enough and there never will be. "Not enough" is a mantra of scarcity. One reason we think there is not enough (and never will be) is that most of us always want more than we currently have. This advertiser-inspired belief ensures there will never be enough. We repeat the "not enough" mantra because society has told us there will never be enough and we should always want more.

Do you want to challenge and change the mantra? We have control over how we save, spend, and give away our money. We control our own "enough." We can chip away at releasing ourselves from this mantra of "not enough" with the counter-mantra below.

PURPOSE PRACTICE 17.1

Repeat this mantra to yourself throughout your day.
I do enough, I have enough, I am enough.

This mantra helps decouple *what we have* from *who we are* and helps create a mindset of abundance rather than scarcity. It also helps us become aware of our attitudes of scarcity around money. It helps us understand that we really do have enough, perhaps more than enough.

The opposite of a scarcity mentality is an abundant money mentality. An abundant money mentality is one in which we know we have enough. We know which expenditures make us happy. We don't grasp more than we need. We know where our money is going and feel good about it. Given our abundance, we have the capacity to share our wealth and material possessions, and we do it.

We can challenge the "not enough" mantra by experiencing a sense of expansiveness and generosity. The gentle yoga pose and heart-opening exercise below can help create that sense of expansiveness and generosity.

> ### PURPOSE PRACTICE 17.2
>
> This pose is called starfish. It helps open the heart. Slowly lie on your back and gently open your legs in a V shape on the floor or bed. Open your arms to a V above the head. Be comfy and relaxed so you can really feel the heart expand while you breathe.
>
> Don't worry about actually looking like a starfish. Breathe deeply and allow the exhale to become longer than the inhale. Begin to picture a light in your heart space.
>
> Now, let the light expand beyond the heart into the space around the body and out into the world. Stay on the floor or bed until you can really see the light around the body. Stay there at least five minutes, just breathing and watching the white light. Then slow the breath even more and return your attention to your body. Eventually, slowly, get back up and resume your reading.

Visualizing the heart opening and emanating out with gratitude and generosity opens us up for more gratitude and generosity in our lives. To begin shifting to an attitude of abundance, we will next explore what affluence means to us.

What Is Affluence?

Everyone's definition of affluence is different. A friend joked in the middle of a big move, "Heck we have two washers and dryers. Now that's affluence!" This joke beautifully articulates that affluence does not always mean more of everything. After all, who needs more than one washer and dryer?

We each define what affluence means, what it means for us to have enough. We can dial down the advertiser, consumer-oriented refrain of "never enough," and the buy-more-have-more attitude to a level of affluence that feels right. In this exercise, you'll create your own definition of affluence.

PART II: THE SYMBOLIC ROLE OF MATERIAL WEALTH IN OUR LIVES

> **PURPOSE PRACTICE 17.3**
>
> What does affluence mean to you? What does it look like, feel like, and allow you to do? Take a minute to write that down.
>
> _____

For many people, affluence means being able to buy something without worrying about where the money will come from, or not worrying when something breaks. My former colleague, Fred Hart, who had eight children and twenty-two grandchildren, had this exact definition of affluence. He said he knew they had finally "made it" when one of their appliances broke, and he didn't have to worry about where he'd get the money to fix it.

For someone who works in a big city, high-stress job and is constantly challenged by ambient noise, traffic, and online distractions, affluence might mean a second home in the country. For someone else, affluence might mean extra time and freedom. Or, affluence might mean being able to help individual people you know with small sums of money, like helping a housekeeper help a relative immigrate. Each person's definition of affluence will differ, and you have the freedom to create your own.

The two exercises below ask you to picture all the things you could do if you knew you had enough, and also to engage in some wild money fantasies about what you would do if you had much, much, much more than enough. Have fun with these. These exercises are highly illustrative and never get old. Your answers change, but the meaning behind those answers does not.

> **PURPOSE PRACTICE 17.4**
>
> Part 1: Stop and reflect for a few moments. What kinds of things would you get to do if you knew you had enough money? Write those down.

> Take a look again at what you wrote and see if you can add a few things. Now look at which of these things are actually worth it or important to you. What do they tell you about yourself?
>
> Part 2: A friend of mine likes another exercise called "pretend you have $20 million." What would you do with it? Try journaling about that one as well.

After you have completed these exercises and written down the answers, see if you can find a friend to do the same exercises. Talk it over with him or her. What do these lists say about what is important to you? How do they comport with your core values? Write a short journal entry on what this list says about your money, your priorities, and your values.

If we put thought into how we use money, our choices reflect our values in real time. Think about experiences and expenditures that have given you real joy. Study after study shows that after the fact, experiences such as travel, get-togethers, and learning new things increase our joy as time passes. Physical possessions, on the other hand, typically decrease in value the longer we possess them. In light of these studies, where do you see yourself and your moments of joy?

Can you use these insights in your own life? Are there plans you can make to travel or experience the world now? What have you always wanted to do? Many retirees find that over time, they have less ability to do the things they want to do, so sooner is often better than later. Also, is there someone you'd like to treat to a trip or experience? What is holding you back?

Our Money Life Sentences

Discovering our own "not enough" stories helps us spend and give more freely. These stories can be so subtle we don't know they are there and can prevent us from rewriting our own relationship with money, what Lynne Twist calls our money mantras.[241]

Our stories, combined with the mantra of "not enough," can cause us pain and destroy any sense of abundance in our lives. Even very wealthy people suffer from their money stories and the mantra of "not enough." Some lack purpose, feel directionless, and wonder what to do with themselves. Others feel guilty. Because excess wealth separates people from others, there can also be a deep sense of isolation.[242] And of course, there is the fear of losing it all. All this suffering can deprive people of a truly rich life with rich human connections.

The "not enough" mantra also leaves us always wanting more, which further destroys any sense of abundance. As Arthur Brooks explains in *From Strength to Strength*, there seems to be an inverse correlation between massive material wealth and satisfaction.[243] As he explains regarding the material obsession of one woman he interviewed, the Mercedes brings her less happiness than the Chevy did at age thirty because now she wants a Ferrari.

Lynne Twist calls our own money stories our "money life sentences." These stories and attitudes are passed on to us from our families. She calls them life sentences because they are hard to shake. Twist shares the life sentences she was told as a child, which include "marry the money, love will follow," "never spend the principal," and "if you have to ask the price, you can't afford it."[244] The one about love is an obvious sexist vestige from the past, but the other examples Twist provides are also terrible advice.

There may be times, Twist explains, when you definitely want to spend the principal. And what you pay for something? Of course the price matters. We should never pay more for something than it is worth to us. That is waste in its purest form. These decisions have nothing to do with whether we can afford the expense. Again, we are the stewards of our money.

Even seemingly positive money life sentences are worth exploring. For example, my husband does not like to use credit.

This has always seemed rather quaint to me. As I said earlier, his family did not use credit for anything other than a house, not even cars. They generally did not use or have credit cards. And so ... the apple fell very close to the tree. He is frugal by nature, never cheap, but always mindful about where his money is going.

I, on the other hand, learned very little about money or my family's money situation growing up. We had bigger fish to fry, such as mental illness. There was no obvious scarcity story but there were empty spaces. I have spent much of my life trying to fill those spaces with stuff. This is a struggle I will always face, but knowing my story allows me to see where my hoarding tendency comes from.

Money rules us all, consciously or subconsciously. We all know people who seem less ruled by money, who even claim to dislike money. Yet they too have a money life sentence. For example, I have a close friend who set out to spend the lion's share of her sizeable inheritance within months of receiving it. She even gave her siblings her portion of a home they inherited. She did not want the money or what it represented to her. But what did it represent? This story demonstrates that we all have beliefs about money that govern us, even if we dislike money. By the way, disliking money is a waste of energy. Money is just a medium and a neutral one at that. It is also power and a powerful tool.

We can all benefit by getting our money on our side and by our side, by finding mindful ways to spend, use, and give it. We also benefit from unearthing our own money stories or life sentences because they help us understand our money habits. These stories likely affect our attitudes and behaviors in unseen ways. This exercise helps unearth these stories.

PURPOSE PRACTICE 17.5

Think back and then write down some of the things you were told by family members about money growing up. Now see if you can tie these stories, some of which may be almost subconscious, to your own habits and ideas about money.

> What do you notice here? What do you see? How might you want to change your own money stories and why?

The Three Money Myths

According to Twist, "not enough" is just one of three myths that permeate our collective money mentality.[245] We talked about the "not enough" mantra in our own lives, but this mantra or myth is bigger than each of us individually. The mantra permeates our entire society. It is built into its fabric. Our society has taught us to believe that there is not enough for everyone, not enough food, money, shelter, resources, and so on. This "not enough" mantra has become a self-fulfilling prophecy. Today, millions of people worldwide and here in the United States go without food or housing, not because there is not enough food to go around, but because of poor, disparate distribution and income and wealth inequality.

The other two money myths are "more is better" and "this is just the way it is. There is nothing we can do about it."[246] In reality, there is enough, more is not better, and there are things we can do. These interrelated money myths perpetuate one another. If there is not enough for everyone, we hoard because more is better, and that's just the way it is. In reality, there is enough, as the next section explains.

There Is Enough for Everyone

Despite what we have been told, there actually is enough. Twist notes that sometime in the mid-seventies, we reached a moment in history when there literally were enough resources in the world for everyone. Everyone could eat and live inside. It's an amazing thought. In terms of resources and people, there was enough to go around.[247]

I think you know what happened next. It didn't work out that way. The rich got richer and the poor got poorer. Why wasn't there enough for everyone? Could it be a lack of capacity to distribute resources? Not likely, since Coca-Cola has found its way to every inhabited part of the world.[248] Rather, greed, corruption, politics, and money myths have kept everyone from being fed and housed. As long as we believe there is not enough, we hoard because more is better, and that's just the way it is.

People often use the failure of foreign aid to feed people as proof of the "not enough" myth. But foreign aid fails because it is a bad model for giving, not because there is not enough. As Twist explains, when we bail out countries with our money, it destroys local farming and other markets, makes local people feel less valuable as human beings, and teaches them they must be victims to survive. It breaks down entire economies and societies. Even when the aid is temporary and does not cause these problems, too often local corrupt power brokers steal the aid and resell it, making the problems worse. Conversely, when societies in need design their own economic systems and solutions and we give money to support those initiatives, those countries and their economies often thrive.

There Is Something We Can Do: Aligning Money and Soul

Regarding the myth that this is just the way it is and there is nothing we can do, there *are* things we can do to help create "enough." We can use the power of our own money choices to fight the two interrelated myths of "scarcity" and "more is better." We can align money and soul.

First, and this is obvious, we are free to use our money as we like. This is significant power in a society that values money as much as ours does. We can use at least some of our money to express our highest ideals. When we do that, the power of our money grows, much like compound interest. How we spend our money may seem insignificant given that we are each just one person or one family, but this insignificance is an illusion. Collectively, these spending habits make all the difference in the world. Here are a few ways we can align our money with our values.

Businesses Worthy of Our Money

Every dollar we spend is a statement about what we value. With every dollar, we are making a statement about what matters to us. If we give this thought, we can slow the flow of money to persons and products that demean life and increase the flow to businesses and people who celebrate and create sustainability and life.

Let's start our discussion with food since we all buy it. We can think about how our food is made and by whom. We all buy some food from huge food conglomerates like Nestlé, PepsiCo, Coca-Cola, Unilever, Danone, General Mills, Kellogg's, Mars, Associated British Foods, and Mondelēz, but we don't need to buy everything from these companies. According to Oxfam, a British confederation of independent charitable organizations focused on alleviating global poverty, these ten companies control nearly everything we buy in a regular supermarket.[249] I call these big corporations *Big Food*.

As this mind-boggling graphic shows, unless you live completely off the grid, you could not avoid these ten companies no matter how hard you tried.

CHAPTER SEVENTEEN

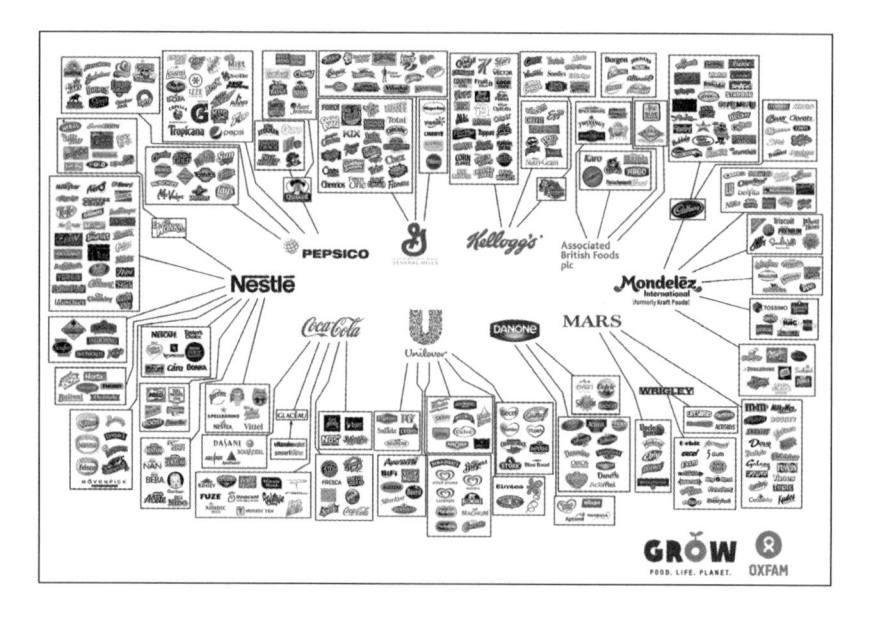

Oxfam put together this graphic and has allowed me to share it because it wants us to know how much of our food supply is controlled by these ten companies. To say their influence is outsized is a tremendous understatement. Why does this matter? For one thing, these companies' cradle-to-grave advertising puts them in control of many aspects of our lives. Second, some of their products contain addictive ingredients and this is no accident. Let's just say they do not always have our best interests in mind. Third, these companies often source foods in unsustainable ways that destroy the planet.

By creating this graphic, Oxfam hopes we as consumers can push these companies to engage in more sustainable practices. In the discussion of nutrition in chapter 8, we discussed shopping the exterior walls of the supermarket for health reasons. This graphic shows us another great reason to shop the exterior walls of the supermarket. No one holds the trademark on bananas and peaches. These foods are not laced with addictive additives or things that provide unlimited shelf life but no nutrition.

In addition to shopping in national chain supermarkets mindfully, we can shop elsewhere. To the extent we buy food from smaller companies, or more natural ones, we can help our bodies and the planet. Buying from local companies has a host of benefits. First, food and drinks taste better when eaten near the source, a French concept called "terroir." For example, we brought New Mexico green chile to Oregon and it tasted OK, but it tastes much better right at its source. Buying local also avoids *big food* and saves transportation pollution and costs as well. Finally, buying local supports local economies and people we know. It improves our communities rather than sending money to already-wealthy far away companies we don't know.

The sourcing of the food we buy is also a statement about what we value. For example, Dr. Joanna McMillan eschews palm oil not just because it's unhealthy, but also because the production of palm oil has destroyed the habitats of orangutans.[250] Dr. McMillan values orangutan habitat and wants to put the power of her money in less harmful hands. Other examples include using thousands of pounds of water-wasting almonds to make almond milk and destroying the Amazon to produce beef.

We can also look at how our food gets to our tables. Some people say a blessing over their food that honors every hand that touched that food. This practice helps us mindfully reduce waste and think about the value of that work, getting us that food. Food waste in the United States is a big problem. A study discussing food waste from farm to fork to landfill found that 40 percent of all food in the United States is wasted.[251]

Being a bit flexible with our eating can help reduce food waste. I don't judge people who eat meat but prefer not to eat meat myself. This is in part because the production of meat has reduced many rainforest habitats around the world and exacerbated climate change. I also don't like to eat animals, and I don't like the taste or texture of meat. Here is where flexibility comes in. I don't like to waste food, especially food for which a live being has lost *its* life. As a result, I will sometimes eat meat that would otherwise be thrown away.

I also think about plants and the people who pick vegetables in the United States. These workers largely lack income and job security, health care, and housing, and they work at the whim of the crop and the master. This makes me want to waste less.

Finally, we can think about how the retailers from which we buy products support their employees. In Bend, Oregon, there is a market called the Newport Avenue Market in which everything in the store seems to cost 50 percent more. If you would normally pay four dollars for something you pay about six dollars, or if you would normally pay ten dollars, you pay about fifteen. The Newport Avenue Market, however, pays fair wages with benefits, hires people with disabilities, and gives over $1 million a year to food insecurity causes. Newport Avenue Market also has a separate building for employees to use on their break, making it a humane place to work. Is it worth it to shop there? Of course, this is your call. You can make that decision knowing the facts, based on what is important to you. That is your money power.

We can use Newport Avenue Market as an example of how our money stories interact with our intentions. Newport Avenue Market caused my own mini-money mindset crisis. This market was located near the home in which we were living when we didn't have a car. It was the only convenient place to buy food. At first, I resented having to pay the high prices. It seemed unfair and even now, I would not rely on it for my every need. But I would shop there sometimes, just as I do at my local food co-op in Albuquerque. I like what these stores do with *their* money power.

These choices do not have to be all or nothing. If it is within our means, shopping at a place like Newport Avenue Market some of the time is a luxury we can feel good about. Shopping there supports the social and environmental systems many of us say matter. The products offered are also more likely to be local or at least sustainably sourced. You get a lot of social and economic bang for your buck by shopping there. This example shows the importance of having an attitude of wealth and abundance. Our shopping choices go far beyond dollars and cents.

In addition to buying from local stores, we can buy from large businesses that support employees and the planet. Businesses that have been lauded for their sustainable practices and good treatment of employees include Clif Bars, Patagonia, Ben & Jerry's, Dr. Bronner's, Seventh Generation, and Tesla. There are many others as well. There are also different levels of support for the planet, workers, animals, etc. Estée Lauder Co., which produces Estée Lauder, Clinique, Bumble and Bumble, Origins, Bobbi Brown, and other cosmetic labels, is committed to solar power and the environment, though some of their brands still use animal testing. Look around, educate yourself, and then make your decisions. You have that power.

And, if you run a business and view employees as people, you will see that we all have the same basic needs and desires. We all want to be happy, we all want to be healthy, we all want to live life with ease. Paying people a living wage that allows them to afford health care and a safe place to live is another way to live life with abundance. It is also a good business practice to pay people well. They are likely to worker harder and better, be more loyal, and stay longer.

This exercise will get you started buying more sustainably.

PURPOSE PRACTICE 17.6

Replace one item you buy with a more sustainable one. Consider this a mindfulness practice and replace new products as you can.

Stop at one local supermarket or co-op and look around. Buy something if you like.

Charities and Other Causes Worth Your Money

Many of us give to charity but don't give the decision much thought. Perhaps a telemarketer calls or you receive a flyer in the mail so you make a donation. That's great, but you can also do some research and support charities that really speak to you, that have low overhead, and that make a lasting impact on society.

You might also look for organizations that empower recipients rather than just giving handouts. In *The Soul of Money*, Twist describes charities in which people receive help but also give something back in return. This creates a true partnership where everyone makes a contribution.

There are many examples of these exchanges in international settings, where foreign communities and organizations know what they need and how to get it. This approach is also powerful here in the United States. Everyone has something to give, and finding that gift is a powerful tool for recipients and donors alike. As discussed above, handouts don't really work. They create a victim mentality, leaving recipients feeling lesser. Handouts may leave donors feeling unappreciated as well.

We can also think about giving to something that will keep giving after our gift. Twist uses the example of her mother raising money for a building to house an orphanage. Generations of families are still benefitting from that building!

In addition to charities, we can help individuals who need it. I have spent much of my forty-year career watching and directing the flow of money by and among both corporations and individuals. Working in the personal finance and consumer credit world, I have seen time and time again that people who don't have money often need just a little bit of help. They don't need a lot of help, but the little help that they need, they need a lot. We can individually provide that little bit of help, often in exchange for something the other person can do for us.

Finally, for those of us who give to politicians, we can support those who support the environment, education, health care, homelessness, nutrition, or whatever we really care about.

The visualization below can help you figure out which causes deserve your hard-earned money.

> **PURPOSE PRACTICE 17.7**
>
> Brainstorm two or three problems in society that you wish you could solve. Who would you help if you had the resources to do it?
>
> Now visualize a sustained solution to the societal problems you identified. See if you can picture detailed tangible ways to help alleviate or solve these problems.
>
> After you have let your visions sink in, research nonprofits that provide the services you visualized. See if you can find one worthy of your money.

Money, Power, and Barter

Money can be a great equalizer in power situations. It is important to pay for the things we receive, but at times, reciprocity and collaboration can be even more powerful. Twist tells a story of how she once played the piano at a party in exchange for getting her brakes fixed. It was not that she needed to barter. She had money, but the partiers weren't willing to fix the brakes unless they had a piano player. This is an extreme example, but a good one. There are many small ways we can help one another without exchanging currency. These are often more valuable and personally satisfying exchanges.[252]

Barter may be even more useful in retirement when we have many skills and talents to trade. We can simultaneously benefit others and ourselves through purpose projects, teaching, and mentoring.

More Is Not Always Better: Unleashing Power by Reducing Material Possessions

Finally, we reach the money myth, "more is better." I wish I could say otherwise, but I love to shop and acquire things. I also know that buying things I don't really want or need has hidden costs. Advertisers use what they call *cradle-to-grave advertising* to get even babies to want their products.[253] This news should make you feel a bit played. It certainly doesn't motivate me to go out and buy their products. There is also planned obsolescence, which is a product design that makes items lose utility in a short time, so we need to buy new ones. The goal behind both cradle-to-grave advertising and planned obsolescence is to keep us buying, buying, buying, to keep corporate profits up.

I still buy plenty of stuff, which is part of my own life sentence, but a few realities are starting to sink in. In addition to all of the woes described above, cheap consumer goods and fast fashion are often made with child labor. Everything we buy requires a lot of the world's energy and resources to make. And, everything we buy ultimately ends up in a landfill.

And then there is the issue of caring for all these things. This takes tremendous energy. Getting rid of some material possessions, especially if we have too many, can be freeing. This is particularly true in retirement, when we need to preserve our energy for things that matter most. When we rid ourselves of unnecessary material possessions, we also give up our expectations about what it is we're supposed to have. Giving up these expectations unfurls energy that can be used in other ways in our lives and in society as a whole.

When we give up some of the material things we don't need, we free up energy, often in short supply as we age. We free ourselves up for more joy as well. Much of this newfound energy is currently being used to care for things we don't need, but that we worry about or fear losing. We can lighten our grip on both things and money. Even people who have layers of financial support, both personally and from family and organizations, sometimes assume they must hoard everything to keep the wealth train rolling in the right direction. This hoarding and grasping is a burden.

When we stop gripping all the things we don't need, we unleash the energy tied up in the chase. We realize that in many cases, we can share what we have because it doesn't really matter if something goes wrong. We can fix it or get a new one. None of this material stuff matters in the end. We don't have to get rid of all of it, but we can at least stop gripping it.

To help release gripping, grasping, and hoarding, try this mantra:

PURPOSE PRACTICE 17.8

I have everything I need.

Now let's start clearing out the things we no longer need in our lives.

PURPOSE PRACTICE 17.9

Schedule a time to clean out some areas of your home and create more "real estate" as we call it. Consider making this a competition with a friend. Who can give away more bags and boxes? Then go to one of the charity thrift shops in your area. This will usually generate a 20 percent off coupon for the same thrift shop. You can then go inside and pick out one or two small things to take home. These items can be given back later.

Consider setting up a quarterly or twice-yearly schedule to do this clean-out.

Money as Freedom

We finish this chapter by repeating part of the exercise we started with. But now, we have a new mindset of money as pure freedom, without burden, grasping, or guilt, just part of our journey to joy.

> **PURPOSE PRACTICE 17.10**
>
> Stop and reflect for a few moments. What kinds of things are important to you? What would you do with your money if you knew you had enough? Write those down.
>
> _____

Now think about these things and how you can accomplish your goals with the money you have. How can you move your objectives forward? Tying this to our discussion of volunteering in chapters 12, 13, and 14, think about how to advance your goals in ways that offer more than just monetary donations. Each of us has more than money to give.

Finally, think about how amazing it has felt when you have helped someone else with a little bit, or perhaps more than a little bit, of money. Using your money not just to support yourself, but to support the species, is one of the most profound things you can do. It creates a sense of joy, accomplishment, and purpose. Giving your time and money creates true abundance.

PART SIX
Conclusion

CHAPTER 18:
PUTTING IT ALL TOGETHER: LIVING THE INSPIRED RETIREMENT

In this final chapter, we distill what we have learned, create a vision for ourselves going forward, and create a system for revisiting these questions as we age. Change happens, and we know it will. Some of the things that will change as we age include our desires, capacities, and dreams.

Like retirement itself, these changes can be scary. If you are feeling unsure what to do next, perhaps fearful of still more change and turbulence, author and fear expert David Ronka shares this advice he got from his own therapist.[254] First, "be curious and spacious." Invoke whatever mindfulness techniques you have developed for calming and exploring. This spaciousness will allow you to explore your fears and use them as motivation. Second—and I love this approach to accepting fear and placing it in the context of our lives—don't tell yourself "I fear retirement," but rather, "a part of me fears retirement." This acknowledges a relationship with fear that doesn't consume all of you.

We'll start this final chapter by exploring the heart and soul of what makes you tick.

CHAPTER EIGHTEEN

PURPOSE PRACTICE 18.1

In your journal, respond to as many of these prompts as you can:

1. Focus on who you are in retirement.
   Come up with three to five adjectives, customs, or habits you'd like people to associate with you. Consider this your brand.

2. Focus on your heart in retirement.
   What do you really love?
   What makes you feel very alive?
   Name five times you have been in flow.
   Start an "alive" section in your journal. Jot down each time today (and perhaps every day) when you feel truly alive. Or, if you wish, reflect on that at day's end.[255]

3. Focus on the meaning of life in retirement.
   What is the meaning of life?
   Where do you fit in to that meaning?
   What does the universe or g-d have in store for you, the rest of the planet, and beyond?

Reread your answers.

Next, we will visualize our lives in our next stage. By now, you have internalized many inspiring thoughts and feelings regarding your future life. Use those in this final Purpose Practice.

PURPOSE PRACTICE 18.2

Visualize Your Inspired Retirement

Spend some time visualizing yourself in your next stage of life doing what you love most with purpose and passion. Now, write a journal entry about what you see. Note your feelings in your body, as well as your thoughts, as you reread this final entry.

When you need a tune-up, reread your answers to Purpose Practices 18.1 and 18.2 above, and consider revisiting Purpose Practices 1.2, 10.6, 17.3, and the exercises in chapter 11. Embrace change as you revisit these questions.

Parting Thoughts on Putting Together the Inspired Retirement Life

You are on your way to living your inspired retirement life. If you are a person who likes structure, go ahead and plan your days. We often think retirement means having no schedule, but most people need structure in retirement. Start with structure, and loosen it up as you go.

Revisit life often. Throughout life, we benefit from reflecting on what we are doing with our lives and where we want them to go. This is never truer than in retirement, when our time on this earth is relatively short, but our day-to-day lives are freer. This combination of scarcity and freedom gives us clarity of thinking and the flexibility we need to create and recreate meaning and purpose as we age.

As we age, we also move from the go-go years of Retirement One to the more relaxed world of Retirement Two. Through all of this, it is like returning to childhood, when we were trying to find our place in the world. Look at these ongoing transitions with childlike wonder. If you get it wrong the first time, you always get another chance to revisit these questions. It is never too late to fulfill your changing retirement dreams.

Things will change, but you have the tools to change your life and your dreams along with those changing times. Your circumstances will change, but your desire to live with relevance never will. Try to stay present and enjoy each step of the way, to balance living in the present with having hope about the future. And lastly, as always, try to goof off and have fun. Best of luck in this messy but amazing journey.

That is it for now. Enjoy your next life.

ACKNOWLEDGMENTS

I am deeply grateful for the sixty or so people who generously shared their retirement stories. I am especially grateful for those who shared the struggles, the uncertainties, and the challenges to ego and heart. What a brave group!

Next, I thank my students of the past twenty-eight years, whether we learned law, yoga, or meditation together. You are my teachers. I also thank the people who have pushed my buttons. You are also my teachers.

I am grateful to so many people at the UNM School of Law. First, I thank my administrative assistants, Cheryl Burbank and Emillee McVay, who made this project possible. I also thank my dean, Camille Carey, for her support, financial and otherwise. Finally, I thank my late mentor, Fred Hart, who held me in the palm of his hand for twenty years, supporting me in every way and admonishing me to develop some interests outside the law school. He would smile deeply if he could see this book.

I thank the people who generously read prior drafts, including Stewart Paley, Pat Marsello, Peter Huang, and Jenny Moore. I thank my prior editor from Cambridge Press, Matthew Gallagher, who sent me down the path of writing about mindfulness and the meaning of life. I thank Pat Marsello again, for her beautiful cover art. I thank Jenny Moore again for her emotional support. We both went through a lot while this book came to fruition, and I appreciate your support more than you can ever know. I also thank Robin Romero for her careful and insightful comments

I am forever grateful for my Beaver's Pond editorial and design team, Laurie Herrmann, Jim Handrigan, Kerry Aberman, Chelsey Burden, and Rachel Blood. You are consummate professionals and helped me overcome blocks and insecurities I didn't know I had.

And finally, I thank Stewart Paley, my partner in life for almost forty years. Are we having fun yet? While retirement is life's greatest adventure, you are my greatest asset and my partner in that next big adventure. Together we can do anything, or if we choose, we can sit quietly and do nothing. That is true abundance.

ENDNOTES

1. "What Does Retirement Really Mean? We asked readers to submit their stories of retirement—to share their experiences, as well as their advice," *New York Times*, June 22, 2024, https://www.nytimes.com/2024/06/20/business/retirement/retire-advice-life-tips.html.

2. Atul Gawande, *Being Mortal* (Metropolitan Books, 2017), 116. While Gawande is speaking about the three plagues of nursing home life, these same three plagues apply to aging in general.

3. Pema Chödrön, *How We Live Is How We Die* (Shambhala, 2023), 2.

4. The classical thinking about financial life in retirement revolves around three sources of income: a pension, personal retirement savings, and social security. Those are the three economic legs of the retirement stool.

5. Arthur Brooks, *From Strength to Strength* (Portfolio/Penguin, 2022), 82–23.

6. Ellen J. Langer and Judith Rodin, "The Effects of Choice and Enhanced Personal Responsibility for the Aged: A Field Experiment in an Institutional Setting," *Journal of Personality and Social Psychology* 34 (1976): 191–98, https://doi.org/10.1037/0022-3514.34.2.191.

7. "What Does Retirement Really Mean? We asked readers to submit their stories of retirement—to share their experiences, as well as their advice," *New York Times*, June 22, 2024, https://www.nytimes.com/2024/06/20/business/retirement/retire-advice-life-tips.html. (Quote of Dr. Michael MacMillan, St. Petersburg, Fla.)

8. C. N. Alexander, E. J. R. I. Newman, H. M. Chandler, and J. L. Davies, "Transcendental Meditation, Mindfulness, and Longevity: An Experimental Study with the Elderly," *Journal of Personality and Social Psychology* 57 (1989): 950–64.

ENDNOTES

9. Michael D. Mrazek, Michael S. Franklin, Dawa Tarchin Phillips, Benjamin Baird, and Jonathan W. Schooler, "Mindfulness Training Improves Working Memory Capacity and GRE Performance While Reducing Mind Wandering," *Psychological Science*, 24, no. 5 (2013): 776–781, http://pss.sagepub.com/content/24/5/776.

A recent study showed that engaging in mindfulness techniques improved graduate record exam (GRE) scores. This study found that mindfulness training improved both GRE reading-comprehension scores and working memory capacity while simultaneously reducing the occurrence of distracting thoughts during completion of the GRE and the measure of working memory. These results suggest that cultivating mindfulness is an effective and efficient technique for improving cognitive function, with wide-reaching consequences. Additionally, one Harvard University study found that spending twenty-seven minutes meditating a day changes the structure of the brain by developing and growing the hippocampus region of the brain and shrinking the amygdala, the part of the brain associated with anger, jealousy, aggression, and even depression.

10. Pema Chödrön, *The Pema Chödrön Audio Series*, lecture 1, 2004.

11. Tim Sharp, Habits for Happiness podcast, episode 1, Audible Original, 2019.

12. Talane Miedaner, *Coach Yourself to Success* (McGraw-Hill 2000), 29.

13. Jack Kornfield, *After the Ecstasy, the Laundry: How the Heart Grows Wise on the Spiritual Path* (Bantam, 2001), 244.

14. "Health Benefits of Gratitude," UCLA Health, accessed March 23, 2023, https://www.uclahealth.org/news/health-benefits-gratitude.

15. Tim Sharp, Habits for Happiness podcast, episode 1, Audible Original, 2019.

16. William J. Broad, *The Science of Yoga: The Risks and the Rewards* (Simon & Schuster, 2012), 43–45.

17. Chip Conley, *Wisdom at Work: The Making of a Modern Elder* (Pantheon Books, 2018), 155.

18. Rabbi Richard S. Sarason, "Why Do We Need This Day of Atonement?" in *Mishkan Hanefesh: Machzor for the Days of Awe* (CCAR Press, 2015).

19. Oliver Burkeman, *Four Thousand Weeks: Time Management for Mortals* (Farrar, Straus and Giroux, 2021), 3.

20. Arthur Brooks, *From Strength to Strength* (Portfolio/Penguin, 2022), 82–23.

21. *Id.* at 51–52.

22. *Id.* at 62.

23. Wayne Muller, *Sabbath: Restoring the Sacred Rhythm of Rest* (Bantam Books, 2009), 1.

24. *Id.* As Pema Chödrön shares, "As long as our orientation is toward perfection or success, we will never learn about unconditional friendship with ourselves, nor will we find compassion." Pema Chödrön, "Signs of Spiritual Progress," *Lion's Roar*, July 18, 2014, https://www.lionsroar.com/how-to-meditate-pema-chodron-on-signs-of-spiritual-progress/.

25. Wayne Muller, *Sabbath: Restoring the Sacred Rhythm of Rest* (Bantam Books, 2009), 1.

26. *Id.* at 1–2.

27. *Id.* at 3.

28. *Id.*

29. *Id.* at 7.

30. *Id.* at 6–7.

31. *Id.* at 67.

32. *Id.* at 68–69.

33. James A. Roberts, *Too Much of a Good Thing: Are You Addicted to Your Smartphone?* (Sentia Publishing, 2015,) 56. Roberts concludes that cell phone addictions are harming our interpersonal relationships, impairing our mental and physical health, and wasting our valuable time.

34. R. Lisle Baker and Daniel P. Brown, *On Engagement: Learning to Pay Attention*, U. ALR. L. R.337 (2014): 36.

35. Cherelle Iman, *How to Show Up and Shine in Law School with Gratitude, Grit, and Grace* (Regal House Publishing, 2024), 106.

ENDNOTES

36. *Id.*

37. *Id.*

38. "Practice the Power of the Longer Inhale," *Mindful*, https://www.mindful.org/practice-the-power-of-the-long-exhale/.

39. Pema Chödrön, "Pema Chödrön's Wisdom for Waking Up to Your World," *Lion's Roar*, April 1, 2024, https://www.lionsroar.com/waking-up-to-your-world-pema-chodron/.

40. Chip Conley, *Learning to Love Midlife* (Little, Brown Spark, 2024), 165.

41. Jon Kabat-Zinn, *Wherever You Go, There You Are* (Hachette Book Group, 2009), 1.

42. "What Does Retirement Really Mean? We asked readers to submit their stories of retirement—to share their experiences, as well as their advice," *New York Times*, June 22, 2024, https://www.nytimes.com/2024/06/20/business/retirement/retire-advice-life-tips.html. (Quote from Paul Matulic.)

43. Paul Wilson, *The Calm Technique* (Thorsons Publishing Group, 1987), 103–04.

44. Jeena Cho and Karen Gifford, *The Anxious Lawyer* (American Bar Association Press, 2016), 5.

45. *Id.* at 167.

46. Paul Wilson, *The Calm Technique* (Harper Collins, 1987), 54.

47. David Friedman, *The Thought Exchange* (Library Tales Publishing, 2011), 166.

48. Pema Chödrön, *The Pema Chödrön Audio Series*, lecture 1, 2004.

49. This form of meditation is also featured in Cho and Gifford's book, *The Anxious Lawyer*. Jeena Cho and Karen Gifford, *The Anxious Lawyer* (American Bar Association Press, 2016) 90–104.

50. Bruce Lipton, *The Biology of Belief* (Hay House, 2006), 172–73.

51. *Id.* at 178–80.

52. Cherelle Iman, *How to Show Up and Shine in Law School with Gratitude, Grit, and Grace* (Regal House Publishing, 2024), 56–57.

53. Carol Dweck, *Mindset: The New Psychology of Success* (Ballantine, 2016).

54. Svetlana Whitener, "The Value of a Growth Mindset, and How to Develop One," *Forbes*, January 6, 2021, https://www.forbes.com/sites/forbescoachescouncil/2021/01/06/the-value-of-a-growth-mindset-and-how-to-develop-one/?sh=151bf3664d2f.

55. Tim Sharp, Habits for Happiness podcast, episode 1, Audible Original, 2019.

56. Bruce Lipton, *The Biology of Belief* (Hay House, 2006), 55.

57. *Id.* at 25–26. Lipton claims that every major illness is linked to chronic stress. *Id.* at 55.

58. *Id.* at 139–47.

59. *Id.* at 55, 65.

60. *Id.* at 149.

61. *Id.*

62. *Id.* at 149–50.

63. Bruce S. McEwen, "Neurobiological and Systemic Effects of Chronic Stress," *Chronic Stress* 1, (2017), https://www.ncbi.nlm.nih.gov/pmc/articles/PMC5573220/#:~:text=Stress%20can%20cause%20an%20imbalance,those%20behaviors%20and%20behavioral%20states.

64. Bruce Lipton, *The Biology of Belief* (Hay House, 2006), 137, 144, 160.

65. *Id.* at 192–93.

66. *Id.* at 192.

67. *Id.* at 209–10.

68. Bruce Feiler, *Life Is in the Transitions: Mastering Change at Any Age* (Penguin, 2020), 71.

69. Pema Chödrön, *The Pema Chödrön Audio Series*, lecture 1, 2004.

70. Bruce Feiler, *Life Is in the Transitions: Mastering Change at Any Age* (Penguin, 2020), 71.

71. Pema Chödrön, *How We Live Is How We Die* (Shambhala, 2023), 65.

72. Jon Kabat-Zinn, *Full Catastrophe Living* (Bantam Books, 2013).

73. David Friedman, *The Thought Exchange* (Library Tales Publishing, 2011), 162–63.

74. Randi McGinn, *Changing Laws, Saving Lives* (Trial Guides LLC, 2014), 137, 139.

75. *Id.* at 143.

76. Guy Winch, "The Important Difference Between Sadness and Depression," *Psychology Today*, October 2, 2015, https://www.psychologytoday.com/blog/the-squeaky-wheel/201510/the-important-difference-between-sadness-and-depression.

77. *Id.*

78. Atul Gawande, *Being Mortal* (Metropolitan Books, 2017), 116.

79. Rick Hanson, *Buddha's Brain: The Practical Neuroscience of Happiness, Love and Wisdom* (New Harbinger, 2009), 40–41.

80. *See* Chris Crowley and Henry S. Lodge, *Younger Next Year* (Workman Publishing, 2007), 71–74, 95–115; Joanna McMillan, Mindfull podcast, episode 7.

81. Alex Korb, *The Upward Spiral: Using Neuroscience to Reverse the Course of Depression, One Small Change at a Time* (New Harbinger Publications, 2015), 33–34.

82. *Id.*

83. Shannon Firth, "Study Finds Emotions Can Be Mapped to the Body: A New Finnish Study Looks at How Changes in Our Bodies Could Shape How We Experience Emotions," *US News*, December 30, 2013, https://www.usnews.com/news/articles/2013/12/30/study-finds-emotions-can-be-mapped-to-the-body.

84. Alex Korb, *The Upward Spiral: Using Neuroscience to Reverse the Course of Depression, One Small Change at a Time* (New Harbinger Publications, 2015), 20.

85. *Id.* at 41–42.

86. *Id.* at 39–41.

87. *Id.* at 39–41.

88. *Id.* at 42.

89. *Id.*

90. *Id.* at 45.

91. *Id.*

92. *Id.* at 46.

93. *Id.*

94. *Id.*

95. *Id.* at 81.

96. *Id.* at 83.

97. *Id.* at 138.

98. *Id.* at 143–44.

99. *Id.* at 147–49.

100. *Id.* at 94.

101. *Id.* at 115.

102. Geoffrey James, "What Goal-Setting Does to Your Brain and Why It's Spectacularly Effective," *Inc.*, October 23, 2019, https://www.inc.com/geoffrey-james/what-goal-setting-does-to-your-brain-why-its-spectacularly-effective.html.

103. *Id.*

104. Pema Chödrön, *The Pema Chödrön Audio Series*, lecture 2, 2004.

105. Mirabai Bush, *Working with Mindfulness* Audio CD, 2012.

106. Bernard Golden, *Overcoming Destructive Anger: Strategies That Work* (Johns Hopkins University Press, 2016), 5–10.

107. *Id.*

108. *Id.*

109. *Id.*

110. Daphne M. Davis and Jeffrey A. Hayes, "What Are the Benefits of Mindfulness? A Practice Review of Psychotherapy-Related Research," *American Psychological Association* 48 (2011): 198, 201.

111. *Id.*

112. Also spelled agita, this is an Italian American slang word

meaning heartburn, acid indigestion, an upset stomach or, by extension, a general feeling of upset. It is derived from the Italian word "agitare" meaning "to agitate."

113. Bruce Feiler, *Life Is in the Transitions: Mastering Change at Any Age* (Penguin, 2020), 92.

114. Chade-Meng Tan, *Search Inside Yourself* (Harper One, 2012), 106. Tan is quoting the Buddha, saying, "Whenever an unwholesome thought or emotion arises in an enlightened mind, it is like writing on water; the moment it is written, it disappears."

115. Jack Kornfield, *After the Ecstasy, the Laundry: How the Heart Grows Wise on the Spiritual Path* (Bantam, 2001), 244.

116. Kristin Neff, *Self-Compassion: The Proven Power of Being Kind to Yourself* (Morrow, 2011), 85–88.

117. Kristin D. Neff, "Self-Compassion, Self-Esteem, and Well-Being," *Social and Personality Psychology Compass* 1 (2011): 5, https://self-compassion.org/wp-content/uploads/publications/SC_SE_Well_being.pdf.

118. *Id.* at 6–9.

119. *Id.*

120. *Id.*

121. *Id.*

122. *Id.*

123. *Id.*

124. *Id.*

125. Chip Conley, *Learning to Love Midlife* (Little, Brown Spark, 2024), 141.

126. *Id.*; see also Pema Chödrön, *When Things Fall Apart* (Shambhala, 1997), 29.

127. Brené Brown, *The Gifts of Imperfection: 10th Anniversary Edition* (Hazelden Publishing, 2022).

128. Pema Chödrön, *When Things Fall Apart* (Shambhala, 1997), 32.

129. Desmond Tutu and Mpho Tutu, *The Book of Forgiving: The*

Fourfold Path for Healing Ourselves and Our World (Harper One, 2015).

130. Jack Kornfield, *After the Ecstasy, the Laundry: How the Heart Grows Wise on the Spiritual Path* (Bantam, 2001), 47.

131. William Ury, *Getting to Yes with Yourself* (Harper One, 2015), 100.

132. Jack Kornfield, *After the Ecstasy, the Laundry: How the Heart Grows Wise on the Spiritual Path* (Bantam, 2001), 50–51.

133. Desmond Tutu and Mpho Tutu, *The Book of Forgiving: The Fourfold Path for Healing Ourselves and Our World* (Harper One, 2015).

134. William Ury, *Getting to Yes with Yourself* (Harper One, 2015), 128–29.

135. Desmond Tutu and Mpho Tutu, *The Book of Forgiving: The Fourfold Path for Healing Ourselves and Our World* (Harper One, 2015). Similarly, in his book *Radical Forgiveness*, Colin Tipping sets out his process for forgiving another person, which is very similar to that of the Tutus. He starts with writing down your story and all of the anger and resentment you still feel toward this person. Colin Tipping, *Radical Forgiveness: Making Room for the Miracle* (Global 13 Publications, Inc., 2003), 217–38. Tipping suggests journaling about these questions one at a time:

Tell your story. Describe the situation causing the discomfort as you see it now.

Explain exactly why you are upset.

Describe and really feel your emotions and tie them to events that hurt you.

If you want to try this, take your time. Describe the events that hurt you in detail and deeply feel what you feel. Then repeat these affirmations, taking time with each:

To accept these feelings: I lovingly recognize and accept my feelings, judging them no more.

To acknowledge that no one can make us feel anything: I own my own feelings. No one can make me feel anything. My feelings are a reflection of how I see the situation.

To take full responsibly for the feelings: Even though I don't know why or how, I now see that my soul has created this situation in order that I learn and grow.

The intellectual mind will fight this last part for understandable reasons. We have been wronged through no fault of our own. Yet only we are suffering. The idea here is to remove the victim (you) from the story and rewrite it. Don't judge yourself for creating this situation, just see if there are any patterns or other lessons to glean. See if you can let go of past hurts with the knowledge that you are the one hurting.

136. Forgiveness is still hard to do. The Tutus are religious leaders and in addition to the personal psychological and physical benefits of forgiveness, they believe that our shared humanity is a reason to forgive. They urge us to put ourselves in the shoes of the perpetrator and recognize that we are all fragile, vulnerable, flawed human beings capable of thoughtlessness and cruelty, and that we all had or have parents, teachers, and relatives who are or were also human. They urge us to see connection rather than separation. They even suggest we consider the life experiences that might have led the perpetrator to cause such harm. This by no means justifies the actions, but it does provide context and perspective.

137. Tim Sharp, Habits for Happiness podcast, episode 1, Audible Original, 2019.

138. William J. Broad, *The Science of Yoga: The Risks and the Rewards* (Simon & Schuster, 2012).

139. *Id.* at 40.

140. *Id.* at 41.

141. *Id.*

142. *Id.* at 102.

143. *Id.* at 43–44. Another study correlated yoga with lower cholesterol and blood pressure and higher levels of testosterone. *Id.* at 44.

144. *Id.*

145. Walter Sullivan, "The Einstein Papers: A Man of Many Parts," *New York Times*, March 29, 1972, https://www.nytimes.com/1972/03/29/archives/the-einstein-papers-a-man-of-many-parts-the-einstein-papers-man-of.html.

146. Chip Conley, *Learning to Love Midlife* (Little, Brown Spark,

2024), 41–46.

147. *Id*. at 41–42.

148. The *Younger Next Year* chapters toggle between the two authors, a medical doctor who is serious about health and believes alcohol is poison, and his lawyer friend who takes most but not all of his doctor's advice. I will stay out of the discussion about alcohol, but let's just say the doctor is no believer in the "one-to-two a day doesn't hurt" philosophy.

149. Chris Crowley and Henry S. Lodge, *Younger Next Year* (Workman Publishing, 2007). (Back cover endorsement.)

150. *Id*. at 71.

151. Alia J. Crum and Ellen J. Langer, "Mind-Set Matters: Exercise and the Placebo Effect," *Psychological Science* 18 (2007): 165.

152. Chris Crowley and Henry S. Lodge, *Younger Next Year* (Workman Publishing, 2007), 49–51.

153. Gretchen Reynolds, "At 93, He's as Fit as a 40-year-old. His Body Offers Lessons on Aging," *Washington Post,* January 16, 2024, https://www.washingtonpost.com/wellness/2024/01/16/fitness-aging-richard-morgan/.

154. *Id.*

155. *Id.*

156. Michael Pollan, *Food Rules: An Eater's Manual* (Penguin Books, 2009), 33.

157. *Id*. at 42.

158. *Id*. at 40.

159. "Put a Fork in Cognitive Decline: Eating Leafy Greens May Slow Brain Aging by 11 Years," December 21, 2017, *Neuroscience News*, https://neurosciencenews.com/leafy-greens-brain-aging-8225/.

160. Maddy Dychtwald with Kate Hanley, *Ageless Aging: A Woman's Guide to Increasing Healthspan, Brainspan, and Lifespan* (Mayo Clinic Press, 2024), 140–41.

161. There are several of these books by the same authors, but this is a good one with which to start: Lisa Swerling and Ralph Lazar, *Happiness*

ENDNOTES

Is . . . 500 Things to Be Happy About (Chronicle Books, LLC, 2014).

162. Atul Gawande, *Being Mortal* (Metropolitan Books, 2017), 116.

163. Maddy Dychtwald with Kate Hanley, *Ageless Aging: A Woman's Guide to Increasing Healthspan, Brainspan, and Lifespan* (Mayo Clinic Press, 2024), 244.

164. *Id.*, citing Dean Ornish.

165. *Id.*, citing US Surgeon General Dr. Vivek Murthy.

166. Chip Conley, *Learning to Love Midlife* (Little, Brown Spark, 2024), 72–73. (Discussing the Harvard Study of Adult Development, instituted in 1938, which follows 734 study subjects over a lifetime.)

167. *Id.* at 73.

168. *Id.* at 79.

169. Florence Ann Romano, *Build Your Village: A Guide to Finding Joy and Community in Every Stage of Life* (Beyond Words, 2023), 60–61.

170. Michael Clinton, *Roar: Into the Second Half of Your Life (Before It's Too Late)* (Atria Books, 2021), 152.

171. Lauren Cahn, "Here's How You Can Look and Feel Younger Right This Very Minute," July 19, 2017, *The Healthy*, https://www.thehealthy.com/aging/healthy-aging/music-feel-younger/.

172. Shlomo Benartzi, *Thinking Smarter: Seven Steps to Your Fulfilling Retirement and Life* (Portfolio/Penguin, 2015), 7.

173. I am paraphrasing a bit here as his intended readers are further away from retirement than most people reading this book. *Id.* at 16.

174. Here I am paraphrasing to focus on the non-financial side of health care. *Id.* at 28.

175. Benartzi calls this second career. I have broadened the concept for an older audience, closer to retirement. *Id.* at 28.

176. *Id.* at 75.

177. *Id.* at 88–95. I have modified the exercise to incorporate mindful contemplation, but the spirit of the exercise comes from Benartzi.

178. Day Schildkret, *Hello, Goodbye: 75 Rituals for Times of Loss, Celebration, and Change* (Simon Element, 2022), 167.

179. *Id.* at 168.

180. *Id.*

181. Alberto Villoldo, *The Heart of the Shaman* (Hay House, 2020), 3.

182. Day Schildkret, *Hello, Goodbye: 75 Rituals for Times of Loss, Celebration, and Change* (Simon Element, 2022), 169.

183. *Id.* at 170.

184. *Id.*

185. Maddy Dychtwald with Kate Hanley, *Ageless Aging: A Woman's Guide to Increasing Healthspan, Brainspan, and Lifespan* (Mayo Clinic Press, 2024), 250.

186. *Id.* at 255.

187. *Id.* at 259.

188. Angeles Arrien, *The Second Half of Life* (Sounds True, 2008), 37.

189. Arrien also asks, "Where do you experience author Federico Garcia Lorca's duende?", a reference to a Spanish word for a fire that burns from the depth of the human spirit, and also asks us to reflect on four fires: the fire of vision, the fire of the heart, the creative fire, and the fire of the soul. *Id.*

190. Mihaly Csikszentmihalyi, *Flow: The Psychology of Optimal Experience* (Harper & Row, 1990), 1–5.

191. *Id.* at 29–35.

192. *Id.*

193. *Id.* at 29–35.

194. *Id.* at 364, 374.

195. *Id.*

196. This exercise has been adapted from J. D. Roth, "How to Find Your Purpose in Life: 12 Powerful Exercises to Help You Discover Your Purpose and Passion," *Get Rich Slowly*, December 12, 2020.

197. Shlomo Benartzi, *Thinking Smarter: Seven Steps to Your Fulfilling Retirement and Life* (Portfolio/Penguin, 2015), 21–30.

198. "The VIA Survey," VIA Institute on Character, http://www.via-character.org/www/Character-Strengths-Survey.

199. "Frequently Asked Questions about the VIA Strengths Test," *Wondrlust*, http://wondrlust.com/knowledge/frequently-asked-questions-about-the-via-strengths-test/.

200. Chip Conley, *Wisdom at Work: The Making of a Modern Elder* (Pantheon Books, 2018).

201. *Id.* at 78.

202. *Id* at 79, 130.

203. *Id.* at 130.

204. *Id* at 79.

205. *Id.* at 104.

206. *Id.* at 106.

207. Connie Zweig, *The Inner Work of Age: Moving from Role to Soul* 318–19 (Park Street Press 2012).

208. Pema Chödrön, *When Things Fall Apart* (Shambhala, 2016), 110.

209. Arthur Brooks, *From Strength to Strength* (Portfolio/Penguin, 2022), 25–27.

210. *Id.* at 27.

211. *Id.* at 26–28.

212. *Id.* at 30.

213. *Id.* at 34.

214. *Id.*

215. Connie Zweig, *The Inner Work of Age: Moving from Role to Soul* (Park Street Press, 2021).

216. Becca Stanek, "4 Questions to Ask to Determine If You're Retirement-Ready," *The Week US*, December 6, 2023, https://theweek.com/personal-finance/determine-retirement-readiness.

217. A legacy project is something that you want to do or change at work before you leave, something that you think will improve the institution or company.

218. Angeles Arrien, *The Second Half of Life* (Sounds True, 2008), 39–40.

ENDNOTES

219. Knowledge workers include editors, doctors, pharmacists, architects, lawyers, scientists, engineers, academics, and people in many other fields.

220. Alex Soojung-Kim Pang, *Rest: Why You Get More Done When You Work Less* (Basic Books, 2018), 62–63.

221. William Ballard, "Only 4 Hours of Creative Power," *Medium*, February 4, 2018, https://medium.com/writing-together/only-4-hours-of-creative-power-b11624f23dd.

222. "Why You Should Work 4 Hours a Day, According to Science," *The Week,* May 9, 2017, https://theweek.com/articles/696644/why-should-work-4-hours-day-according-science.

223. *Id.*

224. Alex Soojung-Kim Pang, *Rest: Why You Get More Done When You Work Less* (Basic Books, 2018), 55–56; Tony Schwartz, "How to Accomplish More by Doing Less," *Harvard Business Review*, December 13, 2011, https://hbr.org/2011/12/how-to-accomplish-more-by-doin.

225. Alex Soojung-Kim Pang, *Rest: Why You Get More Done When You Work Less* (Basic Books, 2018), 69–74.

226. Mitch Anthony, *The New Retirementality* (Wiley, 2014), 31.

227. "About 1 in 4 US Working Adults 50 and Older Expect to Never Retire, AARP Study Finds," *New York Post*, April 24, 2024, https://nypost.com/2024/04/24/lifestyle/25-of-us-working-adults-50-and-older-expect-to-never-retire-aarp-study/.

228. Jon Kabat-Zinn, *Wherever You Go, There You Are: Mindfulness Meditation in Everyday Life* (Hachette Books, 2017); Carl Franz, *The People's Guide to Mexico: Wherever You Go, There You Are* (John Muir Publications, 1975).

229. Maurie Backman, "40 Percent of Workers Plan to Relocate in Retirement. Should You?," *The Motley Fool*, February 20, 2023, https://www.fool.com/retirement/2023/02/20/40-of-workers-plan-to-relocate-in-retirement-shoul/.

230. Bob and Melinda Blanchard, *Live What You Love: Notes from an Unusual Life* (Sterling Publishing, 2005); Bob and Melinda Blanchard, *A Trip to the Beach: Living on Island Time in the Caribbean* (Three Rivers Press, 2001).

ENDNOTES

231. Nathalie Martin and Pamela Foohey, "*Reducing the Wealth Gap Through Fintech 'Advances' in Consumer Banking and Lending,*" U. 2021 ILL. L. REV. 459 (2021): 467–75.

232. *Id.*

233. *Id.*

234. *Id.*

235. E. Percil Stanford and Paula M. Usita, "Retirement: Who Is at Risk?," *Generations: Journal of the American Society on Aging* 26 (2002): 45–46. *See also generally* E. Percil Stanford and Fernando Torres-Gil, *Diversity: New Approaches to Ethnic Minority Aging* (Routledge, 1992); Rose C. Gibson and Cheryl J. Burns, "The Health, Labor Force, and Retirement Experiences of Aging Minorities," in *Diversity: New Approaches to Ethnic Minority Aging* (Routledge, 1992), 53–54.

236. Elizabeth Warren and Amelia Tyagi, *All Your Worth* (Free Press, 2005).

237. E. Percil Stanford and Paula M. Usita, "Retirement: Who Is at Risk?" *Generations: Journal of the American Society on Aging* 26 (2002): 45–46. *See also generally* E. Percil Stanford and Fernando Torres-Gil, *Diversity: New Approaches to Ethnic Minority Aging* (Routledge, 1992); Rose C. Gibson and Cheryl J. Burns, "The Health, Labor Force, and Retirement Experiences of Aging Minorities," in *Diversity: New Approaches to Ethnic Minority Aging* (Routledge, 1992), 53–54.

238. Jae Oh, *Maximize Your Medicare: 2024–2025 Edition: Qualify for Benefits, Protect Your Health, and Minimize Your Costs* (Allworth Press, 2024).

239. Lynne Twist, *The Soul of Money* (W.W. Norton & Co., 2017), 57.

240. *Id.* at 8–12.

241. Lynne Twist, *The Soul of Money* (W.W. Norton & Co., 2017), 44–51.

242. You may have noticed in your own life that the more wealth you acquire, the less you rely on other people. Do you always rent a car when you visit another city? If so, you know what I am talking about.

243. Arthur Brooks, *From Strength to Strength* (Portfolio/Penguin, 2022), 86.

244. Lynne Twist, *The Soul of Money* (W.W. Norton & Co., 2017), 55–56.

245. *Id.* at 43–50.

246. *Id.* at 50–58.

247. *Id.* at 58–62.

248. *Id.* at 63.

249. Kate Taylor, "These 10 Companies Control Everything You Buy," *Business Insider*, September 28, 2016, https://www.businessinsider.com/10-companies-control-the-food-industry-2016-9.

250. Joanna McMillan, *Mindfull* podcast, episode 5.

251. "Wasted: How America Is Losing Up to 40 Percent of Its Food from Farm to Fork to Landfill," *NDRC*, August 16, 2017, https://www.nrdc.org/resources/wasted-how-america-losing-40-percent-its-food-farm-fork-landfill.

252. I noticed a change in my attitude about paying for empirical interviews when writing this book. In my prior studies, I have paid people to talk to me. In the interviews for this book, I discovered that these interviews were conversations, conversations in which I was able to share a bit of my knowledge about ways in which people prepare for their retirement in exchange for other people's wisdom. I also realize that many people really want to talk about their experiences. Sharing valuable knowledge can be incredibly rewarding.

253. Lynne Twist, *The Soul of Money* (W.W. Norton & Co., 2017), 144–45.

254. David Ronka, *The Flipside of Fear: Finding Freedom Where You Least Expect It* (Cliffhouse Press, 2018), 35–36.

255. For me this is teaching almost anything, writing, learning new things, and taking classes.

INDEX

A Trip to the Beach, 248
Addiction,
　devices, 30–31
　work, 26–28
Affluence, 288–90
After the Ecstasy, the Laundry, 80
Ageless Aging, 116–17, 149, 158, 183
Airbnb, 193, 244
All Your Worth, 259–61
Alzheimer's, 140
Anger, 58–63, 72–75
Anthony, Mitch 207–10
Anxiety, 65–67, 68–71
Apologizing, 91–92
Arrien, Angeles, 184, 200–01
Ayurveda, 138–39
Baker, Lisle, 31
Bassan, Bonnie, 37, 88
Being Mortal, 2, 64, 158
Benartzi, Shlomo, 115, 169–75, 187–88
Blanchard, Bob and Melinda, 248
Body scan meditation, 153–57
Breath work, 21–22, 26, 32–34, 43–44, 70–72, 75, 163–64
Bridgers, Janet, 116–17, 125
Broad, William J., 104
Brooks, Arthur, 27–28, 196–97, 291
Build Your Village, 160
Burr, Sherri, 202, 229
Bush, Mirabai, 73
Business ethics, 295–99

Cattell, Raymond, 196–97
Charitable giving, 299–301
Chesky, Brian, 193
Cho, Jeena, 36–38
Chödrön, Pema 3, 33, 42, 58, 72–73
Chronical of Higher Education, 197
Churchill, Winston, 27
Clinton, Bill 95
Coach Yourself to Success, 18–19
Complicated Lives: Free Blacks in Virginia, 229
Conley, Chip, 23, 86–87, 112–13, 159, 193–94, 220, 228
Cost of living, 245–46
Critchlow, Paul, 193–94
Crowley, Chris, 116–17, 123–24, 126, 137
Csikszentmihalyi, Mihaly, 186
Davis, Daphne, 75
Depression, 63–65, 68–71
Devices, 30–31
Dickens, Charles, 203–04
Difficult people, 80–82
Dogs, 159, 183, 247–48
Dr. Seuss, 16
Dweck, Carol S., 45
Dychtwald, Ken, PhD, 106–07
Dychtwald, Maddy, 116–17, 149, 158–59, 183
Einstein, Albert, 105
Emotions, 78–80
　and difficult people, 80–82

INDEX

and the physical body, 67–68
Esalen Institute, 106
Fear, 65–67
Feiler, Bruce, 52–53, 77, 130, 238
Flight, fight, or freeze, 65
Flow, 186–87
Food Rules: An Eater's Guide, 141
Foods for wellbeing, 139–46
   Alzheimer's, 140
   BIG food, 295
   digestion, 129, 146
   trans fats, 140–41
Forgiveness, 83–100
Forward, ix–x
Franz, Carl, 235
Frates, Elizabeth, 116–17, 137, 141
Friedman, David, 41, 60
From Strength to Strength, 27–28, 291
Gandhi, Mahatma, 92
Gawande, Atul, 2, 64, 158
Getting to Yes with Yourself, 96
Getz, Paula, 231–33
Gifford, Karen, 36–38
Gipson, David and Sheila, 222–23, 240, 242, 273–74
Golden, Bernard, 73–74
Gratitude, 20–21, 77, 99–100, 161–65, 288
Gregory, Dick, 137
Greif, 58–63, 68–71
Guilt, 88–91
Harris, Thomas. 42
Hayes, Jeffrey, 75
Health care costs, 246
Health plan, create your own 164–65
Hello, Goodbye: 75 Rituals for Times of Loss, Celebration, and Change, Day, 178–80
I'm OK—You're OK, 42
Income gap, 254
Joie de Vivre Hospitality, 193

Journaling exercises, 14–15, 17–19, 51–52, 79, 96, 160, 165, 169–75, 184–85, 186–89, 191–92, 197, 200–01, 205, 208–09, 248–49, 265, 289–90, 308–09
Joy, xi, 1, 3–6, 16–23, 160–65, 177–80, 290
Kabat-Zinn, John, 33, 34, 60, 135–36, 235
Keleher, Bill, 224
Korb, Alex, 66, 69–71
Kornfield, Jack, 19–20, 26, 80, 94–96
Langer, Ellen, 161
Lao Tzu, 32–33
Learning to Love Midlife, 112, 113, 159
Levitt, Havens, 227–29
LGBTQ+ rights, 227, 231–33
Life Is in the Transitions: Mastering Change at Any Age, 52–53, 77, 130
Lincoln, Abraham, 27, 96
Lipton, Bruce, 43, 48–51
Live What You Love, 248
Lodge, Harry, 116–17, 123–24, 126, 137
Love, 98–100
MacMillan, Michael, MD, 11
Mahfouz, Naguib, 204
Mandela, Nelson, 95
Mann, Thomas, 203
Mantra, 35–38
   for sleep, 151
Massage, 165, 264
   self, 162
Materialism, 301–03
Maximize Your Medicare: 2024-2025 Edition: Qualify for Benefits, Protect Your Health, and Minimize Your Costs, 282
McGinn, Randi, 61–62
McMillan, Joanna, 137, 140–46, 297
Meditation, 33–40

INDEX

body scan, 153–57
breath work, 21–22, 26, 32–34, 43–44, 70–72, 75, 163–64
career transition meditation, 38–40
for the heart, 162–64
mantra, 35–38
Merton, Thomas, 28
Miedaner, Talane, 18–19
Military transition, 218–21
Mindfulness, 12–15, 25–40, 69–80, 86, 135–36, 150–52, 217–27, 307
eating, 135–37
money, 285–303
sleep, 150
Mindset, 41–53, 85, 114–15, 118–19, 125–26, 130–31, 150, 161, 194, 256, 276, 287, 303–04
Mindset: The New Psychology of Success, 45
Mistakes,
learning from, 87–88
Mobility movement, 28–31
Money, 253–304
barter, 301
charitable giving, 299–301
charitable giving visualization, 301
freedom, 303–04
habits, 273–74
life sentence, 290–93
materialism, 301–03
Medicare, 282
mindful spending, 285–303
mindset, 41–53, 85, 114–15, 118–19, 125–26, 130–31, 150, 161, 194, 256, 276, 287, 303–04
money myths, 293–94
money vs. time, 274–75
pensions, 278–80
personal balance sheet, 257–62
poverty guidelines, 258
private retirement funds, 401(k)s, 403(b)s, IRAs, 280–82
saving, 268–73
social security, when to take, 279–80
soul, 294–95
spending, 262–68
three-legged stool of financial planning, 278–83
visualizations, 300–01, 308–09
Motley Fool, 238
Movement, 121–33
digestion, 129, 146
mindset, 130–31
Muller, Wayne, 28–30
Multitasking, 32
Munro, Alice, 204
Murthy, Vivek, 158
Nathanson, Paul, x
Neff, Kristen, Dr. 84–87
Newport Avenue Market, 298
Nonattachment, 111–14
Nutrition, 135–47
cooking, 147
Oh, Jae, 282
Oliver, Mary, 6
Om, Kali, 37
Oregon,
Yachats, 243
Bend, 161, 241, 244–45, 298
Overcoming Destructive Anger: Strategies That Work, 73–74
Oxfam, 296
Petersen, Todd, 61
Physical movement, 121–133
cardio-vascular, 125–27
case study, 131–33
housekeeper study, 126
mobility movement, 128–29
weight training, 127
Picasso, Pablo, 16
Pilates, 128–29

INDEX

Pilates, Joseph, 115
Plutchik, Robert, 78–79
Plutchik's wheel, 78–79
Pollan, Michael, 141
Porchon-Lynch, Tao, 115
Regret, 88–91
Reinvention, 213–234
Relocation, 235–49
  family, 246–47
  social support, 247
  virtual move, 243
Rest: Why You Get More Done When Your Work Less, 203–04
Retirement,
  activities to enjoy in, 187–90
  becoming a mentern, 193–194
  changing careers, 205
  extra time in, 199–200
  flexibility in, 205–06
  identifying character strengths in, 190–91
  identifying forte strengths in, 191–92
  life objectives, 169–75
  loss of identity in, 180–81
  mindful transition to, 206
  nuts and bolts of, 199–212
  planning day to day retirement life, 207–211
  planning time in, 207–212
  productivity in, 202–04
  preparing for, 177–98
  reinvention in, 213–34
  setting life objectives in, 169–78
  teaching in, 196–98
  three-legged stool of retirement life planning, 3
  unfinished business in, 200–02
  volunteering in, 194–96
  working part-time in, 214–16
Richard Morgan case study, 131–32
Roberts, James A., MD, 31
Robinson, Christine, 205–06, 215–16
Romano, Florence Ann, 160
Roosevelt, Eleanor, 33–34
Rumi, 60
Saint Augustine, 27
Sabbath: Restoring the Sacred Rhythm of Rest, 28–30
Sadness, 61–65, 68–71
Schildkret, Day 178–80
Search Inside Yourself, 79
Self-care, 65, 86–87, 113, 160–64, 227
Self-compassion, 36, 83–87, 91
Shame, 88–91
Sharp, Tim, Dr., 18, 99–100
Silver Sneakers, 118
Sleep, 149–58
  mantra, 151
  rituals, 151
  yoga for, 157
Socializing, 158–60
  dogs, 159, 183
Soojung-Kim Pang, Alex, 203–04
Starzynski, James, 230–31
Stress, 160–65
Swami Vishnu-Devananda, 106
Tan, Chade-Meng, 79
The Anxious Lawyer, 36–378
The Biology of Belief, 43, 48–51
The Book of Forgiving, 93–98
The Calm Technique, 37
The Healthy Hedonist, 116–17, 124, 137
The Inner Work of Aging, 195, 197
The Lifestyle Medicine Book, 116–17, 137
The New Retirementality, 207–10
The People's Guide to Mexico: Wherever You Go—There You Are, 235
The Second Half of Life: Opening the Eight Gates of Wisdom, 184, 200–01

The Science of Yoga: The Risks and the Rewards, 104
The Soul of Money, 286
The Thought Exchange, 41, 60
The Top Five Regrets of the Dying: A Life Transformed by the Dearly Departing, 99
The Upward Spiral: Using Neuroscience to Reverse the Course of Depression, One Small Change at a Time, 66, 69–71
Thinking Smarter: Seven Steps to Your Fulfilling Retirement and Life, 115, 169–75, 187–88
Time,
   planning in retirement, 207–212
Too Much of a Good Thing, 31
Transcendental Meditation, 106
Transitions, 32–33, 38–40, 52, 178–83, 206–07, 209–11, 213–34
Trollope, Anthony, 203
Trumpey, Kristen, 113, 131
Tutu, Desmond, 93–98
Tutu, Mpho, 93–98
Twist, Lynn, 286–87, 291–95, 293–99, 300–01
Tyagi, Amelia, 259–61
Ury, William, 96

VIA character strengths test, 190–91
Villoldo, Alberto, 179–80
Vision board, 18
Visualization, 289–90, 308–09
Vrbo, 244
Ware, Bronnie, 99
Warren, Elizabeth, 259–61
Washington Post, 117
Wealth gap, 254–55, 278
Weight training, 127
Wherever You Go, There You Are, 235
Wilson, Paul, 34, 37
Winfrey, Oprah, 18
Wisdom at Work, 193–94
Wizard of Oz, 57
Work addiction, 26–28
Working with Mindfulness, 73
Yoga, 21–23, 60, 70, 76–77, 103–110, 128–30, 151, 157, 287–88
   aging, 104
   classes, 108–10
   history of, 104–07
   philosophy, 80, 110
Yoss, Dave, 125
Younger Next Year, 116–17, 123–24, 126, 137
Zweig, Connie, 195, 197

About the Author

Nathalie Martin is a chaired professor at the University of New Mexico School of Law, where she teaches mindfulness and law, as well as commercial and consumer law. A longtime yoga and meditation teacher and practitioner, she also teaches contemplative practices in varied settings, from hospitals and senior centers to law school classrooms. The author of nine books, this is her first for general audiences.

Nathalie believes in serendipity and lifelong learning. She and her husband, Stewart, are avid travelers who have visited over thirty countries. Both academics, Nathalie and Stewart have taught (either meditation and yoga or law) in many countries around the world. If you don't find Nathalie teaching or taking a class, you might find her birding in Costa Rica or hiking in Northern New Mexico with Stewart and her rescue dog, Mi Hita.

Nathalie's life goal is to help others create vast, expansive lives. Her motto is "Step out of the fast lane and into the vast lane."